Slavery of Faith

Leslie Monique Wagner-Wilson

iUniverse, Inc.
New York   Bloomington

Slavery of Faith

This book is a work of non-fiction. Unless otherwise noted, the author and the publisher make no explicit guarantees as to the accuracy of the information contained in this book and in some cases, names of people and places have been altered to protect their privacy.

iUniverse books may be ordered through booksellers or by contacting:

iUniverse
1663 Liberty Drive
Bloomington, IN 47403
www.iuniverse.com
1-800-Authors (1-800-288-4677)

Because of the dynamic nature of the Internet, any Web addresses or links contained in this book may have changed since publication and may no longer be valid. The views expressed in this work are solely those of the author and do not necessarily reflect the views of the publisher, and the publisher hereby disclaims any responsibility for them.

ISBN: 978-0-595-51293-5 (pbk)
ISBN: 978-0-595-61838-5 (ebk)

Library of Congress Control Number: 2009922648

Printed in the United States of America

iUniverse rev. date: 3/11/2009

Special Acknowledgments

I thank God for having a master plan and never forsaking me.

To the 918 friends and Jonestown residents…you are not forgotten.

To those known and unknown prayer warriors whose prayers that have been upon Jakari and I since November 18, 1978, they are answered every day. I love you.

For my children Jakari, Monique and Demetrius, who have provided me with a reason to live and continue, "Take nothing for granted and live your life well." My granddaughters and their mothers: Honor God,and yourselves. Teach them unconditional love.

To the families of those murdered and injured at the Pt. Kaituma airstrip-I pray that you have found peace and forgiveness.

To my ancestors who are with me always, their prayers and protection keeping me moving.

For Chatfield Hughes my bridge to spiritual enlightenment who taught me unconditional love, I love you.

For Fielding McGehee, my editor, whom we so fondly refer to as "Mac," and Professor Rebecca Moore for your painstaking and unending work of Faith to continue with the Jonestown Institute at www.jonestown.sdsu.edu which provides the world with more content and research on Peoples Temple and Jonestown. Thank you. I love you both.

To Reverend and Mrs. Willie P. Cooke of Shiloh Baptist Church, Sacramento, for being an inspiration and support in my darkest hours and never once giving up on me, I will love you always.

To Dr. Edward Briscoe, my mentor who encouraged and gave me the courage to complete this manuscript, may you rest in peace. Thank you also to his wife Maggie.

For Louise Jones, one of my biggest supporters, thank you and may you rest in peace. For Peter Moyes, of Sacramento, who painstakingly provided me with early editing and the title of this manuscript, thank you.

To Guy Parrish, one of the most consistent people in my life during the last 24 years, thank you for being a friend.

For Charles Kidd of Sacramento and Kidds Gym which helped me change my life, brother I will love you always.

Cynthia Harmon aka Queen Bilquis of Harlem, New York, my sister, Muslim spiritual warrior and designer and artist extraordinaire one of my biggest fans & friend for over 19 years thanks for keeping it real and for your unwavering support… *Send more clothes please.*

To Betty Roberts, of Stone Mountain, GA. a friend for 18 years who continued to encourage me and listen to my ramblings.

To the dozens and dozens of friends and acquaintances over the last thirty years some who knew where I came from, and for those who did not, who touched my life and gave me some sense of normalcy. Thank you.

To-Gwen Rodriques of Sacramento, my friend and sister for over 25 years and the first outsider I shared my history with- I love you and thanks

To my ex's - be well and thanks for the lessons!

To Stephen Weathers, my PSA at IUniverse for staying on top of things and the staff at IUniverse.

Adama @ adamspeaks.com for offering spiritual guidance and enlightment…you are loved. Thank you.

www.slaveryoffaith.com

faithalways@slaveryoffaith.com

Foreword

When I see the photo on the front cover, it is surreal. That photograph was taken a day after my escape from Jonestown, Guyana. I study the image of Jakari with his small hand holding my chin, not understanding the circumstances, as if he were saying, "Thanks for saving me, Mom." We did not know that he was the youngest survivor of the Jonestown massacre. But in fact it was the never ending Grace of the Creator that sustained our lives.

The struggles have been difficult, my faith was tested continually. The survivor's guilt I suffered was enormous. The constant wondering if on that fateful day, my family thought that I had left them knowing what was to come. The thoughts of what the last day must have been like. Of knowing my mother and sister had to watch the death of their children – and the gut wrenching realization that they made a mistake. Why was I allowed to live? Why not my sister Michelle or my brother Mark? Surely they could have contributed to the world more than I. However, through it all I have arrived at a place of peace, forgiveness and hope. The arrival at that state came from numerous people in my life who did not give up on me. Yet, ultimately it came from an arrival of consciousness and finally the ability to love myself. My family will always be missed. For years I searched for another family through marriages trying to replace what I lost. Finally, I came to terms with the hard fact that the family I lost can't and will never be replaced – but they will always be remembered. The deaths of my mother, husband, sister, brother, niece, nephew and a host of people I loved and grew up with changed me. But through it all I prayed to God that my heart would not be hardened – "to please allow me to keep the gift of loving." I believe that is my greatest gift.

I am grateful - I am thankful - I am in awe of the power of the Creator to bring us through any situation if we just believe in the power of Faith, Grace and Mercy.

So as you read this story – my story – I am a Slave to Faith and holding fast to my Faith. As I pray that you can always hold on to your own.

PROLOGUE

Slavery of Faith

"Leslie, Leslie!" I heard a voice I had only dreamed about. As I turned slowly towards the voice, I saw my sister Michelle. "Where have you been?" I cried out. She grabbed my arms and pulled me to her. "We've been looking for you!" she whispered, holding me tight. Within her arms I felt safe and loved. Immediately the fear and pain I had harbored for years left my entire being. Holding her and sobbing, I looked up and asked "Is it really you? How did you make it? Where are Mom and Mark?" She grabbed my hand. "Come with me," she said. "I have something to show you." I took her hand tightly, scared to let go. We walked for a while. I could not feel my feet touch the ground. We came to a building with stairs leading downward to a door. She knocked a series of thumps, as if it was a signal, and as the door opened, I heard the music before I saw the choir singing. I cried, "Oh, my God!" I could barely talk behind the flood of tears. The choir, decked out in their blue dresses I always loved, waved and continued singing. Looking further through the room, I saw a woman approaching me. "Mom!" I shouted, running towards her. From behind her came my brother Mark. The shock of it all dropped me to my knees, and I grabbed my mother's legs, sobbing, crying out, "Where have you been? I have been here all these years by myself!" My heart felt whole again, life again, flowing through my total being, blood pumping into my heart finally, healing. Walking past me were three security guards in their black leisure suits, red shirts and black berets. I shouted at my first love, "Why didn't you tell me?" Matthew and I had reconnected years earlier. From the corner of my eye, I detected a movement. My head turned ever so slightly… There was Jim Jones; surrounded by people I thought had died. He looked at me with his piercing black eyes and nodded his head, his lips slightly curled in a smile. "My God!" I screamed. "It was all a lie."

As I opened my eyes, my husband lay next to me. I snuggled closer to him and with my lips near his ear, waking him with tears still streaming down my face, I whispered, "Baby, I had the best dream."

Chapter 1:
The First Attempt

Before long, Joe and I began having problems. He began distancing himself from me. My thoughts turned every day to ways of escaping. The problem was how? I prayed that God would open another door to help me. Eventually a plan began to emerge – not clearly at first – but it started with a trip to Guyana's capital city of Georgetown. "How can you get there?" I wonder. Then it dawned on me: Hide your glasses. They will have to send you to town to get a new pair! I had been wearing glasses since I was 13. They wouldn't deny me my vision!

I carefully buried my glasses deep inside of my trunk at the foot of our bed. It worked! They approved my request to go to Georgetown. Once I got there, I would find a way to reach the U.S. Embassy and tell them what was really happening in Jonestown. Jim had spies everywhere, especially inside the government, but I knew that as I had sought God's intervention, He would make a way for me. It was just as hard to trust your own family. My resolve was to be able to discern how the Spirit wanted me to move. So, feeling at peace with how I was to proceed, I readied myself for the journey. My faith was still strong and no matter what Jim said about him being God, I knew I had God in me also.

When the day arrived for me to leave, I kissed and hugged my son, Jakari. Right away a tingling went through me creating goose bumps. Déjà vu. I had left him before in someone else's care. But this time I knew what I was doing.

The ride to the boat on the tractor trailer was rough as always. The thought of getting back on that boat was agonizing, and I did not look forward to the possibility of a restless sea.

1

Arriving at the dock, our boat the *Cudjoe* was as I remembered its wooden frame worn from her many journeys. Port Kaituma was surrounded by trees, and as I scanned the little town, I noticed some of the Amerindians watching us. I wondered what they thought of us. Michael told us to unload, and as I jumped from the tractor trailer, the rest of the crew began removing trunks and boxes, walking up the plank to put them on the Temple boat. I gathered my suitcase, stretched my legs, and got on board. The bright light of the sun cast surreal shadows.

Once on board, I looked for a place to sit, finally choosing a spot close to the back of the boat. There were only six of us going into the capital. The others were talking, but I was not in a conversational mood. How would I reach the U.S. Embassy? That was the only thought on my mind.

The engine banged to life, and we began to move. Holding on, I turned to wave to my comrades at the dock. "See you when you get back!" someone yelled. I waved, smiling, although inside I was frightened. As the boat rocked and swayed slowly up the river, I talked with one of the other passengers. Angela was going into the capital to relieve someone who had been there for a couple of months. I think we both knew that she was getting a break and was glad for it. At least at the Peoples Temple house in Lamaha Gardens, she could take a hot shower, use a real toilet with real toilet paper, and enjoy some privacy, all of which were lacking in Jonestown. Angela was part of the regular rotation; she would replace a worker who in turn would return to Jonestown. I had no hope that I would be allowed to work in Georgetown, though. And honestly, I did not want to be far from my child.

As Angela talked, the boat left the mouth of Kaituma River and headed out to sea. I searched for the separation of the water's color which I had noticed on the first trip to Jonestown: it went from a muddy, reddish color to a beautiful teal blue. It was Mother Nature at her best.

I opened the book I brought and tried to read to take my mind off of what I had to do. Someone eventually called out for supper, and I steadied myself as I walked to the galley. I was handed a plate of wonderful peanut butter and honey sandwiches. Living in Jonestown, I had learned to be thankful for whatever food we were given. As we gathered together, we talked about Jonestown and our families. Later, after dinner, I went back to my spot and opened my book again. I read, feeling the rocking of the boat, and as the sun began to set, the beauty of this almost moved me to tears. This is beautiful, I thought. Why couldn't the circumstances be different? Why could I not just go along with the program?

My eyes began to get heavy with the boat's rhythmic swaying. When I awoke, the moon was high in the sky, and the swishing of the water against the side of boat gave me some peace. The quiet was beautiful. Tonight I would not have to hear sirens wailing or Jim on the loudspeaker, telling us to get to the pavilion. Suddenly, sadness enveloped me as I thought about my child, and the others, possibly being awoken in a shroud of fear. Somehow I had to get him out.

The stars shone brightly above us. I thought of Harriet Tubman, leading her people out in the dark of the night, with only the moon as her guide. At that moment, I could feel the desperation they felt, not knowing if they were going to make it or not, understanding only that freedom was worth dying for. My eyes began to get heavy again.

When I awoke again, the sun was beating down on me. Stretching as I did every day as a child, I held on to the side of the boat and bade good morning to those that were awake. I went to the latrine and splashed water on my face. When I looked in the little mirror, I saw a face that looked old and tired. When I went into the boat's galley, the cook was standing over a boiling pot. Rice, I knew. Well, at least we were eating. But then, I smelled what I thought were eggs. No way. I had to be dreaming. Did I even remember what eggs tasted like? "What, we have eggs?" I asked. He turned around and laughed. "How do you want them, scrambled or sunny side up?" "Really?" I asked. "Sure, how do you want them?" "Can I have them scrambled hard?" "Of course, they'll be ready in a minute." Scared to miss out or wake up from the dream, I watched him beat the eggs in a bowl and throw them in the skillet. The smell was divine. As he finished, he put them on a plate and handed it to me. "Here you go." I thanked him, and then took my plate of rice and eggs to show my comrades. They smiled and got up to get theirs. As I sat down to eat, guilt washed over me. No one in Jonestown is eating this. I knew that. My enjoyment of the meal was suddenly ruined. I ate in deep contemplation. This was not socialism: I was having what they were not. What the hell was this? I finished my meal, my stomach full, and took my plate in the galley. "Need some help washing these?" I asked. "No, thanks," my cook comrade responded. "Relax, you probably need it." He knew too, and probably felt the way I and so many others did.

Going back to the deck, I looked for a shady spot on the boat where I could read my book. I slept more than I read and conversed during the 24 hours it took to get to Georgetown. I had not known how tired I really was. Most of us slept and just enjoyed the quietness and the calming of the sea. As dusk settled in, I knew we would be there in another couple hours or so.

Finally, we could see the port up ahead. Even for the time of evening, it was still warm. As the boat moved slowly to the dock, I saw some familiar faces. They greeted us with welcoming smiles. It felt very good to be on solid ground, even though I had enjoyed the ride. We gathered our things as they unloaded the boat. We climbed into one of the vehicles and drove away.

Georgetown looked as I had remembered it, a city of neighborhoods with houses built on stilts. I always thought this was weird. As we maneuvered from one street to the other, I saw people mingling about, and once we got up on them, I felt their eyes on us. I was sure everyone in Georgetown knew about the group living in the jungle.

We arrived at the house as the evening meal was being prepared. We were assigned a place to stow our things and a place to sleep. Some would have to make do with the floor, since they were kind of crowded. No problem, I thought, at least this was a real house.

We were shown the bathroom, and each of us took turns washing the sea salt and smell off of us. When I entered the bathroom, I noticed a lock on the door. Wonderful, I thought. As I got undressed, anticipating the feel of warm water on my body, my thoughts once again turned to the people at Jonestown. Stop worrying, I told myself, they will all be able to experience this again – at least those who want to. Just do what you need to do. We were instructed to limit ourselves to a two-minute shower – well, some things don't change, I thought – but I was still grateful that God shone his Grace and allowed me these luxuries.

When I came out of the bathroom, I was told I could fix my own plate of food. There was fried chicken, eggplant and rice. Chicken, I thought, and remembered the last time I had chicken. I had put my plate down to pick up my drink, and one of the dogs grabbed it. I had chased him, and when I caught him, I yanked my chicken breast out of his mouth, brushed it off and ate it. How long ago had that been? This night, I fixed my plate with small portions, so that everyone would have enough, and sat at the kitchen table. One of the people who had been there for a while sat with me. "How are you doing in Jonestown?" Why is she asking me that, I wondered? Had she heard something about me? "Fine," I responded. "I love it." This was what we expected to say. "Good. Where are you working?" "With Larry Schacht and two days in the fields," I said, smiling. "Oh, that's good," she replied. After I finished eating, tiredness enveloped me. She led me to a room with a couch. "Thanks," I said, taking a place on the floor where three others already lay. I unrolled my sleeping bag and stretched out wondering what the next day would bring.

A moment later – or so it seemed – someone was shaking me awake. "Thank you, God," I prayed quietly, not on my knees but lying down. "Thank you God for giving me another day. Please give me the strength to do this. Please give me the courage to move forward, and please keep my child and those I love in Jonestown safe. Thank you for loving me. Amen."

My stomach was quivering, not from hunger but from anticipation. Today is the beginning of my mission. Find some way to the US Embassy, I kept thinking. During breakfast, we were told what our jobs would be. My eye doctor appointment was scheduled for the next day, and so that day, I was informed, I was going into the marketplace to ask for donations. What the hell are we asking for donations for? I wondered. I received my instructions on what to say: "Tell them Jonestown is a wonderful place and you are of course happy to live in their beautiful country, things of this nature. Don't share anything that goes on there. We have spies everywhere!" Here we go again, I thought. Everything had to be positive but vague.

We headed towards the marketplace, an area of pavilion-like structures, covered tents and lots of tables. There was a sea of women in brightly-colored head scarves, blouses, golden bangles around their wrists, speaking quickly in other languages besides the King's English. It amazed me. All these people of different hues, selling their wares making a living. Why are we begging, I wondered? It must be to put up a front for the government, pretending that we did not have anything. We were warned to stay close to each other as people were known to disappear and as Americans we could be targets.

One of my coaches told me to listen to what she said. She must have seen the apprehension on my face. Following her lead, I approached a Guyanese. "Good morning. Anything for the missionary work?" "Sure t'ing, hon," and I felt the weight of something dropping into my basket. I approached another vendor, received another gift. The Guyanese people were wonderful, always smiling and very friendly. I was offered a Coke, something I had not had in months, and of course I accepted. I drank slowly, savoring the taste. Looking at the vendor who gave it to me, I wondered could he be trusted with my secret. Second thoughts entered my mind, and I decided against approaching him. As I kept begging, I searched the eyes from which the gifts came, looking for a special sign of trust. I procured cassava – like a potato but more bitter – and eggplant, mostly, a bunch of bananas here and there. The women were smiling all the time, happy to be alive. Sometimes their eyes showed wisdom, sometimes they reflected tiredness. All the while I searched for that special person God sent for me to confide in. There were a lot of men looking at me, but I had already decided it would not be a man, since he might have other things in mind. I simplified my plan: just put me near a phone to call the American Embassy.

I heard my name being called. Across the marketplace my coach was waving to me to come towards her. How did I get on this side, I wondered. I smiled and waved back. I maneuvered through the crowd and finally reached her. "You okay?" she asked. "Oh, yes, this is incredible." "Well" she continued, "the van will be here in a few minutes. Let's sit down." The rest of the group was under a tent fanning themselves. It was stifling. Feeling sticky and filthy from all the dust generated from the marketplace, a warm shower – or even a cold one, for that manner – was an appealing thought. We continued small talk until our vehicle arrived.

Back at the house, we showered, talked, ate dinner and went to bed. Exhaustion still wracked my body. Would I ever feel rested? My thoughts before dozing off were of my child and his father, Joe.

The next day I was taken to the doctor's office. He examined my eyes and fitted me for a pair of very ugly glasses. My other ones were better looking, but it was worth the sacrifice, I thought. The other pair hidden in my trunk could never be seen again. The medical assistant told me the glasses would be ready in a week. I thought it was a blessing. It gave me more time to make contact with the Embassy.

And so it went. Every morning after finishing our chores, we would head out to the markets, the streets of Guyana, and beg for food.

One day – a rare day of leisure – I headed into the house's radio room. What I saw caused me to almost panic. There in plain sight on the table was a newspaper from the United States with a picture of Deborah Layton. My hand was shaking as I picked it up. Deborah Layton had not only left the church, she was reporting the conditions of Jonestown, describing how inhumane they were. This was not a good sign. Deborah was very close to Jim and knew so much about the church, including the financials. "Oh, my God!" I thought. I knew my instincts had been right. Why were we not being fed properly when there was so much money in banks? Why was it not used for food? Why are we out here begging, like we don't have anything? This was what I couldn't understand. We were near starving or at least eating as if we did not have anything left. Something was terribly wrong. This information was so sensitive that I did not want anyone to know that I had read it. I was scared. I carefully looked around the room, praying there were no cameras about, placed the newspaper as I had found it, and left the room.

Later that evening, we were told to dress up and prepare to entertain some important people. Someone gave me something to wear, and we got in a car and went out to dinner. The evening ended with a ride up the river with one of the Guyanese officials. He was quite handsome and kept eyeing me. I felt uncomfortable and prayed that he would not ask for me. There were women who slept with men in the government to keep them happy and on the side of Jonestown, but who also gathered and seduced information out of them. I did not have this in mind for myself.

The official came over and asked me my name. I told him. The next obvious question was whether or not I was married and I said yes. That put a wrench in his plan and I was glad he had the decency not to go on anymore. I respected him for that.

When the evening was finally over, we returned to Lamaha Gardens, where there were new arrivals from the States. My heart weighed heavy for them: their journey would not be as they had expected. The next couple of days were more of the same, but I still could not believe what I had read about Deb Layton, and no one was saying anything. This was going to be a bad one; I could feel it deep in my soul.

The optometrist office called to tell me my glasses were ready. The boat was scheduled to take off after my appointment. I had never found an opportunity to contact the Embassy. The boat ride back was not the same for me. I knew it was time to get out of Jonestown. The problem was going to be how?

When we pulled up in the tractor-trailer to the compound, I went looking for my son, Jakari. Joe found me first, but instead of welcoming me back, the look on his face, was one of anger. He told me to go with him. "Where is Jakari?" I asked, following him to the cabin. "You can see him later" he shouted, as he went upstairs. A couple of minutes later, he stuck out his hand to show me what he held: my old glasses. "Oh, where did you did find them?" I asked, trying to appear as surprised as I could. He said "In the bottom of your trunk!" "Really" I said. "Damn, I searched everywhere for them? They must have fallen." "Why would they be at the bottom of the trunk, Leslie?" The way he said my name frightened me. Stay calm, I thought. Remember what Mom said, never admit to anything. "Did you plan this?" he persisted. "What the hell are you talking about, why would I plan it?" He asked me if I was trying to leave. "No, of course not," I replied. "How could I leave Jakari?" I could see he wanted to believe me, but I could also see he was having a difficult time. I was not sure if he would report me or not, so all I could do was pray. I was doing a lot of that lately. Moving towards him, I put my arms around him and kissed him. His body stiffened at first, but finally began to relax against mine. Grabbing my hands, he led me upstairs, where he made love to me, while I whispered in his ear how much I loved him and that was real. Please, God, let this be over, I prayed. Please don't let him tell anyone.

We lay there afterwards in each other's arms, me holding on to him with his back to me as we always did. Later he took me to my son. "Mama," he called. I picked him up and held him close. I had to find a way out. God, I needed to find a way out.

Chapter 2: Childhood Memories

Childhood memories still bring a smile to my face. The visions of my grandparents and sister are still quite vivid. When I look at the surviving photographs of my earliest years, I am very grateful. Dim memories of the little Northern California town of Cottonwood recall our life living on a ranch not many miles from Mt. Shasta. I see my grandmother, Lucille Smith, in the kitchen with an apron around her thick waist, and her gold glasses with pearls on the side. Grandma and Grandpa Smith kept my sister Michelle and me with them until my mother was able to care for us alone. We were well loved.

My mother, Inez Jeanette Fortier, was a divorcee – although we had no idea of what this meant or even what it was when we were children – and lived several hundred miles away in San Francisco. She would visit frequently and, with tight hugs, would tell us she loved us. Then off she would go. The expression on her face carried a hint of something else, possibly sadness or guilt.

Michelle and I had fun on the ranch. We were allowed to run free through the fields under the watchful eyes of one of our grandparents. I remember the cows in the barn and grazing in the pasture. Michelle and I would go out to the fields and play school with the calves. We loved the animals. When Grandpa would kill a chicken, we could not watch, but we would chase the chicks after they were hatched. There were pigs which we had to feed at times, throwing a bucket of slop to them. We helped where we could – throwing feed to the chickens, or looking after the calves, even as we played with them – and we had a wonderful time on that ranch.

There was a creek than ran the length of the property which backed up to a fence and beautiful mountains served as a backdrop to our picturesque scene. Grandma told the story plenty of times – although I don't remember it – of me running one day straight into the creek. She followed me in, fully dressed, to rescue me.

One day a man came to the ranch to pay a call on my grandparents. After he left, they came to us and told us we were leaving. Grandpa had been traveling lately, but we didn't know where and were too young to ask. As they began packing the house up, we asked our grandpa what would happen to our animals. He told me that the animals were still his, but these people were going to rent the ranch and care for the animals. At that age I had no idea what "rent" was I was just happy that we would still have our cows and calves. Soon afterwards, my grandparents, my uncle and a few other relatives packed up the old Ford station wagon and away we went. I didn't know where we were going, but I knew from my grandmother's tears as she told her friends goodbye that we wouldn't be back.

We moved to 18th Avenue in a town called Sacramento. Outside the back gate were railroad tracks. The sound of the metal sashaying across metal still echoes in my ear. The sound of trains was a lullaby to me, the rhythm of something going somewhere, far and distant, somewhere I might never know. Even as a child, I loved to daydream of traveling to far-off places, of trying something or somewhere new.

The grapevines in back of the house produced just enough grapes to fill a few bottles of wine. Grandma spent time taking care of the house, quilting and working in the kitchen, canning homemade jelly, preserves and fruit. Mom still came to visit, and we were always happy to see her. Grandma and Grandpa had a kind friend by the name of Mrs. Hamilton. She lived across the street and made the most beautiful dollies out of crochet. From the covers on the chairs to the pillows, Mrs. Hamilton crocheted everything in her house. Because she only had one leg, she was in a wheelchair, but she did not let her disability stop her. She would use her crutch to knock down plums from the trees in her backyard and share them with us.

Every Wednesday, our grandmother had Mission, a gathering of church women who routinely met at each others' houses for prayer service. She taught us never to ask for anything when she visited her church sisters. My sister and I would sit in our designated seats without saying a word, not even ask to go to the bathroom. As I now look back, I realize my grandparents raised me to respect my elders, not to speak unless we were spoken to, to address them as "Sir" and "Ma'am," and to sit quietly still. Years later I would raise my children the same way.

We attended Sunday school at Shiloh Baptist Church, on 9th Avenue, which still stands. The Reverend W.P. Cooke baptized me when I was four. Shiloh was a large church, not like the mega churches now, but large enough to fit at least 1,200 people inside. My grandpa was a Deacon and my grandmother a Deaconess. Their church responsibilities were important to them. My grandpa would sit in the first two rows in front of the piano on the far left side, and I would snuggle next to him. As the preacher delivered his sermon, my grandpa would respond "Yes, Sir," in a voice you could hear throughout the church. My grandmother would sometimes get into the spirit, and as she began to holler, either Michelle or I – sitting on either side of her – would grab the church fan and begin to fan her. Soon, of course, this would not be enough. She would start to wail, a wail which sounded as if she were in concert with God himself and the angels were singing around him. When this happened, one of us would remove her glasses, so they wouldn't break. Most times her hat stayed pinned down tightly to her hair, but other times the poor thing did not have a chance. Her hat would go flying, sometimes far enough to land in another pew. As Michelle and I hunkered down beside her, she would swing out her arms, and then she really took flight. Out the pews she would go and begin her own personal praise dance to God. In later years, I would find myself so grateful that she was the strong God-fearing spiritual woman and prayer warrior that she was.

Some little girls dream of singing a solo on stage, and I remember the day I realized that dream. The children's choir director summoned me to the front of church and lowered the mike to my height. The only thing I could concentrate on was the sound of my heart. It beat so hard and so loud that I knew everyone could hear it, and as the music began, it only got worse. I looked at my grandpa whose face was beaming with pride. When it came time for me to sing, I opened my mouth… but not a sound came out. Panicked, I turned to look at the choir director. She smiled and motioned to the choir to stop singing. She then came to me and, in the sweetest tone, said "Honey, you can sing this." I summoned my will from somewhere deep inside, forced my eyes to not look at anything but the door to the church lobby, and began again. This time, a sound escaped, almost that of a whisper, but as it kept flowing, the strength inside my little body kept pushing it out, and before I knew it, I was actually singing. When it finally ended, I exhaled a breath of relief. My reward was hearing my grandpa say, "Yes, sir, that's my girl." My goal in life at that age was to make my grandpa proud of me. I loved him more than anything. When I felt that I had made him proud, that made me proud. More than that, it made me beam.

One day, my mother arrived with a white man named Richard Wagner. He was tall and seemed friendly enough. Grandpa told Michelle and me to go in the backyard and play, so we knew that the grown folks had to talk. We did as we were told, and began playing with our German shepherds. After a while, Grandpa came to the door with a look of sadness as he called us in. Grandma was crying. I asked her what was wrong. That was when we noticed suitcases at the door.

It was time for us to be reunited with our mother, to go live with her. Although I felt happy, I also felt as if she were somewhat of a stranger. Grandma and Grandpa mirrored my ambivalence. They were both happy and sad. My place was beside my grandpa. Never had I imagined that I would leave him. Grandpa had been my papa, the one I turned to when I needed – or even wanted – anything. I had been sleeping with him and Grandma for years. And now it was over.

With all of us crying – despite the reassurances of frequent reunions – we climbed into the funny-looking car. Looking through the backseat window, Michelle and I could see Grandma and Grandpa clinging to each other, waving. My mom and the man who would soon be my father told us we were going to our new house. We drove for what seemed like hours. We crossed a bridge and ended in a huge place, with many tall buildings and long streets. This was my introduction to San Francisco. I remember the smells, the noise and oh, all the cars.

We pulled up to a house on Anza Street in the Richmond District. It was much larger than Grandma and Grandpa's. The rooms appeared to loom in front of us. It seemed as if they kept coming and coming. There was a staircase that headed towards the sky. Never had I seen stairs inside of a house. The kitchen was twice the size of the one we just left. Mom and the man showed us the downstairs which they called a basement. Michelle and I looked at each other in sheer amazement. We were surely going to get lost. The whole place was enormous.

They took us back upstairs to show us our rooms, one for each of us. We protested that we had to sleep in the same room, in the same bed. How was I going to smell Michelle's elbow to put me to sleep if we were not in the same bed? Our mother did not understand how really close we were. Michelle, my pretty sister Michelle, was like the other half of me. Mom relented, so my sister and I were allowed to share a room after all. But even as Michelle and I quietly spoke about the beautiful house, we also whispered our fears.

Unlike our grandparent's home where you had separations between houses, the ones in my mother's neighborhood were attached to each other. You could hear the people next door talking through the walls.

We tried to settle in quickly to our new home and to adjust to our life with our mom and the man. Michelle started school, and I went to a kindergarten for four hours a day. This was the first time we had been away from each other and it was not easy. Mom picked us up after school, and after changing into our play clothes, we would go in the backyard and play. Steps led down to the large backyard. I remember the tall building on the other side of us had many windows where people could look down at us.

My mother was very articulate, but when I think about how she had to suddenly fit into a world that she was not raised in, I am amazed - the adaptability of it all. She did not complete the 8th grade. While my sister and I lived in Cottonwood, CA with Grandma and Grandpa, my mother was a waitress at a diner in the industrial area of San Francisco. That is where she met my dad, Richard Wagner. He was a top salesman at Friden Corp. located in the same area. Moving from wearing an apron to work to wearing the best French perfume and entertaining professionals, she made the transition beautifully. Maybe there is a gene for flexibility and adaptability. If so, I believe I inherited it from her.

My mother was very pretty. She had beautiful clothes and coiffed hair, and always smelled wonderful. Her voice sounded like a bird, light and airy. Her laugh made you smile. She kept house – cooked and cleaned – and made us all very happy. Instead of the plaits my grandpa kept in my hair, she would try to style my hair like the Breck Girls. I knew she loved us.

When the man, whom we were told we could call Richard, came home at what seemed like the same time every night, Mom had dinner on the table a few moments later. Richard was kind enough to us. He tried to tell us jokes and even had one of his friends come over and pull coins out of his ear. He was tall, but wore the funniest-colored clothes or an unfortunate combination of a striped suit with a flowered tie. We thought it was funny.

After dinner our parents would take us down to the basement, and mom played the piano while we all sang. Richard tried to join in, but his voice was very funny. It made my sister and me laugh. After we got ready for bed, he would come in with our mother and give us a kiss on our cheeks. He did not smell like Grandpa. In fact, he did not have a scent at all. Still, slowly, we were becoming familiar with him.

Even as we settled into a routine, not one day would pass when I did not think of my grandparents. We talked with them on the phone, but it was not the same as seeing them every day as we had for so many years. I missed Grandpa's laughter and his affirmation of the preacher in church. He was the most special person in the world and remains so, even to this day.

One day, Mom asked us if we wanted to be adopted. Mom explained that we would take the man's last name – Wagner – as our name, and although he was not our birth father, he would be our father for good after that. We could call him Dad. Michelle and I agreed. In the years to come, he would become a dad more than just by name.

Our house on Anza Street was near a very busy intersection with only one set of stop signs. Apparently that was not enough, since there were many car accidents. One day I was at the intersection trying to cross the street. The car turning at the corner stopped, and the driver, motioned with his hand for me to go. I walked out, not stopping to see if any other cars were coming. Wham! I was thrown probably nine or ten feet up into the air and ended up in the middle of the street. I got up, and ran to my sister who was across the street. God was with me even then. Hearing the brakes and screeching, my mother ran out of the house and took me to the hospital to make sure I was all right. The two teenage boys in the second car were scared out of their minds, crying that they did not see the little girl who ran out into the street without even looking. My mother told them that I was fine, that it was not their fault.

My mother became pregnant with my brother in 1962. One morning we woke up to an empty house except for my parents' dear friend, Mercy. She explained to us that our Mom was at the hospital having the baby. Mercy stayed with us and got us off to school.

While Mom was in the hospital, Dad took on the ominous chore of trying to do our hair, the way he saw my mother do. As long as I can remember, I have been tender-headed and hated having my hair done. Mom would set our hair using the rollers with the mesh and snap piece to them. On that occasion, he set my hair in rollers – that was okay – but the next morning, he tried to take them out. His friend had come over to drive to work together. I screamed and screamed, "Daddy, use the brush." It was a sight, two white men, trying to do a little black girl's hair. That day, I went to school looking quite different than usual. There were no curls, just limp hair, in shock! That was the last time my father would attempt to do my hair. When we came home from school that day, we saw the friendly face of our grandmother, and I knew that I would not suffer with my hair anymore.

The day my mother came home with my brother was an exciting one. Grandma called through the house and we raced to the window overlooking the street. Dad opened the door of the passenger side, and as he reached in to help my mother out, we noticed she had something wrapped in a blanket. Grandma said, "Look your little brother." Michelle and I grinned at each other, clapping with excitement. We stood by the front door, and when she came in, we hugged her around her waist. She patted her heads and said, "Look what I have here." Inside the bundle was the funniest little thing. His face was red and he had black hair all over. "What's his name?" I asked. With a smile, she said "Mark." Dad was just as happy. "What do you girls think?" Almost in unison, we said, "Yes." The addition of our brother quickly meant we had a new routine, and we all settled into it happily.

There were difficulties, though. Mark was born with severe asthma, spending days in the hospital on several occasions. Once we almost lost him. My parents were crying and telling us that he was in an oxygen tent, fighting to live. My brother was adorable. Even then he had peacefulness about him, a genuine sweetness, and a smile that was infectious. Mark was my father's heart. The Richmond District where we lived was always cold, so the doctor suggested that we move to a warmer part of the city. My parents got a house on Monterey Boulevard in St. Francis Woods in the Sunset District. It was beautiful, a small mansion. The living room itself appeared to be the size of a ballroom with hardwood floors and windows festooned with enormous green velvet drapes. The house even had a hot house for plants. We lived right down the street from Willie Mays, and Dad would point out his house to us every time we passed it.

My mother wanted the best for us, to give us what she did not have. She signed me up for the Girl Scout Brownies and Michelle to the Blue Birds. When I put on my uniform each week, I had to have my dad help me with my tie. The meetings were fun, and I really enjoyed them.

One day I was called to the office, where I found my mother waiting for me. The woman with her talked about how cute I was, and would I like to be in a book. At that time, I did not really know what it was, but the next thing I knew, I was taken to meet a group of kids my age. This outing happened once a week: we would go to a classroom, where we were instructed on how to act. It would either be to walk along a path with a fellow child, hold hands, play in the park, or pet the rabbit that I thoroughly fell in love with. One time we went to the San Francisco Zoo, and I was able to let a giraffe lick a piece of bread off the tip of my nose. It was fun. It was all for a reading primer called *Let's See the Animals*. Years later I would find a copy of it.

Mom would drop my sister and me off at the movies on Ocean Avenue. Jerry Lewis and Dean Martin comedies were the rage, as were the Three Stooges and Mae West. The movies were still in black and white.

Mom and Dad had moved close to their dear friends, Dixie, who was an artist and had three boys. Although I cannot remember all of them, one I particularly cared for was Gregory, who would be in our lives for a long time after. Dixie began giving me art lessons. She told me to look at an object and then draw it. The first assignment was an apple. I was amazed at how close my apple looked to the real one, drawing it without looking. These lessons would continue even as we moved to our next home.

The move to 10th Avenue between Anza and Balboa – as had been the move to the Sunset – was precipitated by Mark's flare-ups of asthma. But unlike the previous move, I wasn't happy about this one. I loved the Sunset house and I loved the area. Every time I had a set of friends, it seemed to me, we had to move.

This house was large, yet not as grand as the home we had moved from. The neighborhood was very ethnic, and we all got along. My friends included Karen, a Caucasian girl with thick wavy blonde hair, Judy from Venezuela and Peggy who was Japanese. We played a lot and life was good. Dad and Mom's best friends were Fred and Mary Smith. They had a son Fred Smith, Jr. who was the same age as my brother. We spent a lot of time at each other's homes, and we even took camping trips together. My parents loved to entertain. I remember the four of us – Michelle, Mark, Fred Jr. and me –on a staircase listening to the activity in the room below, trying to catch a peek of our parents drinking too much.

We attended a multi-racial church called Foresthill Christian Church. When I was about ten years old, my sister and I went away to summer church camp about 150 miles east of San Francisco in the hills of Auburn. We stayed for two weeks. This was the first time we had been away from home with strangers. Michelle and I couldn't sleep in the same cabin, because we were different ages. She checked on me constantly, making sure that I was okay. This made me feel a little safer. The cottage slept ten camp members, with cot beds lining both sides. The floor was wood planks. This camp was one of the highlights of my childhood. I also had occasion to remember it when I slept in a similar cottage in a South American jungle community 15 years later.

Chapter 3:
And Times, They Are a Changing

Separation? Why would our parents separate? Mom had stayed home, attended every school event any of us had, and in every way seemed like a happy housewife. The evening routine in our house was the same: Mom had a martini ready for Dad when he walked through the front door, and smiling, he in turn gave us candy bars. Mom prepared dinner every night to be served at the same time. They might have argued in front of us twice.

Mom, God rest her soul, was the higher strung of the two. Our father was low-key, mellow. When he moved out, it was as if he never left. This separation was amicable. No yelling, no name calling, it appeared as if they had just both agreed. Even years later I would not know what transpired to lead them to divorce. Dad moved into a high rise apartment near Cathedral Towers in San Francisco, not far away from us. We saw him every weekend.

The first few weekends after he left, Dad picked us up to take us swimming at the Marin County Country Club. We were three children of color, but – as is the case with most children – we did not recognize color. As I think back, I remember we were probably the only non-white ones in the pool. All of a sudden Dad stopped taking us to the Country Club. I believe it was because they asked him not to bring us. We were protected from racism, as it wasn't until years later I realized what had happened.

We stayed at the house for another year and then moved to Acacia Lane in Santa Rosa, a small college town about 40 miles north of San

Francisco. My mother started a personal care home which provided income and allowed her to still be home when we got out after school. My mother was an excellent mom. Mark was still young, a quiet, shy child, and did what a boy did. He spent a lot of time with our father.

Located at the bottom of the road, our house was surrounded by fields. Next door was a horse barn. I loved horses. Eventually we met the owners, who taught all of us how to ride. Even my young brother learned how to ride a Shetland pony. They were so cool. Whenever I saw them go out to feed and care for the horses, I would jump the fences and head over. Eventually they allowed me to ride alone. A friend of mine named Tara had a horse too, and I would ride to her house to pick her up. We would ride together, racing up and down the fields. I rode so often, I became comfortable enough to go bareback. We spent many hours in the fields, jumping the horses. I was eleven years old and happy.

Michelle had become a teenager and was very rebellious. Mom did not like her new friends. They were straggly-looking and looked like trouble. Michelle became more defiant, and out of control. I had no idea what "drugs" were, but I overheard Mom talking about my sister's use of them. Eventually she ended up in Juvenile Hall for running away, stealing Mom's car and wrecking it. When she came home, we had a family therapist come to the home to lead counseling sessions.

One night, I heard a whimpering coming from my mother's room. I knocked, but she did not answer. The door was unlocked and I slowly opened it. What I saw made my heart wrench. My mother was sitting on her couch, her face buried in her hands, weeping. My heart went out to her, and I quietly cussed at my sister. There was nothing I could do but go to her and kneel down to wrap my arms around her. I told her everything would be all right. The truth was, though, Mom had no control over this child who was bent on self-destruction.

My parents, especially my mother, gave more to her than she did to me. I did not need what Michelle did, but still I often felt as if I came last, that I didn't have the place that she did in the family. I spent a lot of time with friends away from the house. I realize now that Michelle never saw herself as beautiful or special. She sank deeper into the drug scene, which in the late 60's meant mescaline, acid, and weed. I truly believe my sister was bipolar, something which was not diagnosed back then.

The Vietnam War was in full force, and songs of protest, rebellion and defiance rang out. Credence Clearwater Revival, Crosby, Stills, & Nash, Janis Joplin, these were the artists we listened to. One Saturday I attended a peace march with my friend Doreen Dornbush. Hundreds of people, many of them college students, showed up. As we marched in our halter tops, love beads, and jeans, we held hands, lifting them to the sky and joined with the marchers in singing the John Lennon anthem, "All we are Saying, Is Give Peace a Chance." Chills ran down my spine as I listened to the hundreds of voices in unison, singing this powerful song. We were losing hundreds of American soldiers in a war we should never have waged. It felt wonderful to be a part of something so important, and I felt like I was doing something to help bring the war to an end.

With my mother's attention focused on my sister's problems, I had a lot of unsupervised time. One of my friends used to hitchhike everywhere, and I remember going up to the Russian River, because there was a big party there. That's where I had my introduction to wine. A wine flask was passed around, and I began to guzzle. I ended up passing out in the river. A dude pulled me out. I slept it off on the beach and awoke, untouched and unscathed. God was watching over me. I was not even twelve years old yet.

Finally I tried the "run-away game." My friend Carol and I took off with no idea where we were headed. We just wanted to be gone. I was in seventh grade and had started cutting classes, forging my mother's signature on doctor's excuses and requests to leave school early. Carol and I ended up over at some friend's house in a barn. Finally, we called my mother, who told me to come home. I told her where we were, and she came and picked us up.

The following week, Mom gave me a choice: Sacred Heart All Girls School in Texas, or back to Sacramento to live with Grandma and Grandpa. I chose Sacramento. Unlike my previous time with them, though, my poor grandparents were in for a challenge. I loved my grandparents – they were sweet and kind – but they ran a very strict house. I moved to Sacramento during the summer to start the new school year in a fresh place. We attended church all day on Sunday. Shiloh Baptist Church became my life.

I attended Fern Bacon Junior High School, in Sacramento. Middle school years are often ones of turmoil, but the brawls that took place in these years weren't personal. They were racial. Chicano students squared off against the Blacks, except when the two minorities joined together to fight as one against whites. Despite the number of food fights in the lunchroom, I managed to stay clear of them. Part of that is due to a friend named Jeannie, who took me under her wing.

But there was something else. Growing up in an interracial family made it difficult to choose just one side over the other. I realized I had problems with the "I hate whitey" call. That was like announcing that I hated my father because he was white. It disowned half of who my brother Mark was. It was declaring that I hated all the people I grew up with because they were not my color. So I refused to form alliances. My friends were Mexican, black and white. It actually worked out. Maybe I was the diplomatic representative of "all one under the sight of God."

My year in Sacramento came to an end, and it was time for me to go back to Santa Rosa as a new and reborn child. When I walked in the door, my mother gasped, not expecting that I could have grown so much. I was fully developed now.

Michelle was still giving Mom problems. One of her friends told her about a place called Peoples Temple which had a drug treatment center for teenagers. My mother thought it was just my sister who needed help. Although I wasn't really interested in drugs, I loved the adventure of my first real feelings of independence and freedom.

Chapter 4:
Redwood Valley, Here We Come

What caught my eye when my mother, sister, brother and I entered the Peoples Temple sanctuary for the first time that Saturday night was the swimming pool at the back of the church. It created an echo and provided the humidity. The service began with a man in dark hair and sunglasses speaking about injustice and the inequality in the world. This went on for some time. Eventually the subject changed to "church business." Two names were called out, and two people – a husband and wife – headed towards the pulpit. The ensuing conversation escalated quickly into name-calling and arguing. People began crying out horrible things to them. Voices were being raised and yet, I still had no idea what they were so upset about. It was after midnight, and most of the folks in the congregation were fighting to stay awake, but this was not a problem for me.

The entire scene was out of a movie. There was so much action, screaming, crying. The minister – Jim Jones – yelled at the man, and the woman joined in. He was called a traitor. A traitor to what? The word "cause" was also bandied about, but still it did not mean anything to me. Cause? What cause? However confusing it was, it was still interesting. It finally came to an end around 1:30 in the morning. Never had I attended a church with so much action.

That night we stayed with one of the members of the church. Barbara Flowers would eventually play a special part in my life. The next morning, after being served a hearty breakfast, we headed back to church for Sunday services.

Although tired from the night before, I was anxious to return to some of the same excitement I had experienced the night before, but when we arrived, the atmosphere had changed. Gone was the electric static of anger and emotion, replaced by what appeared to be a gospel choir and band, and Jim Jones wearing a traditional pastor's robe. As was the case the previous night, though, the audience was made up of many colors, but there were many more of them. A bus had arrived from San Francisco, bringing people who filled the church almost to capacity. There were seniors, young people, older adults and children. They were black, white, Mexican, and Native American. Folding chairs were brought in and lined next to the back of the wall that separated the indoor pool from the the rest of the church. The choir sang high volume gospel, and the people joined in, singing and holding up their arms in the air. Afterwards, a white woman – Marceline Jones, Jim's wife – started singing "My Little Black Baby," a slow melody about a black child. Tears ran down her face as she sang, and many in the audience were crying too. When the song ended, she motioned for someone to come up with her. A tall black boy walked up to her and kissed her cheek. She introduced him as Jimmy Jones, Jr. Oh, I thought, the song is about him. Mrs. Jones explained that she and Jim had adopted this child. The lanky kid was tall for his age and the color of milk chocolate.

My family traveled to Redwood Valley throughout the year to attend Temple services, and in the winter of 1970, we made the move. I was thirteen years old. Our station wagon piled high, Michelle sat in the front seat with Mom, and Mark and I lay on a mattress in the back. I slept most of the way, awakening as we pulled up to a stucco house with a large picture window at the top of a hill. The inside of the house was much smaller than the ranch house we had left in Santa Rosa, but it would do. The backyard was quite large. There was also a cottage behind the house with a kitchen, living area, bedroom and bathroom. It was actually like a two-bedroom apartment.

I spent the first day in my new school finding my classes and feeling my way around. The school was one story, stretching out among several buildings. Behind the school was a vista of beautiful hills and mountains.

The school had very few kids of color, but that was no different than Santa Rosa. All of my friends in Santa Rosa had been white. Here, although none of the European kids spoke to me, a black girl with very short hair approached me and asked me who I was. I told her my name and then asked hers. "Sandi," she said and then added "Are you in the Church?" Confused, I asked her what she meant. "Do you go to Peoples Temple?" "Oh, yes," I responded. She then took me aside and told me that the Temple kids hung out together and didn't associate with kids who weren't in the church. This sounded a little strange to me, and I asked her why. "Jim said that we can only be with each other," Sandi said, "because the other kids are not like us." I still didn't understand but figured I would eventually figure out what she meant.

Michelle was enrolled in Ukiah High School, but when she came home the first day, she said she hated it. She also related the same type of experience I had: a student had come up to her and asked her who she was. We would later learn almost every student of color was a part of Peoples Temple. When they told Michelle what Sandi had told me, she replied that she would hang out with whomever she wanted. This was just like my sister, not following anyone's rules but her own.

Michelle was the same in other ways, too. Her boyfriend from Santa Rosa came up to see her, hanging out with us at the cottage. Mom probably didn't like it, but at least she knew where Michelle was. Whether or not she was still doing drugs I do not know. For some reason Michelle never went to the drug treatment center at the Temple's Ranch. The question was never brought up.

My mother made me attend the Temple's Youth Group meetings every Saturday afternoon, where I saw Sandi Cobb again. We became friends. Michelle came with me the first couple of times, but after that she somehow got out of it. The first discussions were with a few of the college students. Later it evolved into studying Socialism. This youth group was very different than the one I was used to at Forest Hills Christian Church. There we had picnics, went to movies, played tag football. In the Temple's Youth Group, our activities consisted of letter writing campaigns to Congressmen, Senators and judges to plead some political prisoner's case, or to help one of the temple members with a court case. The letter writing often lasted until the wee hours of the morning.

When I first heard the word – Socialism – I had no idea what it meant. Eventually grasping the concept, it made sense to me. Socialism meant that all humans were equal, wealth should be evenly distributed among everyone, not just a few, and everyone's needs would be met. There would be no more hunger, because food would be provided for all. What could be wrong with this?

Our weekly study group on the philosophy of Socialism included tests to check our knowledge. After the introductory class, we went on to Karl Marx' "Communist Manifesto," then to Chairman Mao Tse Tung and his theories. I became very well versed in Communism, Socialism and Christianity. Most children my age had no social consciousness, and the fact that I was in tune with a world outside my own filled me with pride. My thirst for knowledge made me feel as if my life would mean something.

The lessons from the youth group extended into the church sanctuary as well. Just as one of Jim's sermons might have been geared towards Communism, the next service would be geared towards Christianity. We were taught history which we had not learned in the school classroom. It was the first time I heard of blacks having a life before slavery, and it amazed me when Jim talked about my people as if he were not only deeply knowledgeable, but sympathetic. After all, he said, he was Native American, and his people had suffered inhumane treatment.

At this point in my life, I had not experienced racism. Living in Santa Rosa and being exposed to so much, I really did not even grasp that I was black. It was never a subject of discussion, not even brought to my attention.

Jim's constant talk of nuclear war was so prominent in my thinking that we wanted to be ready to defend the cause if needed. The youth participated in paramilitary training in the hills of Redwood Valley. We were taught to run, and tuck and roll. We also had karate lessons so we could protect ourselves. After all, we were the youth, and we had to be prepared. We were training for the ultimate day of destruction, which only we would survive. Jim told us continually about the cave which was stockpiled with supplies we would need to survive after the nuclear war. I was fourteen years old.

I soon learned about the "cause" which had so perplexed me that first night in the Temple: the "cause" came first, and everything else came after. If you had a family member who refused to join the church, it was expected that you would sever the relationship. Nevertheless, for some reason, my mother was not criticized or ostracized for maintaining her relationship with her parents, my wonderful grandparents. Grandma and Grandpa would sometimes come to visit from Sacramento and attend the church services. Grandpa was reserved; whatever he thought he would not voice in front of us. However different than his Baptist Church, I believe that he thought Peoples Temple was a good place. We certainly seemed happy, and that's what mattered to them. They were crucial parts of our lives even then, and because my mother never allowed that relationship to be severed – thank God – they would be my lifeline in coming years as they had been in the past.

High school became a place to complete our educational requirements, and that was it. Most of the other non-Temple students knew that we were in the church. We behaved, and were expected to complete our homework and maintain our grades. Participation in any extra-curricular activities was not allowed. There was no involvement in team sports, dances and proms. Actually, I had no desire to attend a prom, which I considered decadent and bourgeois. The only sport I had a talent for was tennis, and although I did not expect to be approved to play on the team, I did place a request, just in case. I was right. The request was denied, since it would take too much time away from the cause, and my talents were needed at the Temple. My father would play with me when he visited, and eventually I found another Temple member who was not only enthusiastic, but a very competent player. We continued for many years. To this day I regret that I could not compete, because I truly loved the sport and was quite good at it. There were many children such as myself who were not given the opportunity to participate on our high school sports teams.

Even as teenagers, though, we were allowed to travel during the summer on the Temple's road trips. They were never boring and offered us a chance to see the United States. As we traveled cross-country visiting different cities in Texas, Louisiana, Pennsylvania, and New York, the church would gather more flock.

It was one of these trips that I noticed Jim used a decoy. Jim told a congregation in Houston, Texas that he was getting death threats, and one of the security guards, a college student, played his double. He was quite convincing. The honor and duty of Jim's security was to die for him, "to protect the Savior of Mankind."

During our traveling evangelism we usually slept in sleeping bags on the floor, in the buildings where the meetings were held. Some of us slept on the buses, up in the luggage racks or in the aisles if seats were not available. The experience gave me the ability to sleep anywhere. Sometimes if we had contacts in a city we were visiting, people offered their homes, but that didn't happen often enough.

While traveling on the road we became accustomed to changing clothes on the buses. We learned how to dress without a peek of flesh showing, and how to wash up using pre-moistened cloths, but most often we would find a rest stop where we would freshen up before arriving in a new city. Food consisted mostly of sandwiches, but we packed snacks to last us during the trip. We would trade snacks, and once we arrived in a new city, we were allowed to visit a store once to replenish our foodstuffs. For a teenager, the trips were great. I remember the fun we had on the buses, from singing, to playing cards and whatever else you could do to pass the time.

One of the most memorable summer trips was our trip to Philadelphia, where we visited Father Divine's Peace Mission and met his widow, Mother Divine. There were about 200 of us on this trip. When we pulled in front of an apartment complex, we were greeted by smiling black women dressed in navy blue dresses, their heads covered in white scarves. The dorm we stayed in was clean and comfortable. As we enjoyed the hot showers and the warm rooms, we were instructed to rest before dinner. These women were so kind. Their entire spirit was filled with love and reminded me of faithful servants. It was obvious that they knew who they were and what their mission was. Their demeanor brought to my mind that they were humble servants of the Lord.

I took the opportunity to rest – to sleep – and then someone was gently shaking me, waking me up. My eyes opened to the smile of an older sister, who told me that dinner would be ready in 30 minutes. We rushed around the room, trying to iron our clothes with the portable iron someone was smart enough to pack. We freshened up two to a sink, dressing modestly. When our hostess returned, we descended a staircase, arriving in front of a double door. The door opened to reveal tables set with exquisite china and beautiful ice sculptures shaped as Swans. Never had I seen such splendor. The dinner was a five-course meal, and dessert was ice cream in the form of rose petals. It was so delicate I did not want to eat it. It was a fabulous feast fit for royalty, which was exactly as we were treated.

Jim sat next to Mother Divine at the head table, a picture of Father Divine on the wall looking down upon the both of them. I wondered what he would think. His image was that of a handsome black man, strong, burly, yet a gentler side showed through. This man had led masses and still after death had faithful followers.

The next day we were graciously invited to Mother Divine's home, called the Woodmont Estate. In contrast to the modest lifestyle of the Peace Mission's followers, her house was a mansion. Most of us were not allowed to see the inside of her home, but we were allowed to swim. A barbecue feast had been prepared for us and I remember thinking, these were the most hospitable people I had ever met. Later, we were led quietly and respectfully to a shrine for Father Divine.

After all this hospitality and special treatment, I was startled when our security came and told us we had to get on the buses. Mother Divine was not what Jim had thought she would be, and he was upset with her. In retrospect, I can imagine that Jim was inappropriate with her and she asked him to leave. Of course, anything that went wrong was always the fault of someone else, especially if they were an outsider.

Mother Divine was obviously everything Jim talked against. She was white, and all the followers were black. I also recalled the simplicity and modesty of the followers, and the opulence of the leader. The churches taking advantage of the poor, while the pastor lived well: this was a recurring theme in many of Jim's addresses back in Redwood Valley.

We returned to our living quarters in the Peace Mission and packed our belongings. We thanked the sisters, who were still kind, sweet, and humble. We left Philadelphia and traveled a few hours to Washington, DC. Our service there was also packed as it had been all along our trip, but what I remember most was the unbearable heat. I was thinking that the advance crew had really distributed a lot of leaflets to get that kind of turnout, and how hot the work has been for them.

After returning home to Ukiah, I realized that this trip was enough to last me for a while. It would be a welcome routine to resume my daily responsibilities at the church. I also decided to get a job.

One of my first jobs was at the Ukiah Library. It was boring, and I lasted there about three months. When I spoke about it with my high counselor, she lined me up for a job at the Ukiah Chamber of Commerce. My duties there were to answer the phones that barely rang, to open and distribute the mail, and to make copies on the mimeograph machine. After about two months of that, I again requested another position. My counselor sent me to interview with North Coast Opportunities, a non-profit agency which gave out food staples to the poor on certain days of his week. I became the receptionist. The mother of John Biddulph – a college student in the Temple – was my supervisor. She was very strict, but taught me skills that would help me survive in years to come. I worked four hours each afternoon. Minimum wage was $1.65. My first check went on clothes. Although we were often told that the people in the town disliked us, I felt the exact opposite. I was treated with respect and did not feel the prejudice which Jim warned would surround us. I kept the job through the rest of the school year.

During the summer, all the kids wanted to work at the pear sheds. It was not glamorous work – you stood on your feet sorting pears – but the money was good and you could pick a shift that would give you a break from attending so many church services. We had something to do at the church at least five days a week. Although no one would ever speak of that as a reason for working, it was a poorly-kept secret.

When I went to apply, I asked for the shift between 3 and 11 pm, and said I could work seven days a week! We were known to be responsible and hard working, so I shouldn't have been surprised to get the call. Still, I was ecstatic. They even let me have my requested shift. I loved it.

My first night there was exciting. We worked in a large warehouse facility with conveyer belts and a lot of noise. Our orientation included an education in good pears and bad pears. After all, it was our job to distinguish between the fruit presentable for the markets and those that were not.

Sandi Cobb got on that specific shift too, so we stood next to each other and talked into the night. It made the time go by fast. We never talked about the church, though. Father had warned the congregation more than once, never to talk about anything that went on in the church when outsiders were around. That's what we called those who were not members of Peoples Temple: "outsiders." So what do teenage girls talk about instead? The kids you don't like at school, the current music choice, and our all time favorite, Boys!

I had started dating Matthew. I was fifteen. Considered one of the most responsible young men in the church, Matthew was about three years older than me and very mature. He worked at the pear shed's earlier shift, as well as at the drive-in and the Hof Brau. He also owned a car. Months later he got into the Sheriff's Department. Everyone liked him, as he was the "youngest black man" on the rise. He became a youth minister. Somehow he and I were set up on a date, and although I found him crude at times, he had a maturity about him that I found attractive.

Sandi was dating another boy in the church and at times we would double date.

Joe Wilson was his best friend and ended up being one of mine. Joe was the type of person you could laugh with and talk with because he had such knowledge of the world outside the doors of the Temple. The women adored him – white women especially – and I guess he had a penchant for them. I really understood the meaning of friendship when I confided in him that I thought I was pregnant. He instructed me with great authority to "pee in a small jar" first thing in the morning, and he would meet me to pick it up. He had a lover who worked in the Health Department who could run a test for me. There was no one else I trusted with this information, and he promised me that my name would be kept in the strictest confidence. I believed him. Thank God the test was negative. My reputation was still intact.

At that time I was still living with my mom who had moved downtown into an apartment. We shared a room so my brother Mark could have his own room. I left my mother's house shortly after my sixteenth birthday. By that time, I felt I did not have to live under the rules of a parent. I had been three years in the church, and matured in many ways.

Sandi Cobb, by now my best friend, had the responsibility of taking care of her three younger siblings, while her mother worked in

San Francisco. Her brother attended college out of town. Two other sisters also attended college out of town. Sandi and I took care of the baby. Her mother would give us money for groceries and we would cook and care for the children. We were tenth graders in high school.

Taking care of a family at sixteen was not difficult for us. After all, we were not children but revolutionaries. When we traveled out of town, someone from the Temple would make sure the children got off to school okay. Since neither of us drove, we depended on fellow Temple members to get us from one place to another. Everyone helped everyone. It was a community.

After taking a break from summer traveling one year, I was ready to go again, and volunteered to be on the advance crew to Seattle, Washington. Since we were told Seattle was a Bible-touting city, we went through grueling hours of learning the Bible scriptures and lessons. I remember during one of these sessions which one of the youth pastors led, someone asked me when I got saved. I said, "When I was hit by a car at five, Jim saved me, even then." Everyone started laughing. I sat there with a blank look on my face. "What's so funny?" Mike interrupted the laughter to tell me that "saved" in the Christian sense meant to "profess that Jesus Christ is my Lord and Savior." "Oh," I said. "Now I understand."

On the way to Seattle, we spent our time preparing: learning more scripture, drilling each other on what to say if we got in a bind, what not to say, etc. By the time we arrived in Seattle, we thought we were ready. We stayed with a family who had space enough for the ten or so of us on this trip.

The feeling was one of joy and teamwork. We felt wonderful knowing that we were doing the work of Socialism, leading the masses to the real truth. All of us, black, white, working together, side by side, with the same mission. We had a message to bring to the world, that "God" truly meant us to live together as one, with no regard to color or social status. We were working for the rise of a new humanity, one that would give every person equal rights, freedom, and most of all, love.

It felt special to be on the advance crew. I was giving of myself. This is what we were taught, unselfishness. It meant you were living the right way and those other people's petty worries were not ours. We had moved to a higher level of consciousness, performing God's work.

I was proud to be a Socialist, not a victim of capitalism and greed, not caught up in a world where money meant everything. We had climbed above that, we knew how to make personal sacrifices. Even recalling that I had not been able to join the tennis team did not evoke bitterness within me. It appeared that I had more important work to do. I was being counted on to stand up against capitalism and to spread the word of humanity and love between all people. What greater work was there?

The first morning we got up early and hit the streets of Seattle. The city was very large, and the weather was very cold. We found a street corner and worked it. We stayed on those corners until it was clear we couldn't reach any more people. While we passed out literature, we also solicited donations, asking people to support the orphanage in Brazil. We spoke of the arrival of Jim Jones in Seattle at the end of the week, hailed him as a man of God who had been anointed by the Holy Ghost to live the life of Christ on earth, and testified to personal healings that had taken place. I used my accident in San Francisco as my testimony. It made me feel good that I could speak as a devout young woman.

The night of the meeting finally arrived. It coincided with the worse snowstorm in Seattle history. As people began to fill the auditorium, we received word that all the buses – including Jim's – were having problems getting through the snow. If Jim were all he said he was, though, how could he allow a little snow get in the way of a man who ignited a crowd by laying hands on a cripple and then they walked, who healed people of cancer by making them spit their growths from their bellies? Where was his power then? These thoughts were never spoken aloud, and I pushed them out of my head as soon as they came to mind. My fear was that Jim would hear them anyway, and then – I knew! – on the carpet I would go. I told myself that I was being negative. What I did not know was how many more had the same thoughts. And that truth would have set us free and would have awakened us to a horrible realization. It is amazing how you can actually talk yourself into something even though your heart may be telling you something completely different.

About an hour after the meeting was to start, the choir – of which I was a member – began to sing. We were able to get people on their feet and dancing for joy. As we sang, I began to shout as if I were in the church, as my grandmother did. It might have been put on at first, but also I felt a devotion and joy that was real. This little shout from a small teenage girl got the audience to forget about the delay and join in. The audience danced, sang, clapped and had a good time. Diane Wilkinson, whose voice would send you crying to your knees, sang as if all of our lives depended on it.

Jim finally arrived about fifteen minutes after my performance. After the meeting, he motioned me to him. I was nervous as I approached, but he said, "I heard what you did. You are my little Angela Davis for the cause of Socialism!" I felt as if I had been given a Nobel Peace Prize. Whatever it takes for the cause of Socialism, I thought. I beamed so much joy that I thought I would burst. After that, my dedication to the church was more concentrated. Although we were young – and we listened to music, went to the drive-in, and dated – my life looked different.

The choir of which I was a part was the smaller of the two in the church, consisting of approximately ten singers who had strong voices. This was the choir that made the Temple's album, *He's Able*. The experience of this recording was unforgettable. The choir director rented a recording studio on the Sunset Strip in Los Angeles. We went to L.A. three days early and were in the studio, working every day, sometimes four to five hours. Each group – sopranos, second sopranos, and altos – laid their track. I sang alto. Afterwards, we put on headsets and listened to the previous recorded tracks and sang along. The blending was great.

Back in Ukiah, I was asked to be on the Testimonial Committee, along with Sandi and Andrea. Jim had begun referring to himself as Father. I had no idea what that meant, how blasphemous it was. After Jim performed each healing service, our job was to go the people that were touched and ask for permission to use their testimony in any way the church deemed appropriate. Feeling blessed by what they had just witnessed or experienced, all of them signed. Jim's healing touch became the most popular part of the church service.

One of my most vivid memories of that period was of a service in the Los Angeles Temple. A man was in a wheelchair. His hands and fingers were twisted. He appeared to be in extreme pain. Jim went into the audience towards the man and bent down to whisper in his ear. Tears began streaming down the gentlemen's face, and his body began racking with sobs. Jim was sharing something special with him, I thought, and my eyes filled with tears. Jim stood upright and told the audience that this man had been infected with syphilis which had had gone untreated for years, and the disease had rendered him crippled. It saddened me that America would allow someone to suffer this type of crippling because they were poor. Jim laid hands on this older man, praying for him and calling upon God to come in and touch him. He touched the man's back, neck, legs and hands. Music was playing in the background, and people reached their hands out to this man, praying for him to move. Jim challenged the man to stand up.... and slowly, that man began to rise. Jim kicked away the wheelchair and beckoned the man to come towards him. Taking little steps and crying, the man began to walk, slowly at first, but undeniably putting one leg in front of the other. The church was now in a frenzy, some people grabbed by the Holy Spirit began shouting. I had memories of my grandmother. As the music got louder, people began singing, clapping, and praising God, I stood in awe. The blessing of Father had brought joy and healing again. The feeling I had is indescribable; it was watching a miracle in action. The room was filled with a power, a power of prayer, anticipation, hope and love. Joy overcame everyone who witnessed this. To this day I can say only that I believe prayer works, that the power of hundreds praying their pure prayer together can cause the blind to see and the crippled to walk. How could a man so evil, turn away from what appeared to be so real? This is something that would take me years to understand. I still believe that when power of prayer and power of healing is in one place, it can move mountains. I believe that the universe has given special gifts, gifts of healing and gifts of destruction. It is difficult to comprehend that these did not take place, and I will not say they did not.

There were many instances of healing. Whether Jim had a gift or not, I will never know. What I can testify to is my own witness of many people, pushing back wheelchairs and walking. They believed. Jim would reveal things to them that they only knew (or so we thought). This is all I can contribute to this subject. Whatever Jim became in Jonestown, the power that he presented in the United States was mighty, and it made people believe they could receive a miracle. My belief in the Universe, the God within us, the I AM, and the power of prayer still believes that all things are possible. They indeed expected a miracle and, I believe, were provided with one.

On Sundays in Redwood Valley, there would be a grand feast after church service. People would bring different dishes as they had been assigned. I was on the serving committee, and we would bring food from the kitchen and place it on the tables for everyone to eat. This was during the time that people could still fit into the church. Sundays was always a good time.

But Sunday was not the only day the church was in use. Catharsis sessions took place on Wednesday nights, but your prayer during those was that you did not do anything wrong to get called up on the carpet. Some Saturdays the church would be open for us to swim in. The pool still served as a place of baptism and recreation during the week.

Mr. Muggs lived in a cage on the property next to Jim's house. Everyone adored this funny-looking chimpanzee, but Joyce Touchette handled him more than anyone. After one service, she asked if I wanted to hold him. I was thrilled. I had a love for animals, and this chimp was very close to human. As she placed him in my arms, he shifted unexpectedly, and before I knew it, he bit me in the area between my thumb and second finger. I screamed and she grabbed him. I was rushed to the church where a nurse patched me up, and within hours I was at the hospital getting a tetanus shot. Good old Mr. Muggs.

About that time Jim told the congregation that he was beginning to receive death threats and that he might have to look at a car that would provide him more safety. I remember him mentioning a Mercedes. That struck me as strange because this was considered a very bourgeois car, and I thought we were against the mainstream, bourgeois idealism. I pushed that thought from me and decided if it meant his safety, then maybe he would have to look beyond the status symbol of the car.

The church in Redwood Valley was outgrowing itself. The greyhound buses which the church owned would drive up from San Francisco and fill the church to its capacity. Eventually the contingent from San Francisco was bigger than ours, and we reversed direction. At least twice a month, we would travel there. The church held its meetings at Benjamin Franklin Junior High School in the Fillmore District, the heart of the city's black community.

With this shift, the Youth Group began to form teams on Saturday mornings to travel into the inner city to pass out leaflets. I remember when we entered a project called "The Pink Palace" in the Fillmore. The building was scribbled with graffiti in the elevators, and the powerful stench of old urine inside overwhelmed our nostrils. In teams of one female and one male, we passed out leaflets in the building, knocking on strangers' doors to share the wonders of the ministry. My testimony was that my sister had been on drugs, but after she was sent to rehab in Redwood Valley, she had been clean ever since. We were ministering to people of all ages, as old as my grandparents, as young as me. If we were not passing out literature, we were downtown on Market Street asking for donations for our missionary work. I often collected more than a hundred dollars, and not once did the thought of dipping into the till even cross my mind. I would happily turn over the money, since it was my declaration of faith in Father and the church.

As the following grew in San Francisco, Jim began talking about purchasing a permanent place of residence to call our own. It was referred to as "the San Francisco Temple." Located right on Geary Street, one block down from the junior high school which we had leased for meetings, the building seemed to become officially ours with the erection of the sign "Peoples Temple."

The Fillmore was also the home of the Islamic Temple of the Nation of Islam, two doors down from us. During this time, the Nation of Islam practiced Black Nationalism, which Jim spoke of many times. It was not a friendly relationship. The Brothers at the Mosque Temple looked at us as sellouts. Here we were following a "White Man." Most of the time we tried to stay clear of them.

Our new facility was huge. Communes had already been started in Redwood Valley, but this church would house not only Jim Jones and his family, but members of the planning commission, the finance department – most of whom were on the Planning Commission – and other key members. Rooms were converted into living areas and three meals a day were served there. It had become the nucleus of the operations of the church.

We also acquired a church on Alvarado in Los Angeles, and the congregation had begun to grow there as well. Sundays were packed. I did not participate in passing out leaflets in Los Angeles, but there were crews which worked the streets there as we had done in the San Francisco. Nevertheless, I believe more of the marketing was done via word of mouth and radio broadcasts.

No matter who we were in the Temple, we were instructed to always carry a form of identification. The church might have had a reputation as a growing institution, but the reputation of the Los Angeles Police Department – its racism matched only by its brutality – was even better known than ours.

Chapter 5:
The Teacher
and Lover

Matthew and I dated for more than a year before we broke up. We didn't speak for about a month. In the meantime, Joe was working at the Ranch and used to come by and hang out at my mom's house. My mother had moved to a two-bedroom house in Redwood Valley right down the road from the Ranch, and I had returned home when I was seventeen. She and I shared a bedroom, so my brother Mark could have the second to himself. My mother liked Joe, and he would come by often.

The Ranch served as a drug rehab center. Joe would tell us of the people going cold turkey. He described in detail the vomiting, sweating, screaming. He used to sit with some of those coming off. Those who really knew Joe liked him, but he had such a bad reputation.

Before one of the biweekly bus trips to Los Angeles, Joe called to see if I wanted to go to a movie while we were there. I looked forward to it, because Joe was always so much fun. After the church service, we caught a bus downtown to the theater. When the movie began, I was shocked. *Felix the Cat* was not the children's cartoon I was expecting, but rather animated pornography. Instead of getting up and leaving, I laughed nervously through it, but felt very embarrassed. Pretty soon I feel Joe's arm circle around my neck. I really did not know what to do. Matthew was the only boy I had ever been with, and I was trying to figure out if this was cool or not. Naive was my middle name, and Joe was a well-traveled veteran.

After the movie, Joe and I caught the bus back to my church apartment. I rattled on nervously, and as always he listened. I kept telling myself that Joe was my best friend, my ace in the hole. Even then I realized that this was going to be a difficult situation. We got off the bus, and he walked me into the apartment complex. In the hallway, I told him goodnight, but he leaned in and kissed me. The bad part was that I responded to his kiss. I was so confused, but because it felt good, my knees weakened and my head spun. Oh, no! What was going on? He certainly couldn't like me in that way. Panicking, I broke loose and scurried into the apartment. My face was noticeably flushed, and my friends asked me what happened. I could only whisper, "Joe kissed me." They started jumping up and down, screaming. "Joe Wilson has the worst reputation," they told me, "you know how bad he is." But I couldn't hear them. I still felt his soft but firm lips on mine.

The next day when I saw Joe at church, I was slightly embarrassed. When he asked me to sit with him on the way back to Redwood Valley I just nodded. From then on we were the couple of conversation. No one could stop us. My mother – who liked him well enough as long as he was not with one of her daughters – was very upset, and in the months that followed, my relationship with my mother deteriorated even as Joe's and mine became stronger.

Six months after my seventeenth birthday, I moved in with Joe. Home was now a single trailer in downtown Ukiah, with a tiny bathroom that would greet you with an electrical shock when you touched anything in it. We slept on a single chair that pulled out into a bed. I had a car and a job, and continued to go to high school. Joe worked odd jobs and worked at the ranch. We ate Kraft Macaroni and Cheese, four for a dollar. I cooked for him and he ironed my clothes for me. I was happy. We were in love.

On the next Temple summer trip, we went to Atlanta, Georgia, Joe's birthplace. We had a meeting in the Martin Luther King Center for Non-Violent Change. We only got to see a small portion of Atlanta, the place Joe used to call home. As we traveled down Auburn Boulevard, I tried to imagine what life was like during Jim Crow, and what exactly integration has accomplished. When we went down to the street that housed black businesses, I wondered if integration had helped or did it add to the detriment of black-owned businesses. Why did people stop supporting their own? This would be a question which would remain with me years later. But the underlying issue of being discriminated against because of color was something I could not grasp. It made me appreciate the church even more, because we were color blind.

I had learned that Joe had a temper, but during this trip, he was fighting more than usual. It seemed like every time I turned around he had his fists just about in someone's face. I did everything I could to try to talk him down. He would get so upset, and then he would want to fight.

After we returned to Ukiah, Joe resumed working at the ranch. He also worked part-time at Masonite Corporation, the largest employer in Ukiah, and struggled to get on permanent. Somehow Joe was also put in charge of scheduling the security shifts at the church. We all had to participate.

One day would make me mature more quickly than I wanted to. When I arrived home one day after school, one of our neighbors, who was also a church member, said Joe had been rushed to the hospital where he was in the suicide ward. He had taken an overdose of pills. I remember feeling as if my life was coming to an end. I called Michelle, who picked me up and took me to Ukiah General Hospital. When I looked at him, his eyes filled with tears. "I am so sorry, I couldn't take it anymore," he said, and then I found out what had troubled him so much. My mother had threatened him with statutory rape. Joe was 20, and I was 17. Joe had kept a lot from me, but he was also catching a lot of grief for being with me. He was my protector. This was kept very quiet. After his 72 hours of observation ended, our friend Keith and I went to pick him up from the hospital. We never spoke of it again.

Following Joe's release from the hospital, we felt we needed a change. We moved a little further out of Ukiah into a small two-bedroom house with hardwood floors. It seemed to be made just for us and our little extended family. Keith, who had been staying with us at the trailer off and on for a while, came along. He was working at a dental clinic training to be a dental assistant. Later Chris joined us. Joe told me Chris had been sleeping in the church. I never asked why. Joe was always helping someone, and our house was always open to whoever needed it.

My family now had four people in it: me, Joe, Keith and Chris. We all worked and went to school, except Joe. During the summer, the house had been extremely warm, but during the winter, we slept in our clothes and heated pots of water on the stove to get the house – or at least the kitchen – warm. To help pay the rent, Joe would go out in the wee hours of the morning and milk goats. He asked the three of us to help. Milk goats, I thought? I was not a country girl. But our love for Joe made us place our city attitude aside.

This was a particular long and cold winter. The first morning he got us up, it was freezing outside. Snow was on the ground. We piled on clothes and marched out to the barn. Joe showed us how to grasp the udders and get the milk. We were out of our element, but we tried. He also told us to stay away from the back of the goat because it could kick the heck out of us. And sure enough, I moved behind the goat and wham! She threw her hind legs up and landed one on my shin. I screamed out in pain. Joe told me to go on inside and put some ice on it. I bent down to the ground and grabbed a handful of snow. The stinging and subsequent bruise hurt a lot. My leg turned black and blue in no time, and Joe, loving me as he did, told me my goat-milking days were over. I was relieved, because to tell the truth, that one morning was enough for me.

Since we did not have a car and there were no buses that ran by us, we had to depend on other people for rides. We did not have a problem assisting others or – for that matter – asking others for assistance. We were all expected to and did so without regret. It made us feel good to help. After all we were family.

One day, I decided to paint the bathroom. And not just any color, but I chose dark brown. At a Temple meeting soon after, Jim called me up on the floor to ask what got into me, to paint a bathroom dark brown. I told him it needed painting, and it was the cheapest paint the store had. He had to laugh, because my intentions were right. The landlord did not care too much for the color, and left express instructions for Jim that when we moved I would have to paint the bathroom white again.

Joe began having serious problems with his knee and had to travel to San Francisco to visit an orthopedic doctor there. The fluid constantly building up on his knee caused problems for him, even to walk. When he came home from one of his visits, he told us that he had to have surgery. We were stunned and scared because we were so dependent upon Joe.

About a month later, Joe traveled to San Francisco for his surgery. I was still in high school and holding down two jobs: the same receptionist job at North Coast Opportunities, and also at McDonald's after work, from 5:00 to closing. Keith had graduated but was working at the Dental Clinic full time. He and I decided that we did not want Joe to have to keep milking goats every morning, and the only way to do that was to find a new place for us to live. Our love for Joe was very deep. He was the head of our family, our rock. We needed him, and we depended on him. He was there always for us and anyone else that needed help. Joe provided an incredible force of love and light. Past the tough exterior was a real man, one who knew how to love and give. He was the quiet in the storm, the encourager.

Keith and I searched until we found a new apartment building for $190 per month. It had burnt orange carpet, two bedrooms, and one bath. We applied for the apartment and they gave us the okay. Chris, Keith, and I were so excited. It was special and it was for Joe.

When Joe called to say he was coming home, we gave him directions to a new address to come home to. We asked how he would get home from the Greyhound station in Ukiah, and he said not to worry. He was always so independent. About fifteen minutes passed before the doorbell rang. There he was standing at the door on crutches, with his suitcase tied around his neck with his belt. This was the man I fell in love with, the strong, can do, and didn't complain kind of man. He was wonderful. I cried when I saw him, cried because of his never-ending strength and cried because I was so happy to have him home. My love for Joe was enough to turn my back on anyone who opposed us. This man taught me to be strong, and showed me the importance of sheer will and determination. This man stood up and meant what he said.

Due to all of the work credits I accumulated from my two jobs, I was scheduled to graduate early in January 1975. My father sent me $100 to buy my graduation dress. While in San Francisco for the church services, I traveled to my favorite store, Casual Corner, and found a black knit long dress, buttoned down the front, with gold trim and gold buttons. I loved that dress. My father came to the graduation, but would not come into the house. Even then he had an aversion to Joe. Dad never explained why, but as time went on I assumed it was because Joe was so dark complexioned. He thought I should marry white as my mother and sister did. Joe also attended my graduation, but stayed clear of my father.

At Wednesday night catharsis about a week after graduation, I was called to the floor. The charge was purchasing the dress. I was asked about the cost of the dress. I answered honestly, because Father had powers and he would know how much it cost anyway. Once I admitted I had spent $100, I was called a capitalist, materialistic and bourgeois.

The confrontation had been brewing for a while. My mother had warned me about the clothes I had. Someone had told her that I appeared to spend a lot of time on my appearance. Not heeding her warning, I continued to shop and had more fashionable clothes than most my age in the church. But my comrades informed me that I had spent the money frivolously, wasted it, that it could have gone to a better cause. When I told them my father had given me the money as a graduation present, they replied that I still did not have to spend that much. I could have purchased a less expensive dress and given the remainder of the money to the cause. Knowing I was beat, I apologized. My punishment was to turn the dress in so that it could be sold at the thrift store run by the church.

I was angry and hurt, not only because of the dress, but also because someone had snitched on me. And the only one knew about the dress was my best friend Sandi. I felt betrayed.

During this time in my life, the only people I associated with closely were Joe, Keith and Chris. I had outgrown my childhood friends because I had broken all the "good girl" rules; living with a man, having sex out of wedlock and asserting my independence. What I still wonder about was why Joe and I were allowed to live together. We continued to pull our weight at the church, but we had a lot of freedom.

Joe and I traveled to San Francisco one weekend to meet Eddie Crenshaw and his girl (later to be his wife) Francine. We all went to a place called the Soul Train Club on Broadway. It was there that I had a Pina Colada – my first drink – and saw Chaka Khan and Rufus and the original Whispers. Never had I had so much fun. I kept telling Joe we were going to get in trouble, but he told me not to worry, that no one would know. And he was right. Apparently, no one ever found out.

Two weeks after high school graduation I turned the magical age of 18. Joe and I could now get married without parental consent. One night Joe called me into the bedroom and told me he had something to tell me. He began by saying that he loved me, but because I was now at the age that I could legally marry, he wanted to come clean. As he held my hand, he quietly and gently confessed to affairs he had been having with two other women. A numbness came over me and deep pain followed. I cried out and told him to leave. He tried to calm me down, but my heart felt as if it had been hit with a sledgehammer and shattered into a million tiny pieces. Immature as I was, I could not then appreciate the fact that he had been honest with me. He wanted me to make a decision based on the truth.

My world was suddenly crumbling. After he left, I swallowed about five of his pain pills. I lay on the bed, and as I was slowly drifting out, someone came into the room and found the bottle of pills next to the bed. I was shaken until I groggily opened my eyes. Joe and Keith pulled me into the shower and turned on a stream of cold water. They made me drink salt water to induce vomiting. Finally, wet and sick to my stomach, I was allowed to come out of the shower and lie on the bed. I had vomited as much as I could. Both stood guard throughout the night.

I called in sick from work for one week. Joe did not want to report this because he knew what damage it would do. But the incident did not deter me from the painful decision that I could not be with Joe anymore. I left the apartment and moved in with Sylvia Grubbs, a Temple member who was like a surrogate mother. She was honest and always had good things to say. Her gift was relating to young people.

During a trip to Los Angeles about two months later, I awoke one Sunday morning sick to my stomach and started vomiting. At first I thought that the hamburger from the night before must have given me food poisoning. Someone gave me saltine crackers and Seven-Up to settle my stomach. And then a friend of mine asked me if I could be pregnant. I angrily, emphatically denied it. A few days later back in Ukiah, I woke up one morning throwing up again. Sylvia, who arose every morning at 5:00 a.m. to apply meticulous, perfect makeup, heard me in the bathroom. Again the question: was I pregnant. "I don't think so," I told her, but I wasn't so sure anymore. My body did feel a little strange, and my breasts were beginning to hurt. My period was late by two months, but this was not unusual, as my cycle was never regular.

Sylvia worked at the Family Planning clinic and – as Joe had instructed when I had had the earlier pregnancy scare – told me to pee my first morning urine in a cup. When she came home from work that night, she gave me the news: yes, I was pregnant.

From that moment on, it was somewhat of a blur. I wanted my baby. Abortion never seemed a choice. My love for Joe had not wavered. I still loved him, but the pain of his infidelities was something I still could not handle at that young age.

My mother and I had not reconciled our relationship at this time, so my first boyfriend's mother Barbara asked me if I wanted to stay with her. We were very close and she supported me through this transition. She allowed me to cry as we talked about my pregnancy.

One evening during the Wednesday night Catharsis meeting, Jim called Joe and me up to the floor. Jim asked me point blank if I was pregnant. How could I think I could hide it from Father? I wondered. He knew everything! I told him I was. He then asked Joe if he wanted to marry me. Joe answered with a resounding NO! I lunged at him and hit him in the face. His nose instantly began to bleed. As he grabbed for me, security managed to restrain him. I ran quickly down the aisle, humiliated and ashamed. I humbled myself to go on.

Chapter 6:
And Now There Are Three

Lethargy. Depression. Anxiety. Anger. Not a wonderful combination for a pregnant mother. A few days after my confrontation with Joe, Barbara came to me and asked me if I still wanted him. I replied yes, I still loved him. Speaking with the wisdom of women who have been around a while, she told me what to do: Ignore him, she said. Well, that sounded easy enough. How could I not ignore him? He had just told the whole church that he did not want to marry me. But Barbara was right. One day, Joe approached me wanting to talk. I followed my wise woman's advice and ignored him. Pushing back my chair, I just rose up and walked away. He kept this up whenever he saw me, but I continued to act as if he did not exist. It actually worked. The more I ignored him, the more he pursued me. I was really getting a kick out of this. He really was chasing me! Oh, had the tables turned. Eventually, I began to feel sorry for him, and loaned him my ear. He professed his love for me, explaining that he was scared, but he loved me. He was still working at Masonite and could afford to maintain a family. It was then my arms went around his neck quickly and I hugged him. Within a matter of days, we had found an apartment on State Street. This is one man who did not procrastinate. Of course, he could have acted quickly out of fear of changing his mind, or concern that I would change mine.

We moved in our new apartment a couple of weeks later. The only furniture we owned was a twin bed. The apartment was upstairs from a Real Estate office, across the street from A& W's. There were four apartments set up like a quad, with two entrances on both sides of the building. The apartment had two bedrooms and one bath. The rent was $140 per month. It was really cute.

One day, Joe came home hauling a couch upstairs. I was ecstatic. "Where did you get this?" I asked, happy and looking at him with love and affection. "You know me, the hustler!" he responded. On his second trip up, he brought the love seat! A third trip, a coffee table. We were in the apartment for about one month, when he arrived with a king sized bed! So, we left the twin and moved into the master bedroom.

We were finally married in San Francisco Temple. Jim made a quick pronouncement. Tim Stoen, the church attorney, signed our marriage license. We were husband and wife. My Joe, I loved him more than life itself. Our relationship was like no other in the church. We were independent and strong. We took care of ourselves and had so many opportunities to leave the church. But we never spoke about it. Joe's parents would have taken us in, provided us airfare to get away, if we wanted, with just a phone call. We just never did. As I look back now, I realize how dedicated we were.

My belly was getting bigger and bigger. My grandparents were not happy about my pregnancy, nor was my mother. On one visit my grandparents bought us a used crib. Joe and I sanded it down and painted it blue. I knew this child would be a boy. As the pregnancy developed we readied our child's new room.

Young people from the Bay Area knew that Joe and I had the spot, where all the young people from out of town would stay. We had a stereo – yes, Joe hustled that up too – and played all the goodies: Earth, Wind & Fire, the Ohio Players, the Chilites, Blue Magic. We did not own a television. We were a young, dedicated and responsible couple. We had it going on.

I continued to work at North Coast Opportunities, which hired me full time after I finished high school. Joe worked swing at Masonite, from 3 to 11 p.m. When he got home, he had a hot dinner waiting on him. There was no more macaroni and cheese. With both of us were working, we had enough to have a nice amount of groceries. Joe's temper had waned or – more accurately – he had more control. He was a shift leader for security at the church and he handled that position well. One of my jobs was to call people and remind them of their security shift. I spent many nights with him, walking the grounds and talking. He would rub my belly and place his head in my lap to hear the movement of our child. There was no doubt in my mind that he would make a great father as he made such an excellent husband. I delighted in the glow of him.

My first trimester brought me a lot of morning sickness. My job was only about eight blocks away and I would walk the distance every morning. It did me good and kept me in shape.

One night while Joe was at work, I heard a loud knocking at the door. The man on the other side of the door was as upset as he was drunk. He banged and yelled that he knew I had someone in there. I called Joe's job and asked them to tell him that someone was trying to break into the house. The person at the other end of the line told me to call 911, which I did. About 15 minutes later, I heard someone yelling and falling down the stairs, as well as sirens in the background. When Joe unlocked the door, I fell into his arms. Shortly after, the police arrested the guy. Apparently, he had been knocking on the wrong door, thinking our apartment was that of the woman next door, and while she heard the commotion, she did not do a thing. She never said a word to me after that. She was a coward.

Joe and I attended Lamaze class together. I wanted my baby to be delivered under the water, but my doctor did not practice that procedure. Joe and I did a lot of reading about children. We thought we were prepared for our new arrival. I was looking forward to a natural childbirth, and since I knew I had a high tolerance of pain, I'd convinced myself that after the first labor pain I would be able to deal with the rest of them.

During the latter term of my pregnancy I went over to the house of Rheaviana Beam, a Temple member, so someone would be there with me when I went into labor. This lasted about two weeks, until one evening when my water broke. Joe came over immediately, and when he arrived, the dress I had on was soaked, and water kept coming out. I was scared. We went to the apartment for a change of clothes, but it was no use. I kept getting wet. He grabbed my bag and off we went, him driving like a madman.

The nurse led me to the delivery room while Joe lingered to fill out the paperwork. They undressed me, put on a hospital gown, and hooked me up to a monitor. The first labor pain struck about 11:20 that night. I can only tell you, the Lamaze had not helped at all. I tried to focus on one central point, but the pain was hard. Sweat broke on my forehead. At one point Joe was almost on the floor as I squeezed his hand. But he didn't say a word! That was my Joe, a trooper no matter what! I began screaming for him to get out! "Don't you ever touch me again!"? I remember saying that over and over.

My mother came about from San Francisco four hours later. She was a rock. Even though she did not approve of my pregnancy, she was there for me. She fed me ice chips and rubbed my forehead with a cool towel, and prepared me for the next contraction. Tears ran down her face as they ran down mine.

The labor lasted 23 hours. At one point, the nurse came in to check the monitor, and then suddenly wheeled to slam her fists into my stomach. I must have cussed at her and cried out. Hearing me scream, my mother came in to find out what was wrong. What was wrong was that my child's heart had stopped beating, and the nurse started it up again with that slam-dunk on my stomach.

The labor continued until the next night when the doctor finally recommended an emergency C-section. I was not dilating. The idea of a C-Section scared me; I was concerned more for my unborn child than me. Joe came to tell me what would happen next, but they had already sedated me and I was getting sleepy. When I emerged, Joe was at my side and told me what I already knew. We had a son. He then said they had named him Michael John Wilson. I screamed my protest. His name would be something that meant something. I found a name in a Swahili book I had found: Jakari. Our son's name would be Jakari Lafayette Wilson, and he would have would have the same initials and middle name as his father. My mother was a little disappointed, but Joe was relieved.

Jakari was voted the "Most Handsome Baby" in the hospital, but my suspicion was he was also the first black baby to be born there, hence the award. After a week in the hospital, I was finally allowed to go home.

My mother, who was working in San Francisco at Pacific Bell, had had to go back to work. Joe had to return to work at Masonite, where he was now on the graveyard shift. This was one job he did not want to lose. I spent my first night home by myself. But when I held my new son, it was heaven. I sat in an old rocking chair that Joe and I had found and that he had painted it for me. As I rocked this precious baby, my heartbeat accelerated with my overwhelming sense of fear that I could not protect him from all the pain in the world. I fell asleep with him in my arms, sitting in that rocking chair.

When my mother arrived two days later, I was nursing my baby. I was glad to see her. She made me rest when the baby rested. She cleaned the house and cooked for us. She'd been angry that I'd become pregnant so young, but she loved me and loved her grandson as if there had been no bad history between us. This was my mother.

After six weeks, I showed up at the church with my little black Baby. Everyone gasped and exclaimed. My old high school chums offered congratulations, but I did not think that they meant it. I had left them behind, and I now detected some envy and disgust.

One night, after I had put my baby to bed, a sharp pain began in the center of my stomach quickly knocked me to my knees. I crawled on the floor to the bed to reach the phone. I had to call Joe. This must be from the C-Section, I was thinking, or it wasn't, something terrible was wrong! I was gasping for air. The person at Masonite who answered the phone must have heard the stress in my voice, because Joe was home in about ten minutes. He wrapped Jakari up and took me to the emergency room.

The diagnosis was not life-threatening, but it had sure felt like it. My doctor found hundreds of tiny gallstones the size of sand pebbles. He had never seen so many gallstones in someone so young. The prognosis was good, but I would eventually have to have my gallbladder removed. In the meantime, I had to modify my diet to eliminate lettuce, cabbage, and all other roughage.

Joe's parents wanted us to come visit them in New Jersey for Christmas and bring their only grandchild home. We submitted the request to the Temple and it was approved. Our tickets were waiting at the airport. This was the first time I had been on a plane, and I was petrified. Our seat had a built-in bassinette attached to the wall in front of us. We were able to lay Jakari down when he slept. In retrospect, I almost marvel that we did not even think of leaving the church. We could have gone then.

We had a great time in New Jersey. Joe took me to a nightclub where we danced the night away. Like me, Joe loved to dance. We drank and had a great time. I did not want to leave. My mother-in-law took us shopping. And everyone wanted to hold Jakari, both of Joe's sisters were home, and of course, Joe's parents did all they could to spoil him. The only time Jakari got to cry was when Mama and Pops went to work. Mama would even change his diaper holding him. We stayed for two wonderful weeks and when it was time to go, I cried.

After returning home to California, my surgery was scheduled to remove the gallstones. Joe, who'd taken Jakari to Ukiah while I was convalescing from the surgery, called to tell me we would be moving to a commune with Jimmy and Alice Cooper. I settled in as best as I could. Our room was nice, and we still had a great relationship. But I was also worried about money. I had been laid off my job because they did not get the funding to keep me. Masonite was also cutting back, and Joe was not working there anymore. I helped Alice, but I was beginning to get bored. I spoke to Joe about moving to the city where I could find a job. My sister Michelle was working at the Hilton as a purchasing secretary, and she'd told me she could probably get me on. Joe agreed.

This was the beginning of my descent into hell.

Joe had agreed I could move to San Francisco, but he wanted to stay in Ukiah and he wanted to keep Jakari. Alice Cooper became his surrogate mother. I moved in with Michelle at Westlake Village in the Daly City area. She was really out there, and I believed that she was still using drugs. She and I did not see each other that much except for work. True to her word, she'd found me a job at the Hilton in the cashiering cage. I met a lot of people, and with that of course came more exposure to this outside world which the church had taught me could give us nothing but trouble.

Michelle took me out one night to a club called Dance Your Ass Off in North Beach. She was going to meet someone, but introduced me to the bouncer and told him to keep an eye out for me. He agreed, looking me up and down as if undressing me. She got me a drink, told me she would be back by 1:30 a.m, and left. I had no choice but to try to enjoy myself.

After that first night, I became a regular. I was only 19, but the bouncers all let me in. They were all Puerto Rican and Cuban, and they thought I was Puerto Rican even though I did not speak Spanish. The energy in that place made me forget about everything else. The room was huge, the disco ball glittered at the ceiling, the music pulsated through my blood, and I often felt I was in a trance. I was attractive enough for everyone to want me to join in the fun. I found that this was something I could have only imagined. The beat and rhythm of the music allowed me a freedom I had never known, and I became addicted to the nightlife. For years afterwards, dancing allowed me to escape my problems.

By this time, Jakari was living with me. Joe did come down on some weekends and stay. My mother lived in another part of the complex, but when she wasn't available to look after her grandson, I had a babysitter I could call upon while I was at work. Mom also took Jakari to Sacramento when she visited Grandma, and that would also give me a break. She loved her grandchildren. My sister's first child Dawynelle was staying with someone else in Redwood Valley. Both of us had given up our children at one time or another.

I didn't last long at the Hilton. My attendance was really bad – it just didn't seem important to show up – and I was soon fired for not reporting for work without calling. Money was not a problem, since the church had taught us to live with only our barest necessities. My mother would contribute when I needed extra, and even Michelle helped to support me.

My big sister was beautiful. Her life was carefree and without the hang-ups of what others thought. As far back as I can remember she did her own thing. She also had the personality to stand out above the rest. I will never understand her insecurities. She was giving to me, although she was jealous also.

Michelle had a boyfriend who took care of her. A member of the Temple, he worked in Los Angeles and also served on the Temple security team. He was older and he adored my sister. He used to come up and visit staying weekends. He bought her a green Camaro, and we suddenly had transportation. Michelle still hung out, but she still was more particular as her new boyfriend was very jealous. Of course this did not stop me. Later, I would find out that he had no problem putting his hands on another woman, but she hit back. She never won, but she would go down swinging. This wonderful trait must have been passed down through the strong women in our family, and I too would be tested in this very same way. As Joe was becoming more and more involved in the church, I was becoming more and more uninvolved.

Chapter 7:
The Tables
Had Turned

In an attempt to save our marriage – and to save me from myself – Joe moved down to San Francisco. As I found myself putting distance between me and the church, it appeared that Joe was given more responsibility, taking on major security assignments and becoming a part of Jim's entourage.

As Jim strategized his political career in San Francisco, we also hosted the Who Who's of San Francisco's political elite on a couple of occasions.

One particular time the church hosted a banquet. I was one of the young women chosen to serve our distinguished visitors. We were given lessons on how to serve their food and pour their beverages. That evening of the event the church of course was full to the brim, even the balcony - as all members knew attendance was mandatory. The talent of Peoples Temple performed. One of the highlights was the African Dance troupe; most of my friends were members. The visitors were always entertained, and I pretended that everything was fine.

By this time Peoples Temple was considered a political force in San Francisco. Hidden were the public beatings which consisted of boxing matches and spankings. My husband would sometimes be the aggressor and anyone who was called forth for this discipline knew better than to fight back - whether they were a physical match or not. Discipline would be handed down for small incidents such as falling asleep in church (even if you had worked a shift where you did not rest) or you made a comment to another church member that was considered negative. The public humiliations were hidden from the outside world. Those who touted the Peoples Temple as great, only saw what they were allowed to see – because behind those doors laid a dark secret of self - humiliation, an ongoing strategic plan to tear down self-esteem and incorporate intimidation in the name of Socialism!

Signing blank pieces of paper was normal, a sign of dedication to the cause. We were also instructed to write fake confessions incriminating ourselves in activities we never engaged in. All this done in the name of Jim's Socialism.

At some point I wondered why my mother was still involved in the church. The church as a whole did good work – providing legal counsel to those that could not afford it, healthcare services and community work – but the sinister side of Jim Jones was even more obvious then. My brother, Mark thank goodness was still spending court ordered weekends with my father – at least he had somewhat of a childhood.

Church meetings were becoming more frequent and of course the more services that you attended, the odds went up that you were going to be called on the carpet for any number of reasons. I learned to stay out of as many meetings as I could- using work as an excuse – I am sure there were many more attempting to do the same.

The church provided us with an apartment that it paid the rent on. However, the apartment also came with roaches. They would meet you at the door and crawl on you at night. We decided to move to the commune on Steiner Street. The little room held a set of bunk beds, a TV, and not much else. Jakari was with me and I felt better, but it still was not the same. I had a couple of lovers outside of my marriage by then, but my principal condition was boredom.

It was easy for me to get into the club called Streets of San Francisco on Mission Street, even though I wasn't 21. One night, I had just sat back down at a table with a woman friend after dancing and was having a drink. Fanning myself with a napkin and trying to cool off, I hear a voice near my ear ask, "Do you want to dance?" I smiled and turned, until I saw that the man standing there was my husband. My friend Becky's face reflected the fear I felt. Joe whispered, "Get your coat and let's go." He did not have to say it twice. He escorted us to the door and into the car with him. I was so embarrassed. At first I tried to figure out how he had found us, but as I thought about it, I realized that he had been out to party too, and had seen us. However he did it, I got the brunt of it when I got home. Joe never laid a hand on me. Sitting me down as he so often did and he asked me what I was trying to do. I told him we just wanted to dance. As he softened, and I lay in his lap while he shared how worried he was about me, telling me he did not want me out in the streets. Joe always made me feel loved.

However, I was trying to escape the church. Every time I set foot in the building, I felt as if I were living a lie and suffocating at the same time. Here I was 19, and it seemed as if my entire life was built around the organization. I was told when to eat, how to dress, and had to live two lives; one for the public and one for the church. Working in the outside world, lying about your life, I was exhausted of being controlled.

Finally, Joe got tired and moved out to another commune. He had a girlfriend, which he deserved. At that time I was so lost. When his mother and sister Toni said they wanted to come out for a visit, we had to pretend that we were still living together. All I was told was that we were going to have to pull this off.

We went to pick up Joe's mother and sister from the airport appearing to be a happy family. As we drove to the new apartment, my mind was racing, because I had to pretend that this apartment – where I had never been – was my home. I didn't even know where Joe was going. We pulled up in front of a four-story building on Fillmore, and Joe opened the car doors. He unlocked the front door of a big apartment complex, and I stood with Jakari waiting for his lead. He began to explain where everything was in this very nice old Victorian apartment. This was better than the one room in the commune, I thought. As we settled in, Joe left us to work the security night shift at the church. I was disappointed.

Maybe Jim had hopes that we would find our way back together, so he would not have to worry about me anymore. For the moment at least, we were a family again. Toni looked like a lighter-complexioned version of Joe. Their resemblance was amazing, and their closeness made it even more special. Joe truly adored his younger sibling.

Joe's mother and sister stayed for two weeks, and much of their visit included attending church services. After they departed, I stayed in the apartment. No one said anything, so neither did I. I stayed there for two or three months before I received the infamous call which would send me on another journey.

I had applied for a job at the Hyatt Regency Embarcadero as a PBX operator on the swing shift. As before, the reason I sought that timeslot was so I would not have to attend Wednesday night services. Unconsciously – or perhaps not – I was trying to pull myself out of the church. I admit it was only because I was not ready for all that responsibility at the time. I wanted to keep partying with all that freedom. I was the perfect example of what Jim always spoke about: a very self-centered young woman.

Still, my plan worked. Usually by the time I got off of work, the church meeting would have been ending or at least close to ending. The Hyatt Regency was one of those places always bursting with business. A four-star hotel, their guest list included many celebrities, and almost all their messages – the calls for all departments and guests – came through the PBX room

At work one night I received a call from a Temple member named Emmett saying Jim wanted to see me. Even though this was the infamous Wednesday catharsis night session, I didn't think Joe would get up there and knock the daylights out of me in front of everyone. Still, my friend Becky had warned me that people in the church had been talking about me and my lack of participation.

I told Emmett that I could not leave my job. He replied they would come and get me. I told him to do what he had to do, but they could not drag me from my job. Now I was really rebelling. If they did not know before, they knew then that they had a problem. I was away from Joe, away from the church, even away from Jakari. I missed my son, but at this time in my life, I felt he was better off without me. I wasn't much of a Socialist.

While working at the Hyatt, I had met a young woman about my age, a single mother of a mixed child, black and Filipino. She had a one-bedroom apartment in the Mission District. We immediately clicked and a friendship developed. She began taking me out with her to all kinds of clubs. She was a girl after my own heart. And we had fun. She introduced me to Bacardi 151.

One night after work we went to a club, where we met a man with a Jamaican accent. Carlos sat with us, bought all of our drinks, and even sent us home in a cab which he paid for. I was smitten by him and gave him my phone number at work. The next night he called and asked if he could pick me up for dinner. Of course, I agreed. He showed up at my job in a limousine. We went into Chinatown. He was so articulate and well-mannered, suave, tall and dark, very attractive in a rugged way. He told me that he traveled the world and he owned an Import/Export business. This was fascinating, I thought. He was someone who – among other things – could get me out of the church. He dropped me at the apartment, said good night and returned to the car.

Carlos called the next night inviting me and my friend Karen to join him and a friend of his. So, after work at 11:30 PM. we walked out of the Hyatt Regency, looking for our dates. And there they were. We couldn't wait for this night to begin.

Once we were in the back of the limo, Carlos pulled out this little package. He opened it, dipped a corner of a card inside and pulled out some white powder. He carefully placed it near his nostril and sniffed. The look on his face made me laugh. His face just lit up, his eyes were brighter. After he serviced the other nostril, he beckoned me to follow his lead. I asked him what it was. "Happy powder," he said with a smile. Being the adventurer that I was, I let him put the powder close to my noise, and blew. The stuff flew all over the place, a lot of it on Karen and her new friend, some of it on the floor. Carlos looked at me in pure shock. "No, hon, yah got to do it like thes," he said, and showed me again. This time I sniffed the right way, into one nostril and then the other. And then I felt my head open up. This surge of energy went through my body, and everything looked brighter. I felt light, happy, and exactly where I wanted to be.

Karen was waiting her turn. She was obviously not new to this and understood the value of this happy powder. When we had all taken turns again, the limo stopped at a club, and we were all ready to move. The beats were loud and my heart began racing. This is the kind of life I wanted, a constant party where I did not have to think or remember.

As we all danced, laughed and drank all night, I felt as if I had arrived. To what, I had no idea, just that this was the greatest. Carlos motioned for us to take the powder and go in the bathroom for another blast. We did. Karen was feeling no pain and neither was I. We finally left the club about 1:30 and headed for Karen's place. There was a danger about him, a mystery, just as I had a mystery about me. These people didn't know who I was or where I had come from, and I didn't know about them, and no one cared.

I got a call at call from Carlos the next evening about seven o'clock. He wanted to see me again that night, telling me he would only be in San Francisco for another couple of days. At 11:00 p.m., as I hurried to meet him outside, I had no idea what I was in for. We went to get Chinese take-out and ended up in his hotel room. I was surprised. The location was not the Hyatt, or even like the Hyatt. It was sparse and located on an alley, deep in Chinatown. As he opened the door, I told him I had to use the bathroom. As he pointed to the door, he told me to leave the door open. As weird as it was, I did as I was told. On the back of the toilet was a big clear plastic bag with a lot of white powder in it. I didn't ask any questions when I came back out, but I could tell from his expressions that he was little suspicious. I didn't know why. We were intimate together and afterwards we fell asleep. When I woke up he was gone. On the dresser was a note with his Los Angeles phone number and address. Beside the note were that little white envelope and two one-hundred dollar bills. I knew that I would never see him again. It wasn't until years later that I realized what the import/export business was, and why his passport was stamped in and out of Columbia so often. Of course, my guardian angel was looking out after me because I had been in the company of an international drug smuggler who had hundreds of thousands of dollars worth of cocaine sitting on the back of a toilet.

The package he gave me contained "happy powder" which lasted Karen and me for more than a month. We had really become close friends, and not just because of the cocaine. She was another version of me. My life was really beginning to change.

By that time, I did not want anything else to do with the church. I didn't disown it, I had just lost interest. My agony was over Jakari. I knew that Joe would never let me have him, but being totally off of the path of Socialism and the Cause, I also felt Jakari was with better people than me. I was living a lifestyle that went against everything I was raised to be. I had become a traitor.

Smoking reefer went along with this new lifestyle. The turning point came when I went on break one night and went out to smoke some reefer with a guy I thought I knew. I took a couple of drags, but I didn't feel much at first. When I headed back to my department, I felt this weirdness comes over me. I felt dizzy. I made it back into the telephone room, and even though the room was spinning, I found my seat. My supervisor asks if I was all right. I told him I felt sick and then slipped out of my chair. I heard someone scream, but I don't think it was me. There was no time between the space I was in and the distance I seemed to have traveled. I heard a paramedic ask where my purse was. My senses were clear. I could hear but I could not speak. When they lifted me onto the stretcher, I thought I heard someone mention suicide. Hell, no, I wanted to say. Kill myself, and float out there for an undeterminably amount of time? Not me! Before I knew it, we were headed out the front door of the Hyatt.

When they placed me in the ambulance, I thought I heard someone say, "Take the long way." Was I hearing correctly? Soon enough, the guy in the back said, "Look at these big mamma's." I felt his hands slide under my sweater and to my breasts. I began to panic, but I could not move. I felt paralyzed. I felt a hand slide up my skirt and pull down my pantyhose, and I knew what was next. He was going to rape me. His fingers entered me roughly. "My God," I thought, feeling the tears streaming down my face. He probed within me for a while. I could feel his breath on my chest, as he rubbed my breast with one hand, pulling my nipple. He pulled my skirt over my waist and I felt his weight on me. As one hand spread my legs, the other rammed his penis inside me. The force was so great that it pushed me further up the gurney. He was forcing himself in me and all the while asking me how I liked it. I was scared. He pounded away at me for a while, while the driver told him to save some for him.

The ambulance pulled to the side of the road, and I heard the door open. The first guy got off, and the driver traded places with him. His breath was on my neck, as he whispered that I was going to enjoy this. He felt bigger than the other guy, and as he shoved himself in me, he had more stamina. The tears still ran down my face. *You deserve this,* I was telling myself. *You deserve this, you traitor.* I had rebelled against the cause of Socialism and I was no longer under the protection of Jim. Still I could not will my eyes to open. I wanted to see my punishers. He kept on pushing himself harder and harder into me. Finally, I heard him groan, and the weight was lifted off of me. *You are a lousy mother and a bad person,* I was telling myself. When they pulled me out of the ambulance, I prayed for the strength to open my eyes and look at both of them. Jim gave me that strength, and I saw them. Never will I forget those faces.

When I finally awoke, my mother was at my side, as was my husband Joe. My hands and the space between my fingers were sore and bruised. My mother explained that they had tried to waken me by pressing their fingers between mine. That seemed really stupid to me, and they had bruised the area between my fingers. My mother said the hospital thought I had tried to commit suicide. I laughed weakly. "No Mom, I smoked a joint and then I was out of it." The doctor in attendance disagreed. "PCP," he said. I looked at them both confused. What was PCP? The doctor said it was a powerful drug that people sometimes laced in their weed. It was particularly strong, and although I felt weird, he said most episodes are really wild. It was embalming fluid.

I apologized to my mother, who hugged me and held me. That's the kind of mother she was. Even though I had messed up big time, she always had love for me... unconditional. Joe was there too, and I could tell he was very upset. But he understood. He was remembering how he'd overdosed on those pills when we first got together and how I still stood by him. I loved him as I always had.

Upon my release from the hospital, I went to my mother's and she took care of me for a couple of days. She told me that I could not go back to the apartment. I told her I had to until they found me somewhere else to stay. I had to try to be better. And I *was* getting better. My mother was always a source of inner strength. These strong women were few and far between. But she was one, coming from strong stock. She was a tough and spirited woman.

Joe's love for me, by comparison, seemed transient. After his brief appearance in my life following my ordeal, he continued his affair. I tried to win him back, but he rejected me. Not only was it a blow to my ego, it scared me: this was a man who had at one time truly loved me, who had been there for me as I had been for him, and now he did not want me anymore. But I also thought he had good reason. I would not have wanted me either. I tried desperately to seduce him and his disgust of me cooled even his libido. His disappointment in me hurt, and I walked away even more defeated than before.

The effect of this, unfortunately, propelled me even further away from the church. Who would I call to rescue me now? I had tried to come home, but it was not working. Attending church services made me feel out of place, as if I did not belong any longer.

We got word from Jim that the New West Magazine article was to be published. Jim was angry because what the article would expose was some of the inner workings of the church. It was actually an expose' fueled by former temple members—even a couple of the college students.

There is no doubt that the telephone campaigns were activated to "save the reputation" of the church. The horrible publicity pushed Jim to leave the United States. He was a coward even then. (http:Jonestown. sdsu.edu/AboutJonestown/PrimarySources/newWestart.htm)

Then Joe approached me one Saturday evening with the news that when Jim left to go to Guyana, he was taking Jakari with him. I angrily told him no. Joe tried to reason with me, and said that Amber would be traveling with our son and would watch over him. And I relented. Amber was part of a family and I trusted her. To this day I do not know what made me agree to the removal of my child to a place so far away. But it was not the first time during my life in Peoples Temple era, or even after the massacre. I also did not know then that sending Jakari to South America was a ploy to bring me back into the fold. Not wanting to see the truth – because then I would have to face my own inadequacies – I said yes. I was 19 years old, and I still did not believe the manipulations.

The evening my son went away, I sat alone with my fear, guilt, and relief. I thought it was okay for a child to be raised by the "community." I remembered my child waving goodbye, through his tears and mine. He was only eighteen months old, still in diapers. They would not even let me go to the airport. I cried that night. Then I went and had enough drinks to forget my pain and regret.

About two months later and still living in the apartment on Fillmore, I got the call from the Temple: I was scheduled to be in the next group leaving for Jonestown. The first thought that entered my mind was *if you don't go you will never see your child again.* God had spoken. I said I would be ready. I was given the date and prepared for the journey south.

Chapter 8:
Going Over Yonder

We boarded one of the Temple buses in San Francisco and traveled across country. Temple members were leaving for Guyana from Miami so as not to raise any red flags at the San Francisco airport. We arrived early in Miami, so we found a park near the beach and went for a swim. I was shocked at the difference between the Atlantic and Pacific Oceans. Where I'd grown up, the water was always cold. This water was warm, a huge Jacuzzi. After we swam, the heat of the evening quickly dried our clothes.

The first group left for Guyana the following morning, and the rest of us waited our turn. That evening we said goodbye to our bus driver and headed for the Promised Land.

We had a brief layover in Puerto Rico, where the air was damp and thick with the rich smells of spicy food. Humidity was high. We broke out into a sweat as soon as we stepped out of the little airport. On the second leg of the journey, I met people from all over the world. When we arrived at Trinidad, our escort announced that there was a delay in boarding the flight to Guyana. The supervisor wanted to know why all these people were leaving the U.S. with a one-way ticket to a socialist government. We were told the airport would put us up for the night while they researched this strange occurrence. Our escort called the US and explained the situation. Someone was working on it.

We were driven to a hotel, where we each had our own room. After washing away the grit and grime from a week on a bus and two airports, I slept soundly. The next morning we were treated to a big breakfast of eggs, rice, meat and goat's milk. It was lovely. By that time, the situation had been straightened out, and we were booked on the next flight for Guyana. Thank you, Father! We exclaimed. We were on our way.

As the plane began its descent, we looked out the window at what would be our new home. My heart beat with a mixture of fear of the unknown and anticipation of seeing my child Jakari. We disembarked at Timehri airport outside Guyana's capital city of Georgetown, where people from the Temple's greeting committee welcomed us. Once again, I was both overwhelmed and excited by the unfamiliar surroundings. Parts of the city looked worn. The people were all nationalities. The Guyanese Liberation Army stood strong and intimidating, all these men of color in their uniforms. It made me proud to have made it.

We rode to the Temple's headquarters at Lamaha Gardens, a house that stood on pillars raised off the ground. I saw my old friend Sandi. She had lost her child due to toxemia since the last time we'd met, and I commiserated with her. There was another couple there from Los Angeles who had turned over $125,000 to the church, and you could see the look of anxiety on their faces, wondering if they had made the right decisions. They were weary from the flight, and now that they were here, they were also distressed by the meager servings of food and the sleeping arrangements. I felt sorry for them. Sandi would not tell me too much about Jonestown, except to assure me that I had to see it to get the picture. I wasn't worried, but I was curious.

A few of us went to the dock to see the *Cudjoe*, the boat that would take us to "paradise." Joe was there. Sandi did not tell me that Joe was here, I thought. I had not expected to see him, and my heart began to race. He was cordial but cool, as if I was the only one who had betrayed the other. I noticed how great he looked, his deep chocolate skin glistening in the sun, an earring glittering in his left ear. Feelings of longing engulfed me, and I realized that I still loved him. I could win him back, I thought. His girlfriend was still in the states, so I would have no interference. After all, we were going to be together, Joe, Jakari, and me. This time it could work. The guilt rose up in me as I focused back in time at this man who was kind yet stern, who loved his son, and was still as dedicated to the Temple as ever.

I asked how long it would take to travel to Jonestown, and was shocked to hear the answer: "24 hours." On the water? In that boat? Well, I thought, we are going over yonder. We would be leaving in the next few days, waiting for more arrivals we were told. I wanted to ask Joe when he was going, but decided against it.

That night, we all stayed up as late as we could. As Sandi and I sat outside remembering old times, Joe stayed far away from me. "Sandi," I began. "What is Jonestown really like girl?" She shook her head and said "Really, you have to see it to get the full picture." The more I pressed for an answer, it became obvious that she was not going to share anything.

We arose early that morning to a nice breakfast. As we quickly gathered our things, we loaded into the vehicles. Once we arrived at the dock, my anxiety dissipated soon after we boarded the Cudjoe. The group along with me began singing songs. "Going over yonder, going over yonder, going over yonder, to be with my Father." There were big cockroaches accompanying us, but I tried to ignore them.

The early morning ride was not rough. As night drew near, I began feeling my stomach getting queasy, but thank God there was Benadryl. That helped to calm my stomach. As we headed farther and farther from Georgetown, I felt no fear, but rather amazement that I was in another country on the way to build utopia. Away from any city – away from any civilization – we watched the sky darken into deep night and slept out under the stars. The elderly couple slept inside on the bunks.

As we approached land again, I could see a line dividing the water by color, one side green blue and grayish on the other. It was a sign of beauty, Mother Nature at work. We ate sandwiches and drank Postum, a coffee substitute. Finally, the captain of the ship pointed to where the sea narrowed into a waterway that would take us to our destination of Port Kaituma. As we pulled up to the dock, I was ecstatic that I would see my son again, but I wondered if he would still call me Mama. Maybe he called Amber Mama now. Again I had competing emotions, both guilt and fear as I thought back on the selfish moves I had made, the self-centeredness that possessed me when all I thought about was freedom, freedom from a husband and freedom from a child. The lurching in my stomach now had nothing to do with seasickness. I realized how close I had come to truly abandoning my child; my child with big brown eyes, and cheeks to match, the child I had cried over when he was placed in my arms after his birth, the child I had vowed to protect from as much hurt in the world as I could. I was almost there. My prayers were answered.

I saw familiar faces as we disembarked, and could only imagine what I looked like. There was a tractor hooked to a long trailer. Was this what we were to ride on, I wondered. As the crew began to transfer our luggage from the boat to the trailer, I noticed people – small in stature, dark, with colorful clothing – standing around, looking at us. Some were smiling, others just stared. They looked like they were from the deep jungles of the Amazon. Later I would learn that they were Amerindians, natives of the interior with a rich history all their own.

We boarded the trailer, finding open spaces along the side, and held on as the engine roared to life. We were lurching toward the Promised Land. Taking in the scenery, holding on for dear life, we were silent. The jungle was deep, the humidity was thick. I could feel the sweat pouring down my back. Thank God I did not have any makeup on; I would've looked like a vampire.

Thick bush mixed in with strange-looking trees. I could hear crickets singing. Was this their welcome song? The tractor ride was rough by any measure, and dirty. Dust billowed up off the sides of the truck, us breathing it. *Like I need more dirt,* I thought, and then admonished myself to change my attitude. All of a sudden, the sign loomed ahead: Peoples Temple Agricultural Project. There was a guard shack, and I recognized one of the security guards. I waved, wondering why he had a rifle strapped to him. I thought we would be safe here.

We turned off the main road, passed under the sign, and bounced along an even more deeply rutted dirt road towards the community itself. As we came around a bend, the project suddenly appeared in front of us, and I heard cheers coming from my fellow comrades. We're almost there, I thought. The shouts increased moment by moment. Butterflies were swimming in my stomach. I searched for my child, and my beautiful niece, Dawynelle, my sister's first child. I couldn't pick them out of the crowd, but I saw I saw countless faces of those who were the chosen.

It was just about dark when I found Jakari in Amber's arms. I ran to him, crying... *my baby, my baby.* He held on to Amber, searching my face, trying to recall my voice. Suddenly he grabbed me and said "Mama." I cried tears of joy and relief. "He remembers me," I thought.

His fat cheeks, jet brown eyes, and smile made it all worth it. This – he – was the reason I had come. To try to make up for all the wrong I had done, the drinking, the partying, and the selfish life. Would I ever be forgiven? Would I ever forgive myself? I vowed then to live a socialist life, to sacrifice as all my comrades had done, to leave the other world behind and start afresh. Thank God, my son remembers me.

People started around us, "Welcome, Welcome All of You, glad you are with us." This was Jonestown. I was here at last, here with the people that love me without condition. It felt wonderful. There were probably about 500 people there at that time. I saw the many familiar faces and felt grateful. I'm lighting the way for the rest of my family, I thought, for my sister and my mother who had yet to come. I was the first one here. Don Fitch, Dawynelle's dad, brought my niece to me, and I hugged her, tears streaming down my face. Dawnyelle was a beautiful child. I told her who I was – Auntie Leslie – and she finally smiled. Don asked about his wife – my sister – and I told him she was doing okay. He'd heard she had another baby. There was some hurt still in his eyes. Yes, I told him, Daron, a little boy. Oh, he said. I could tell he was probably wondering how she could give up one child and have another. My heart ached for him. I knew that Jakari and Dawnyelle knew each other. *Everyone raises the children,* I thought, trying to ease my own guilt.

There was a table set aside for us to drop off our personal items. As each of our names was checked off a list, we surrendered our passports, which were placed in a wooden trunk. "You won't need this any longer," the sister said. I smiled. I sure won't. Another sister began going through my suitcase but left it intact – I had no contraband – then someone took my trunk to my cabin. Trunks of supplies were taken elsewhere.

That evening we were shown into the pavilion and assigned to a room. Although Jakari was staying in the nursery, I asked if he could stay with me. I was told yes. Our escort showed me to my cabin. It held nine bunk beds, and someone slept in the loft. I liked the loft and hoped that I could have that. It reminded me of the room Joe and I had in the commune, with the beds built in to the wall. We'd slept on the bottom and company slept on top. Amber, who was already there, suggested I take a shower. She said she would watch Jakari.

The building with the showers took me by surprise and made me uncomfortable. With about eight shower heads on each side of the wall and a large open space with benches to put your things, the whole set-up reminded me of pictures I'd seen of Auschwitz. I was puzzled why there was only one handle on each shower, but when I turned it on, I understood why. The cold water shocked me awake. Oh well, I thought, as hot as it was here, who needed a hot shower anyway.

On my way back to the cabin, I asked someone where the restrooms were. They pointed to another building. As I opened the door, I had another sickening shock. Inside were about ten seats, basically holes cut in long, wide boards. Good God, I thought, this was nothing more than a primitive outhouse.

Finally making my way to the cabin, I put my things away and reached for my child sitting in Amber's lap. His head was against her chest. She had taken good care of him. We sat up late in the night talking. I was so grateful for her for taking care of my child. She said she knew how different it was from the States, but I would adjust, and if I did not like it now, I would eventually. I wasn't concerned about that, I said, this was where I wanted to be. Jakari finally dozed off in my arms, and after Amber and I said goodnight, I went to my bunk and lay down with my child hugging and kissing him. Happiness engulfed me like flames. *I can finally be a good mother; I can finally be a good mother...* the refrain kept going through my mind. Guilt is difficult. It eats away at you, but when you try to fix the mistakes you made, this is called Grace. God had brought me to Jonestown for a purpose, even if I had no idea of what it was at the time. As I looked at my creation made of love, my heart swelled with happiness.

The next morning a knocking on the side of the cabin stirred Jakari and me out of our sleepiness. I had to take Jakari to the nursery and get back to the cabin to get ready to work. I had an hour. When I left Jakari at the nursery, he looked at me as if he were afraid I would disappear. Mama will be back, I told him, but I could see his doubt. It reminded me of the days when I was not there for him. I swore that from that day forward, I would always be there for him.

I quickly used the bathroom – there were more people in there this time – finished my business, and went to the showers to wash my face and brush my teeth. A monitor yelled we had only two minutes. I was sweaty already, so neither the cold nor the brevity was a deterrent. When I finished I hurried back to my cabin, dressed quickly and headed for the pavilion.

Someone stopped me to ask if I had eaten, then took me to the dining area. The aroma of fresh baked bread warmed and comforted me. People had plates of biscuits and syrup. When I went to the serving window for my plate, the person there greeted me and asked how my family was. I told them we were great. I sat down next to one of the seniors. We talked about Jonestown and how much I would love it.

My first work assignment was on the banana crew. "Great," I exclaimed, even though I had no idea what the banana crew did. The woman making assignments looked to my feet and noticed my stateside shoes – they were plastic and inconsequential "jellies" – and even though she didn't say anything, a look of mischief danced in her eyes. Being the disco queen that I was, I did not own a pair of jeans, tennis shoes, t-shirts, no casual clothes at all.

The foreman of my crew was Jeff, someone I had known from the states. He welcomed me and gave me a long sword-like weapon. It was a machete, he explained, and we use them to cut down bananas. Okay, I said. He also warned me that it was very sharp and that I had to be careful with it. Okay, I said again.

The other crew members – all familiar to me from the States – greeted me. Most were young, people I had grown up with. I felt right at home.

Our first task of the day was to dig up the roots of a stump. I began trying to cut some of the area around it, but stopped when I heard a giggle. A sister behind me with a big smile offered to help. She started to dig around the earth, handed me her machete and pulled at the plant. The stump finally gave way, the force of it almost knocking her down. It was big and round. "There," she said with a proud look. I asked what we were supposed to do next. We have to replant it, she said. A banana tree only produces one bunch and it takes approximately two years to grow. To think I never knew this, and this was one of my favorite fruits.

We dug up a couple more before Jeff called for a lunch break. By this time I was not only dirty, but dripping in sweat. The feeling that I was in a sauna – steamy and hot – had returned with a vengeance. Jeff found a spot in the shade and handed out peanut butter and honey sandwiches. They tasted very good. We had a lot of water with us, and we all drank. After a short rest, Jeff called the lunch shift over, and back we went to pulling stumps.

It felt wonderful to be working this land. My bourgeois attitude had not lasted long. Even on that first day, I felt such a surge of pride that the old world looked downright nasty.

Later in the afternoon, the sky began to darken and I could see heavy, ominous clouds gathering above us. Someone cried out, "Monsoon," and the first drop of rain to hit my skin was followed by a thousand more. Solid, hard rain. I had never experienced a downpour like this. Ten minutes later, it stopped just as quickly as it had started. We were all soaked; even though we had taken cover under some trees, the jungle canopy was not thick enough to keep the rain from soaking us. One of my new comrades let me know it was really going to get hot, and after about twenty minutes, the sun was blaring down again, hotter than ever before. Steam rose from the earth. It felt almost wicked.

We continued to work. My wet clothes had dried after the rain but were now drenched in sweat. My hair fell, and I knew I did not have a curl left in it. Gosh, what am I going to do with my hair, I thought. During our caravan days I had resorted to two big French braids on either side of my head. I thought braids would be the only way to look halfway decent.

As I worked, I thought about both Jakari and his father. The fields were a refuge, a place to think, to work the land and see the results of your labor. It was not like working for some corporation where you were treated as stock, but you were active member, making a way for the community to survive. Still, to say I was exhausted would be an understatement. Although I was physically in good shape, I had never worked this hard. Jeff called shift over, and I dragged my sore body back to the compound. We had about a little over a mile to go, and I felt I would just drop and die. My feet were killing me, sweating under the plastic. I had walked into a mound of red ants and been bitten for my trouble. One of my crew members told me I needed to go and get some boots. No kidding, I thought. Still, I believed as if I had accomplished something and this was special. I wanted more. We met other crews on the road heading home, mingling and talking among ourselves. Not one negative word came out. I did not complain. Someone remarked that I would get used to it. They were right. I did.

As we approached the compound I saw people playing basketball and volleyball, having fun. I noticed my husband sinking a jump shot, his beautiful chocolate skin glistening under the hot sun. I immediately wanted him in my bed. *Soon, I will have him back*, I promised myself. It was a wonderful picture. Some folks were lounging, engaged in deep conversations, while others assisted a senior, and others just watched us all come in from a long day of working for the cause. A wave of tremendous pride welled up within me. This was worth it, I thought. I felt honored to have the opportunity to make up for my past sins and start anew. Where else but Peoples Temple could you just go home and be forgiven? The looks on all of our faces said that we were in the right place, doing the right thing.

We placed our gear in the equipment shed. While others returned to their cabins, I went to the store and asked for field gear. I was handed five pairs of jeans, five shirts, socks and rubber boots. The jellies I had on would not see another day. Heading to my cabin, I could not wait to hit the showers.

As I walked along one of the paths lined with young palm trees, I noticed the toddlers and spotted my child laughing and playing. I called out his name. He turned to look, then ran towards me, arms outstretched. "Oh," I protested, "Mama's dirty," but then he was in my arms, and the feeling of having his small hands around my neck, made me know without a doubt I was in the right place, doing the right thing.

When I arrived at my cabin, greeting people along the way, I again felt exhilaration, that I was a part of something incredible, something that made a difference. I grabbed a pair of pants, a shirt, bra, and panties. I found a towel, soap, a toothbrush, and toothpaste, and headed for the showers. Modesty was out, the shower line was long. The shower monitor was again reminding people of the two-minute rule. I undressed, wrapped a towel around me, and waited for a shower to become available. In the meantime, I washed my face and brushed my hair. It was still hot and sticky. When it was my turn, I dropped the towel and headed in. The cold first bit into my skin, but as I got used to it, it felt very good. And then it was over.

Using the bathroom was what I dreaded. This would take some getting used to. It offended my nostrils. Newspaper substituted for toilet paper. I wondered if I was going to have ink in my private parts. I noticed people rubbing newspaper together as they sat on the toilets, and figured out that this would make the paper softer. I soon mastered the task myself. Conversations went on while you used the restroom as if there was no such thing as modesty or decorum.

I returned to my cabin to put my things away. Father was on the loudspeakers, reading current news from the BBC. As I readied to go back and see my son, my best friend appeared at the doorway. She was married to someone very close to Jim. She asked me how I was, "Well what do you think?" she smiled. "It's amazing that we built all this." I said. Growing up in the church you learned a little bit about what to say and what not to say. She had more to say about Jonestown when we talked in Georgetown, but never breathed a word about the outhouses, the showers, any of the things that she thought would make me not want to come. So, I followed her lead and said nothing negative. All was well, she said. I hugged her, letting her know that she was still like my sister. I had just grown up faster than her.

We found Jakari at the nursery, and as I gathered him in my arms, I noticed his father heading towards me. I was not sure how to approach him so I waited for him to make the first move. He asked how I was. "I'm assigned to the banana crew." He just looked at me and said okay. I felt awkward, but hoped that would pass as time went on. It was important for me to be able to feel a part of Jonestown quickly. My assimilation had to be quick. Joe reached for Jakari, who beamed at the sight of his father, and the four of us – my family and Sandi – began walking towards the dining room.

Dinner that night consisted of rice and gravy and bread. It smelled delicious and there was no doubt that it tasted as good as it smelled. We all sat down with our plates and as Jakari sat on my lap, Joe to my right and Sandi to my left, I felt that everything would eventually be okay. We talked more about our previous lives in the States – nothing serious – and laughed a lot. Joe's leg touched mine, by accident or on purpose I did not know. All I knew was that it felt good to be next to him. His build had changed and he looked different, even though he had arrived in Jonestown only a day ahead of me. Jakari was more familiar with his father, because it was his father who had raised him. I could not take credit for that. While I was running the streets, Joe was raising his son. He loved that child and I loved him for it.

After emptying our plates and stacking the utensils in the areas to be washed, Joe, and I walked together with Jakari and talked for many hours. We did not mention our relationship except towards the end when I asked him to forgive me. It was important that he knew that I was sorry, for I had hurt him deeply. He said that he understood my restlessness and that at one time he had been the same way. I thought back to the time he decided to come clean, and I had tried to take my own life, hurting from the betrayal. I loved this man who always looked out after me and his son. As night fell, we took Jakari to the nursery and kissed him as we laid him in bed. I wish my son could sleep with me, I again thought. I asked but was told that all children stayed in the nursery with the other children. The first night was a treat. It would not be a habit.

Joe and I both felt the emptiness of not having our son with us. This child had endured a lot and still had come through it all. He was a warrior from conception. Look at his dad and look at me. Not only did he get our temper, he also inherited our passion for life. What we had created was a mini version of us. This we both knew.

Joe walked me to my cabin and bade me goodnight. It was almost like a first date; do we kiss or not. He was still my husband, and I was still his wife, but it felt awkward. He did not kiss me, and I had to confess to myself that I felt relief as well as a little disappointment. The night was quiet, except for the sound of crickets. As I drifted off to sleep, I actually looked forward to another day.

The 5:00 a.m. knock on the side of the cabin slapped me awake. Gathering my toiletries, I set out for the bathroom, then to the showers to wash my face. It was wonderful to see people milling around in bathrobes, rubber zorries and tennis shoes, heading for the showers relaxed and readying for a day's work. It was the most natural thing in the world. Those who had lived a communal life had prepared for this; those who had not were probably having a hard time. This was not a Club Med. It was straight out jungle, new territory, un-chartered and raw.

As I dressed for the day in my new jeans, shirts and boots, I felt ready to report to my crew at 6:00 a.m. It was still dark. Breakfast this time was biscuits with eggs. They were good. I ate quickly and went to find my crew. We were issued our machetes, and a couple of the guys handled the water jugs and the cooler which kept our lunches. We talked and laughed as we walked. When we got to our spot, we began the work for the day. Again, it was hard and I was a little sore, but we worked the land as a farmer worked his.

Every day became more and more like home. The seniors would clean rice under the senior tent. They appeared happy and I would frequently hang out with them, trying to fill the void of my grandparents. There were sewing classes and basic medical classes. In the medical training classes we were taught how to take blood pressures, pulses, and temperatures. I knew then that I wanted to be a doctor, and my friend Corliss told me she wanted to be an optometrist. We were given an option to take a job in the medical office with our doctor, and I seized it. I began working in the office three days a week, and stayed in the field the other three days. The flexibility allowed me to challenge my mind and to work for the common good. It was worthwhile work, and – by extension – my part in it made me feel worthwhile. We worked Monday through Saturday. Sundays was rest day and it was then that the ladies in the kitchen would make up the best peanut butter fudge. I would barter for fudge all the time; a hair barrette, a shirt, whatever the person wanted and I did not, giving it up for another big piece of peanut butter fudge. I loved it.

The dentist periodically came to Jonestown from Georgetown. My first visit with him for a toothache was not pleasant. As he opened my mouth and put an instrument I could feel him grab my tooth and tug. My eyes opened up wide, and I tried to say "wait a minute" What about a shot? "No shot" he said with a heavy accent. "Won't hurt much." He took the tooth without any anesthetic. Was the decision intentional or situational? Did he not have Novocain, or did he decline to use it because we were socialist, so it could do nothing but make us stronger? That is probably the reason. My mouth hurt for days. The long term consequence is that I have yet to go to the dentist on a regular basis.

I recall a day out in the field when I felt something crawl up my leg. Jeff told me to keep still, that it was a snake. Oh, no I thought. I could only imagine how big it was, that I did not want it around my private area. He told me to remove my boot, and I did. He kept telling me that it was not poisonous, but I wasn't sure if he really knew what he was talking about or was he trying to keep me calm. What he did not know was I had no fear of snakes, or of lizards or frogs. Since I was not scared – since I didn't feel that my life was in danger (and the realization of this gift would be given to me later) – I was able to take the other boot off and started to wiggle to try to get that snake out of my pants. Finally, I disentangled myself from my pants, and everyone started laughing. The snake was as scared as I was – he probably more than me – as he wiggled out of the pants and went about its way. I must have been a sight, standing in my panties. I did not care. Modesty had died a long time before. I was also happy no one thought to kill the snake. After all, we were in its territory. Receiving hugs from my comrades, I laughed and thanked Jeff for trying to keep me calm. He was sweating more than me. No one had been lost on a crew yet, and he did not want to be the first one. We were warned about some critters, but with the land cleared and us not traveling deep into the jungle, we were okay. Those natural inhabitants stayed in their areas, and as much as we could, we stayed in ours.

After work, I retrieved my son and played dominoes with a friend. Joe joined us, and we spent the rest of the evening together. I felt that Joe was finally looking at me as he used to. It would take some time I thought, but I think he truly loves me. Later that evening, we spent some time alone. As painful as it was, we talked about our failed marriage. He told me he was getting a cabin full of boys. This was just like him: always picking up strays and helping those he could. He was a good father figure. He walked me to my cabin, no goodnight kiss again, and as I laid in my bed, I basked in pleasant thoughts of the evening, I fell asleep.

Most days were like this. We worked and we played. Joe played a lot of basketball and I would sometimes see him working construction, heaving two-by-fours. His dark skin glistening with sweat made me smile and remember our love making sessions. I missed him. A month had passed already.

One Wednesday night we had a catharsis session. Jim began as he had stateside, exhibiting a frightening paranoia. He spoke of a traitor within. On this particular night, someone was called up on the floor for a sexual liaison they were having. Jim still spoke about his sexual needs. Suddenly it seemed as if we were back in the States, as if this would never end. I was hoping for more of a teaching evening, as the BBC was on quite a bit. The meeting lasted about four hours and about 9:00 p.m. we were allowed to leave the pavilion and go to bed. Most of the children were already asleep in someone's arms. The evening was comfortable, not too hot, yet not to cool. I dropped Jakari off and returned to my cabin.

I got to sleep in the next day, since I would be reporting to the medical clinic, and it didn't open until 8:00 am. The clinic was very close to Jim's house, with the pharmacy next to it. Across the walkway was the infirmary. There was also a small first aid area for minor scrapes and cuts behind the kitchen.

My excitement was I was finally going to get a chance to work with our doctor. I knocked on the door, and Larry Schacht opened it to welcoming me with a smile. We spoke awhile about what I wanted to do in medicine. Once he found out I wanted to do OB/GYN, I think he was satisfied. The clinic was well organized, with an examining table close to the sink and countertops. In the back of the clinic was a table and chair, and along the south side of the clinic was a long counter that was much like a built in desk. There were bookcases and a ladder leading up to his loft where he slept. Curtains in the windows gave it a more personal feeling, not only for the patients but probably for the doctor as well, since this doubled as his home. It was quite nice and comfortable.

Larry and I got along well from the start. My first day was a typical one for him – a series of medical appointments – but he not only examined patients, he had me assist. "If you want to be a doctor, you have to do more than observe," he would say. He had me take blood pressures, and if he was examining someone's abdomen, he would take my hand and guide it under his to feel what he felt. From that day on, I knew I would be dedicated to medicine, and I thank Larry Schacht for being a fine teacher.

The days I spent in the medical office were the best. I loved medicine. My passion for it would keep me up nights, studying. For the next several months, I had learned enough to perform pap smears and take cultures on my own. I got to assist with the delivery of a baby, an incredible experience, even as I thanked God that I did not have to deliver a baby like that. When I could not assist with a procedure, Corliss and I would take our place in Larry's loft and watch the procedure below.

As time went on, I noticed that Larry seemed to be getting increasingly irritable, and at times I thought he was sinking into a depression. His bedside manner was becoming more and more abrupt with the patients, and sometimes even his treatment of me was harsh. Most of the time, though, Larry and I would talk about a lot of things, and I thought he really trusted me.

Some of our discussions were quite personal. He once told me that I was not vain because my build has never been super thin, and I was not overly obsessed with my body. I did not take offense to his remark. My body had always been on the curvy side. I believe Larry Schacht's ideal shape for women were those pencil-thin women who were close to Jim. His taste in women seemed to lean towards women with boyish figures, very small-breasted. It was an interesting analogy.

Finally, Joe made his entrance back into my life and asked me if I wanted to get back together. Elated, I told him yes. I had heard that he got a letter from his girlfriend in the states, saying that she did not want to be with him once she got to Jonestown. Since I had confronted her in the states, and she was scared, I contributed that night to her making a decision, before she got to Jonestown. It would not be any better in Jonestown. He told me we would have a cabin full of boys. We were the only couple that was allowed to keep our child. Curious about this, I asked Jim's wife Marceline, who told me very quietly and very lovingly that Jakari needed both parents and we truly needed him. This answer was strange to me. What about the other parents and other children, I wondered. So as not to appear disrespectful, I said, oh, I see.

Our cabin housed eight boys, their ages ranging from eight to 13. Joe worked them hard. The cabins had simple wood floors laid on top of dirt, and one of the boys' jobs was to keep the floor clean. All of our boys had chores. There was a faucet right outside of our cabin where we would sometimes wash things out by hand, instead of carrying loads up to the washhouse. At the wash house, there were teams working in three shifts around the clock. Even the soap was handmade from scratch like the old days.

Time continued, one day into the next, no sense of time, or dates, or the outside world. My days began to blur together as they were much the same. We were getting to the point of being nothing more than tired. I was still in the fields and still in the medical office. But the best part was that Joe and I were together, and we were happy. We slept in our cabin's loft. It was as if we had never been apart.

Chapter 9:
The Color of
Socialism

One day, while I was working in the doctor's office, Jim's wife
Marceline Jones – known as Mother to some –asked me to step outside
for a moment. She had an old high school chum of mine, a woman
who'd been on the tennis team with me. I laughed to myself, recalling
how angry I'd been with her because she joined my tournament team,
even though she could not play tennis at all. I had to play like hell to
cover her lack of ability. No one knew how important tennis was to me,
although she might have figured it out from my testiness. I remember
telling her to just stand back and let me try to get every ball.

Welcoming her to Jonestown I asked how she was doing. It was
more than just a greeting. She looked sunburned, the color of baked
salmon. Since Pam burned easily, Marceline said, she could not be
expected to work out in the field. And that meant Marceline wanted
me to go out into the field two more days a week and allow Pam to
work in Dr. Schacht's office.

It felt as if Marceline had slammed me with a two-by-four. Looking
at this overweight white baked salmon and Marceline, and for the first
time in my life, I felt discriminated against. I almost wished Marceline
had lied and said Pam was too sensitive to heat, but not that she burned.
With as much calmness I could muster, I asked Marceline "And I don't
burn?"

I had not completely drained sarcasm from my voice. Marceline's
face reddened. She angrily accused me of being insubordinate and
selfish. And again, I asked her, why is it okay if I burn and not her?

Her answer changed from a request to an order: "You will go out to the fields two more days a week, young lady, and I don't want to hear another thing about it." I screamed my rage in my head, but replied "No problem." But it was a problem. It meant that I would have only one more day in the medical office. There is no way to explain the injustice that I felt. Did Marceline forget I was studying to be a doctor?

I must have cussed under my breath for the next two hours, and was still angry when I went back into the clinic, Larry finally came back from Jim's house. He was upset too. He knew how hard I had worked to familiarize myself with medicine. I had studied into the night many times, long after the clinic had closed for the day. Many times Larry would sleep down at Jim's house because he would be sick sometimes, so I had the clinic to myself. We were treating many patients and I loved it. This was what I was supposed to be doing. We had even talked about me going to Cuba to pursue my studies.

The most common ailment in Jonestown was skin ulcers. I had several on my legs because of the heat, but mine were mild compared to some. One of my patients was an elderly sister whose top of the foot was just about eaten away by an ulcer. Three times a day it would be treated, gently cleaning it I would talk to her and assure her it would heal. After a while I began to wonder if it would. Ointments and aloe would be applied, and it was filling in, but very slowly. She said the pain was not as bad which was a good sign. But I worried about her. Severe athlete's foot was also a common. Rubber boots and sweat just don't mix. Sometimes a case would be severe enough to take the person out of the fields, and put them in the tent to clean rice with the seniors (everybody worked if they could).

The mass exodus continued from the states, and more and more people were arriving. It seemed that Jonestown was changing, and not for the better. Some people – especially we young people – were getting restless, because once you finished your day's work, a lot of us had nothing to do, except play basketball or volleyball, talk, listen to music and have sex. We needed more to do. Even though I was married, I was also only 20 years old, and I wanted more entertainment. I began to think about college and if I was actually going to have the opportunity to go. When I began to really think about it, I started asking a few of my young comrades if they wanted to go to college. Most said yes.

So I asked myself when they were going to let us go. After all we had graduated from high school and I was already 20 years old. However, I did not feel comfortable asking anyone but the doctor. Knowing how moody Larry was lately, I knew the time would present itself that I could actually approach him with the question.

Jim yielded to the building pressure and allowed us to have a dance. Someone brought their big stereo unit… fondly called "ghetto boxes" and we had so much fun. Some of the adults joined us, dancing the jitterbug and such. I think they needed some fun also. We laughed and it took so much stress off of me. Suddenly a sinking feeling of hopelessness came over me, and I could not describe why. I felt as if I were going to suffocate and I had to fight it. It left just as quickly as it came… but it shook me, for I did not really know what it was.

Everyone shared music, passed around tape cassettes, both pre-recorded music and homemade dubs and compilations made by our comrades. Music seemed to move us somewhere else, to let us reminisce about the States. At least that's what it did for me.

Still, problems were beginning to mount. A couple of children supposedly tried to escape and were placed in a small box for punishment. Other children sent to the infirmary were given medication – Thorazine, according to Sarah – to control rebellious behavior. The side effects put them into a walking comatose state. It scared me. This was not normal. A couple of people were reported missing, never to be seen or heard from again, and Jim told us on the rare occasions we had more than the typical plain gravy that the meat we had eaten that night was human. I didn't find that funny.

At one point, Jim began talking about us going to Russia. The Guyanese government was turning against us, he said, and we needed to make contingency plans. The talk was bolstered with the arrival of visitors from the Soviet Union, who gave us Russian lessons. It was impossible for me to learn this language. I thought it was too different and besides, what about Cuba and medical school? What about my dreams? Then, as quickly as the Russian appeared, he left.

But it was undeniable; Jim was becoming more and more weird. The Wednesday night sessions were more like gripe sessions. Sometimes we stayed up all night. People talked about other people not doing their jobs and still messing up. Jim complained about people wanting to have sex and the lack of women on birth control. He also offered sexual critiques: A man who had to brag of his sexual talents was either homosexual or had inadequacies in the bedroom. I wondered if he were speaking from experience, because he always reflected on his sexual appetites and his ability to "go on all night." I did fear that he would call upon me for a sexual liaison, but of course he did not sleep with black women. This was probably because most black men would not allow this type of invasion, socialist or not.

It was about this time that I "lost" my glasses – to give me a pretense to go to Georgetown to reach the American Embassy – and that Joe "found" them in my locker. After this incident, Joe began to act a little different, as though he knew the truth that I wouldn't admit. My friend Sandi also asked me about the trip to Georgetown, and said there were rumors about me trying to escape. Of course I denied it, and wondered if Joe's truth – that he could not admit – was that he was the source of those rumors.

My mother and brother arrived about this time, and although I was happy to see them, I was very disappointed that I could not warn them not to come, or at least to delay their trip until things improved. When I had arrived, it was great, the food was plentiful. Every Sunday we had a quarter chicken and either peanut butter fudge – which I loved – or cinnamon rolls. We worked six days a week so people could move out of the mindset of weekends as we had stateside, but Sundays were also our days of rest. With the addition of more people, though, the portions of food at mealtimes began to shrink, and we rarely had chicken now. Rice and gravy was the mainstay for dinner. The fields were not producing as much. And the cooks seemed to take less care. I remember chicken soup with feet sticking out of it. I could not eat that. I was the lowest weight I had been but I was also in good physical condition.

Joe and I talked about what would happen if Jim were killed. Joe said chaos would ensue, but we would go back to the States and raise Jakari.

The first real White Night began in the middle of the night, with the sound of gunshots ringing out. The PA system came on, and Jim cried, "Wake up, everyone to the pavilion." I started from a sound sleep. Joe jumped up, went downstairs and roused children. I grabbed

Jakari. We dressed quickly and ran to the pavilion. Jakari was crying. He was scared. Everyone was scared.

Jim was already in the pavilion, and the area was surrounded with security. Joe left the boys with me and went to his security area. Each had some sort of weapon. There were crossbows, rifles and hand guns. We were under attack, Jim warned, we had to stand and be vigilant. This went on into the daylight hours. We were so juiced that staying awake was not a problem. As the day wore on and the attack did not come, Jim dismissed the group and gave us the rest of the day off.

The next crisis was a personal one. Several weeks earlier, I had written a letter to my best friend, and concluded it by asking her to tear it up as soon as she read it. This would prove to be a big mistake.

At a Wednesday night meeting soon after the first White Night, Jim announced, "I have a letter here from someone saying they wanted to leave Jonestown." I could hear the crowd murmuring. Who was it? Call them to the carpet. My stomach turned as Jim turned to look at me, his glasses on his nose. "Leslie Wilson, front and center." Oh no, I thought. How did he get the letter? I could barely walk, but I could hear the people whispering my name, I made it to the front of the stage, and my family began coming up as they knew they had to. Jim did not read the entire letter, just the part saying I wanted to leave. Thank God for that. He then asked me why. Did I want to become a traitor? Someone came up and whispered something to him, and his glare deepened. "I have just been told that your trip to Georgetown was an attempted escape and that your glasses were found."

"No Father, that is not true," I stumbled. "Yes, my glasses were found, but I did not try to escape. I would never leave my Jonestown family or my child." I answered appropriately, apologizing, saying I had a weak selfish moment. I love Jonestown and I loved him. I could have won an Oscar that night.

Then, as was typical in a catharsis session, my family had to join in criticizing me. Joe went first. "Are you crazy? As much as we have been given, you want to leave?" He reached out as if to grab my neck, but someone restrained him. I began to cry. *I can't do anything right,* I kept telling myself, *I am really selfish. But I want my child out of here.*

My mother went next, "Leslie, after all Father has done for you, you would rather go back to the capitalistic states? I am ashamed you are my daughter." Then my brother: "You should be thankful to Father. Look what he has done for us." I adored my baby brother, and that one hurt the most. "You are right," I said, "it was horrible to say. I ask for forgiveness."

Then the final act. Jim looked at me and pronounced my sentence: "Two weeks on the Learning Crew." Okay, I thought, that's doable. The Learning Crew was just that. You were assigned chores that no one else wanted to do. You had all of your privileges taken away and had to stay in a cabin just for the bad folk. As I moved some things from our cabin that night to report to the Learning Crew, Joe would not even look at me. I wondered if I had lost him again.

However, the Learning Crew was a hard crew to be on. We ate after everyone else. We had to run everywhere. It did not matter if it was to the front gate three miles from the pavilion, walking was not allowed. We ran to work, ran to the toilet, ran to the showers, and ran home. No one was allowed to look at us or speak to us, nor could we speak to anyone who was not on the learning crew. We were all quiet around each other as well, in large part because we knew that we could not trust anyone.

Our project was to build an outhouse in the area where the new cabins were. We were given shovels and began digging a hole ten feet wide and twenty feet deep. We dug and dug, but the first day we got only two feet down.

I missed my baby, and when he saw me he would cry out for me. Tears welled up in my eyes, and I had to turn away, it was so painful. And if I didn't, Joe – who had him most times – would turn Jakari from me or even walk the other way so he would not get upset. *God, please don't let Jakari think I have left him again*, I prayed. This hurt me more. When Mom ran into us, she had to look down as well. Same with my brother. It hurt, but I had caused it again. How had Jim found the letter? I tried hard not to think that my friend would rat me out, so I put it in my head that it had fallen out of my pocket, although I knew that was not the case.

Physically I was in excellent shape, so the work did not tax me. It was the longing for my family. Working like we did, the two weeks went by fast. Finally, at a Wednesday night service, my name was called out. I had been released from the learning crew. I went straight to my child, my mom, brother and finally to my husband. Or at least I tried to. He was cool towards me.

The truth was Joe was disengaging himself from me. Things were changing quickly, and although I could not put my finger on it, I felt it was time for me to try to place myself in a strategic place. I needed leverage, something to protect myself. My solution came in the form of a sexual liaison.

One of my dear friends and I had resumed our friendship. She would confide in me regarding the problems she was having with her husband, someone very, very close to Jim Jones. My friend and her husband had separated and he had shown an interest in me. It was reciprocal. My guilt was diminished knowing that my friend was not getting along with her husband, nor I with mine.

One night Tom and I had a conversation. He asked me to his cabin. "Be there at 10:00 p.m." "What am I going to say to get out of the meeting?" "Come on girl," Tom began, "you know what to do, get cramps." I laughed. As it was a Wednesday night there would be a meeting going on. Joe had security all night at the front gate, so I didn't have to worry about him. Shortly before 10 p.m., I left my cabin, dodging between ten or twelve other buildings to get to his. His cabin faced the back of the jungle – the bush, as we called it – and there was never a lot of activity around there. I tapped quietly on the door, and he opened it slowly, pulling me in, kissing me before we made it to the bed.

This affair went on for about three or four months. Time was not something you really paid attention to in Jonestown, where every day ran into another. Our liaison was mutually satisfying. I longed for him all the time. We had chemistry together, but I had to be careful not to fall in love with him. It would have been easy. Tom was always a great guy, nice, friendly with a great sense of humor. When Joe was at the front gate, Tom would come to my cabin and sneak upstairs to the loft and wake me. I would get dressed and follow him to his cabin. At times I wondered how he knew that Joe was gone, but Tom scheduled Security detail and Joe was scheduled at the front gate.

I thought about myself and who I had become. I also did not want to hurt my friend, but she was already protected by whom she was married to. Finally the affair ended. I believe Tom found someone else, and I now was in a state of just pure survival. My senses were keen and everything I did was centered on watching my back.

While working at the medical office, I had befriended a young woman named Sarah, who worked in the pharmacy. We would make jokes about something, careful not to disclose too quickly our dissatisfaction with our lives. As we became closer, I learned she was just as unhappy as I was. Sarah had a serious asthma problem and she had shed most of the one hundred extra pounds she carried.

Jim's paranoia was increasing. It did not help that the Government of Guyana was threatening to serve him with custody papers from the States. Grace and Tim Stoen, two high profile Temple defectors, wanted their son John Victor Stoen out of Jonestown, but Jim claimed that he had sired the child and that John's place was with his father. Eventually Tim Stoen and the Concerned Relatives – which Tim now led – became more and more the subject of Jim's ramblings, and the madness accelerated.

One afternoon, Jim brought up the subject of revolutionary suicide, and we had our first suicide drill. A potion which appeared to be a fruit drink like Kool-Aid had already been prepared. Jim spoke quietly into the microphone. "Who has the courage to take the test? Who of my children would die a revolutionary death?" Several people stood in line. He began to walk around the pavilion, asking people if they were ready. As I saw him near me, my heart raced. He looked down at me and said "My little Angela (referencing the first time he called me his little Angela Davis at the church service in Seattle) are you ready to commit revolutionary suicide?"

"Yes, Father, of course!" I replied as convincingly as I could.

So why did I do that? My belief that Jim could read minds was gone, so I knew he couldn't see my lie, and my respect for him was also gone. What else was I to do? If I hadn't agreed, I would have had to go through the public humiliation, the calls of traitor and perhaps a beating that no one would have stopped. So I told him what I knew he wanted to hear. Thank God, he did not call me up to actually test my loyalty. I was not ready to die.

Three people in line drank the "poison" and sat down, waiting to die. Nothing happened. Jim then praised them for their loyalty.

But they did not bask in the compliment. Rather, they had looks of disappointment on their faces. Maybe they were just tired of Jim too.

Jonestown was getting very harsh, but not yet unbearable. If we had been allowed to live without Jim's constant harangues, threats, and interference, Jonestown may have worked for those who wanted to be there. Like anything else, when there is a group of people, there have to be rules of governance, but Jim's was becoming more paranoid, erratic and selfish, and his demands were increasingly unreasonable, draining and – more discouraging of all – tiresome.

Joe and I finally separated and he began an affair with someone very loyal to Jim. She did nothing to hide it. Jakari remained with his father, about two cabins down from me. He was becoming increasingly removed from me, and perhaps others and it showed in his face. Whether he was depressed or on drugs, I could not tell. One night I was at his cabin, playing with Jakari, and Joe and I got into an argument. He became very upset and pulled out a gun from under his pillow. Moving too quickly for me to react, he grabbed me and, with his hand around my throat, put the gun to my temple. He has lost his mind, I thought. My mouth racing ahead of my good sense, I decided to call the bluff. "Pull the damn trigger!" I had never seen him this way. He was ranting and raving, a different Joe, replaced by someone else, someone alien to me.

I lived through that episode – and felt lucky afterwards that I had -but I began to worry what his new lover was doing to him. She was very close to Jim, and her influence on Joe probably reflected Jim's influence on her. Every day I saw my husband, the more agitated, inpatient and explosive he seemed to be. Something was going on, even if I could not pinpoint what it was.

It is my belief that Joe never learned of my affair. I know that he was so agitated that I was fearful of saying anything to him. I truly believe that if God had not been looking over at us, Joe might have blown my head off that day.

Joe's lover continued her manipulation of him, but she could not even look at me. Her husband had left for another, younger woman. Joe's lover had been like a sister to me, but I understood. Her jealousy of her husband's new lover had just about destroyed her and there was not much else she could do. Her husband's new lover also had lupus. This is the way it worked – or seemed to work – in Jonestown. She used to come to the medical office to see Dr. Schacht and even though her condition required more than the clinic could provide, they would not allow her to go into town for medical treatment.

In spite of the turmoil between us, Joe remained a loving and devoted father to Jakari. He never let anyone come between himself and his son, or – for that matter – between me and my son. For that, I am forever grateful.

The next "attack" on Jonestown was much more serious, not only in its duration, but how it affected the community.

The wail of the sirens seemed louder than normal. This meant trouble. That sound was madness to me. It always meant we were close to death. People streamed from everywhere – the fields, the gardens, the cabins, the kitchens, and the clinic – towards the pavilion. Jim sat in his big chair as usual. Today's message was about how the Guyanese government had turned its back on us. The U.S. Government had been applying pressure on the weaker socialist country, and it was not holding up. He'd sent Temple women to seduce Guyanese officials, to keep them loyal to us, but that was beginning to fail. And so, Jim said, we were about to be attacked. Our paradise had gone to hell, but we were going to defend it to death. He ordered the children to the nursery. The rest of us gathered in a line in front of the compound with any weapon we could find. Most of us who worked in the fields carried machetes. The guards were already armed. We found our places, sitting knee-to-knee waiting for an attack by the Guyanese army. Jim remained on the P.A. system, telling us that treacherous family members in Concerned Relatives and traitors from our ranks were the cause of this. His rambling droned on and on, and eventually, we just tuned it out. You responded when everyone else did and otherwise placed yourself in a state of detachment. This is how we survived.

The first night was bearable. Our bodies were in good enough condition to stand unusual punishment. My comrades and I sat and talked about the old days. We tried to remove ourselves from the fate that may be ours. It was somewhat like an all-night slumber party, without the sleeping bags. My brother sat next to his girlfriend, about three people down from me. I got to talk to him, too reassure him that everything would be all right. My brother was a true gift from God. There were many like him in the ranks of Jonestown.

The second night came and went without incident. My fellow comrades stood strong and brave. My thoughts were how I would die. A quick bullet, or a lingering, tortured death. I was recalling all of the methods Jim told us about tortures in Chile, Cuba, and Vietnam. They would torture you to the point of unconsciousness. After it endured the limit of pain, your body would shut down. The bamboo sticks under your nails, the dripping water, the constant light in a room for days at a time, women having their vagina shocked by electrical currents. The more I thought about these, the stronger I got.

The third day, we were still alive.

On the fourth day, I was near exhaustion, talking myself into going on and staying awake. Eventually, I began to spot illusions on the horizon. I thought I heard gunfire, or thought I spotted someone lying on their bellies. I spotted my husband and wondered what he was thinking. My eyes were tired. Fortunately I sat next to someone who was somewhat trustworthy, and even though I could not be 100% sure of that, we worked out a plan to take catnaps while on the front line. Five minutes at a time, that's all we needed to refresh our bodies. I told them to go first. After they took their nap, I felt they were on the up and up. Through the rain we sat, holding our machetes, ready to die.

My mother found me and asked if I was all right. I could see in her eyes that she wished we were somewhere else. "Of course, Mom." I tried to sound strong. "I'm fine." She placed her hand on my shoulder, squeezed and moved on. She was assisting with the seniors. I was glad she was not out there.

By the fifth day, my body was numb. We all managed to keep up the fight. Food was brought to us and we were allowed to go to the bathroom. But when we went, we had to run. Then we returned to our spot, resumed our position. Several of my comrades had not lasted. Jim was still rambling on. I was beginning to get really, really angry. Mr. Powerful, with no power to stop this. If I ever get out of here, I thought, I am going to tell him what I really think. I had not seen my son in five days. Joe was still walking around. I bet the security team got to sleep. They finally sent my Mom on the line too. And still we remained vigilant, waiting to die.

Six days later – smelly, tired, dirty, and pissed off – we heard Jim's announcement that the ordeal was over. We cheered and waved our machetes in the air. I imagined my machete leaving my hand and cutting his head off. It would be considered a freak accident. By this time, my anger had overtaken me. His death would have been great news to me.

During the time on the line, through the rain and the heat, we sat out there sometimes cold, sometimes hot, always dirty and dusty, and infinitely tired. We told stories about earlier, happier days, and we talked about death. My thoughts went to my family: to my mother and to my grandparents whom I loved dearly, especially Grandpa, the light of my world. I regretted that I would never see them again. It's amazing how the fear of death leaves you when you have been close so many times. I thought about what the papers would print about us. Most of it probably negative, because they did not see the people, only crazy Jim Jones. I wanted him to go away, either by death or just leave. But he would never leave, so it would be death. If he would just die, I thought, this would be over. Why doesn't someone just kill him? I thought about this too. How could I get close enough to knock him off without anyone knowing it was me?

We were the chosen ones, I thought, because this madman was choosing to have us killed over his ego. Let John Victor Stoen leave with his parents. Let the Concerned Relatives come in and take their family members. Let those who want to leave, leave and those who wanted to stay, stay. Or maybe he would do it on his own, to let those of us who wanted to leave, go. He did not do anything but berate us like we were never good enough. If that was the case, why wouldn't he want us to get out of the way? After all, he was GOD. If you are GOD, why can't you do something? We had made this work. We built Jonestown, kept Jonestown running. He didn't do a thing but suck the life out of it. He was a leach.

My faith in the real God did not waver. Jim had taught us that there were discrepancies and errors in the Bible, but the basic Ten Commandments applied to everyone. This is what I kept close to my heart. It provided a blueprint for a good life, for a peaceful and loving world. Why could people not follow it? I remember the end of the siege. In my mind's eye, the sky revealed life and hope. I thanked God for getting us through it.

The atmosphere in Jonestown became increasingly withdrawn. It showed in my brothers' and sisters' eyes. Everyone was losing hope. We were trying to be motivated and happy, but the dream was turning into a haze. People's bodies were not tired on a daily basis; rather their spirits and emotions were crumbling from long-term exhaustion. As Jonestown divided into Jim's die-hard followers and those who had had enough, I wondered if we had made a mistake that was too late to repair.

White Nights were being called at least two to three times a week, more and more often for all-night meetings. It was formal for me to sleep in my clothes and shoes, and sometimes many nights would pass without the comfort of sleeping in bed clothes. When we were allowed to get some rest, we crawled our way to the showers to clean up, and brush our teeth, and then we staggered to our cabin for as much sleep as we could get before that awful siren began to howl. It's as if we slept with one ear still awake, waiting to hear the howling of the horn and Jim's voice rasping over the sound system: "White Night, White Night, everyone report to the pavilion."

The worst part of the White Nights was the screaming and crying of the babies and children. I remember running to the dining area and turning over tables to cover the babies for protection, and I remember the frightened looks on their little sleepy faces. Half asleep and teary-eyed, most would cry out for their mothers, while others just whimpered. They didn't know what was going on but they could sense danger. It was horrible. They were traumatized.

With a decent night's sleep so rare, most of us learned to function on three to four hours rest as we stumbled around the camp. Uncertainty permeated the air. At times Jim would not emerge for days, but apparently he still had the P.A. system hooked to his cabin, and all night, he would fill us with the only news he wanted us to have. And when he was too tired himself to speak, he would play a tape of a newscast from earlier in the day or week. We were being brainwashed, slowly but surely, our spirits destroyed every time his slurred voice intruded on a decreasing sense of normalcy.

I remember the day I saw Shonda dressed in a hospital gown and looking like she had been through hell. Sarah knew a lot of what was going on, because she worked in the pharmacy. Word was that Jim had taken Shonda as one of his lovers. She had not done well and was now being given Thorazine to keep her quiet. That was the last straw. This man who we called Father, Father God, and Jim had disappeared into a madness that was beyond understanding. Shonda was not only younger than I – and I was 20 – but she was one of his son's girlfriends. He had taken advantage of his power. I am sure he did not think that her reaction would be as it was, but the fact is, he stole her trust and shattered her. This was the state of mind he was in. The young women wondered who would be next. I prayed it would not be me, because I would have to try to kill him. Then I would be dead and Jakari would be stuck in Jonestown.

No one was safe anymore. The community that I rejoiced in at first was turning into a swamp of suspicion and paranoia, all because of one man with his sickness and negative ego. Jim had always preached about doing away with ego, but it appeared as if this was all he was consisted of. His rambling boasts about his sexual liaisons made me sick to my stomach. How dare he continue with this socialist utopia when he had removed himself from it? How dare he talk about us as if we did not consist of flesh, bone, soul or heart? He screamed at us for being lazy, inconsiderate and uncaring, whereas the truth was, it was he who wore those clothes.

And yet we couldn't trust each other. We knew the Concerned Relatives, the Stoens, and Deb Layton worked against us, and other potential defectors were among us. Distrust was rampant. People looked at their mates and families as potential spies or traitors. Gone were the days of laughter and joy, beautiful songs of peace and brotherhood. My only agenda was trying to figure out who I could talk to and who I could not.

Thank God, Sarah and I continued to become very close friends. We would talk ever so slightly about different happenings. We were still feeling each other out, trying to see if we could trust one another. Finally taking a chance, I confided in her about my unhappiness and the horrible things that were taking place. A few weeks later, she confided in me her plans on leaving. I told her that I wanted to go too. She said that there was a group, known only to her and her husband Basil, who wanted to leave. Basil had been planning his way out from the moment he had arrived six months earlier. She said that she would ask Basil, but she was concerned because she would have to tell the others as well. They would consider it a risk. Everyone knew I was married to Joe Wilson, and they would probably think it was a set up. I explained to her that it was not a set-up, and hoped she – and they – would believe me.

One day, Jim had a new reason to be paranoid. The Guyanese government would no longer protect him against our enemies in the U.S., he said, so we might have to blow ourselves up. He was concerned, however, that while some would die, others would survive and be maimed. He was looking to tweak the plan so that that we would all die. I wondered what it would feel like, to be blown up.

Jim had us line up to take showers to prepare for the death. What flashed before me were the films we saw on the holocaust. It was as if he was repeating the gassed shower scenes from all the Third Reich movies we had seen.

The sad part was we did not know if Jim was just talking or if he was serious. At this point death was spoken about so much, you really began to wonder what death would actually feel like. Here I was 20 years old and did not think I would live to see 21. That was my reality. And what about the children? I didn't want this to be my son's reality. I had to get him out and tell everyone what was really going on in Paradise.

One night I looked up to the stars and the moon, and said as loud as I could to God, without as much as a whisper escaping my lips, "This will be our last year here." This would be what brought me to understand truly what faith really was. As I spoke from my lips to God's ears, I did not know how long, or what it would take, but the strength that I mustered up was enough to know in my heart of hearts that my prayer would be answered. What I still had was Faith.

Although I saw Sarah every day, I did not want to mention the escape until she was completely sure that I was telling the truth. She finally said that Basil talked to the others, and they were deciding now. I begged her to try to convince them. I was taking Jakari with me. Why would I put him in danger if I did not want to get out? I asked her. She again said that she would talk to them.

The worst was yet to come: my sister arrived with her twenty-month-old son Daron. I was not happy to see her. I had not wanted her to come, which is why I never wrote. I hoped that she would get the hint. My brother was there and finally had a girlfriend, a Latina named Pat. I liked her. She was older than Mark but she made him happy. At least he had some type of normalcy.

When Michelle arrived, I went to her and hugged her. I asked why she had come. She said that her husband was abusing her so much that she had to get away. Michelle tried to get in the swing of things. She opened her trunk and showed me all the beautiful clothes she had made. She had a talent I would never have. Her garments looked as if they came from Macy's or I. Magnin. They were high end designer wear and the sewing was impeccable.

My sister was happy to see her daughter Dawnyelle. Daron was a beautiful child and so was Dawnyelle. Her father Don Fitch was white with red hair, and with fine long curly blond hair and fair skin, Dawnyelle did not look as if she had a drop of black blood in her.

With Michelle's arrival, her two children were both in one place. It just happened to be in Jonestown.

Chapter 10:
Liberty or Death?

The word spread through Jonestown like a brush fire: The Concerned Relatives had joined forces with a California congressman named Leo Ryan, and they were on their way. Not just to Guyana, but to Jonestown. They were going to come and talk to their families in person. All would be done under the watchful eye of Ryan, his media entourage, and of course, Jim Jones.

That afternoon, out in the back of the compound working the bush, we heard the buzz of a plane overhead. It looked like a twin engine. In the same moment the siren went off and summoned us to the pavilion. I am so tired of this, I thought. Lord, please find me a way out. And so He did.

At that moment, Sarah came up to me and gave me a pair of new sneakers. They would be leaving tonight, she said, and I could go. I hugged her and thanked her. I ran to the kitchen area, stole a butcher knife, and stuck it in the front of my pants, its handle hidden under my shirt. I then went to the pavilion where Marceline was addressing the crowd. She told us that the Concerned Relatives would be in the compound that night, along with the U.S. Congressman and a news crew. Jonestown residents with families in the Concerned Relatives must say the right thing. I wondered if my father was with them. He had not been happy when my brother left, and I knew he wanted to see his son. I prayed he would not be with them, because then people would watch me closely to see what I would say, risking my escape. We sat for about an hour, listening to familiar instructions on how to look happy, how to show that we loved Jonestown. When we were dismissed, I went and took a shower. I hid the knife in my trunk and found some comfortable traveling clothes to put on. I had jeans, a shirt and a sweatshirt around my waist. I got an outfit for Jakari ready to wear. Nothing extra was taken, only what we would wear.

The community was quiet, unsettled. When the tractor arrived with the visitors, my father was not among them – thank God – and I remained in the background. There was an elaborate feast prepared. As I looked at the plates before us, I wondered where it had come from. Sarah described it as the feast before the slaughter. I looked at her, hearing but not hearing. We have been living off of little portions, and this was all of what was left. I was angry again.

I recognized Jim Cobb, my surrogate brother, among the visitors. I wanted to go over to him, but didn't dare. They would think I was trying to be sympathetic and then I would never find my way out. As I watched from a distance, the Cobb family gathered around their brother, trying to hide their happiness at seeing him.

Congressman Ryan spoke to the residents, and of course we clapped and cheered. Jim addressed the group. This lasted a good couple of hours. We did not know where they were going to sleep, but I was sure it was not going to be in the compound. By the time it was over, the news had traveled around that someone had slipped a note to one of the reporters saying that they wanted to get out of Jonestown. We did not know who for sure, but I heard it was Vern Gosney. Selfishly, I thought, this will increase security and make my own escape that much more difficult.

I found my mother, told her what I witnessed working in the medical field and expressed my belief that things were not right. Her eyes spoke to me before her lips. "I'm tired, sweetheart," she said. I knew then that it was up to me to get out and then come back for everyone else.

I retired to my cabin, forcing myself to lie down so I'd be alert for the next day, but I only catnapped. Sarah told me earlier that we were going to leave the next morning and to meet at the kitchen area at 9:00 a.m. I asked her how we were going to get out. "We'll say we're going on a picnic," she said.

When daybreak came, I hurriedly dressed and put on my new tennis shoes. We had breakfast. I went to Joe's cabin and got Jakari washed up and dressed. Later when I saw Joe, at the kitchen area, I told him I was taking Jakari on a picnic. He said, "No, not today. Today is not a good day." My heart was in my throat and I was sure he could spot my tension, but I assented. Joe took Jakari from my arms and headed toward the guard station on the compound. How was I going to get my son back, I kept asking myself. Don't panic, I kept answering, you have time. Walking to the kitchen, there was a strain in the air. The atmosphere had changed and it was charged with something different. A stillness accompanied by something else. Later I would understand what it was.

The rest of our party had gathered at the kitchen area, when Joe came to me suddenly and said "Take Jakari. I have to go. No picnic," he added as he left. "Okay," I said. The others were motioning me to come. I mouthed "Hold on," and scurried to the library where my mother was. "Mom," I told her, "I'll be back. I'm going to the piggery for a picnic." "A picnic?" she asked. Maybe knowing but not knowing. I hugged her tight and told her I loved her. She held Jakari for a moment and the look in her face told me she knew I was leaving. Please don't say anything, I silently pleaded with her. She smiled and said, "I will always love you." I left before I began to cry.

I was surprised to see who was in the group. I knew about Basil and Sarah, but I was surprised by the others in the group.

As we began our journey, I was so nervous I could barely keep my footing. Sarah had prepared some fruit punch and measured out enough valium in it to keep the children calm. We trekked past the banana field, my heart beating wildly. We were fully exposed to anyone who might happen to glance up, and I kept thinking, someone is going to see us. I prayed to God to please get me to the top of the hill, and when we got there sudden warmth engulfed my body from head to toe, and I heard a voice say to me, "Everything will be all right." The fear left immediately. I knew God had us, not the crazed man below, but the higher force of love and Grace. God had his arms open holding us and guiding the way. What I realized also was that the angels had placed a sheath in front of us, a wall of protection to carry us home. *"Faith without works is dead,"* I thought.

We headed down the other side of the hill and walked for approximately a mile before stopping. Basil had hidden some items we would need for our journey. As he began digging on the side of the road, we heard a tractor coming up. There was Stan. "Hey you guys, where you going?" he shouted from the tractor? "On a picnic!" Basil called with a wave and a smile. Stan called back to us. "Don't be away long. The congressman will be coming back in soon." "Okay," we said, and waited for him get out of sight before Basil resumed looking for the items. He cursed bitterly. "They aren't here," he said. Sarah urged him to forget his parcels, but Basil would not give up until he finally found one of them.

It was then that we picked up our pace. If we got caught we would wish we were dead, knowing that the discipline would be intense. The sound of another vehicle drove us into the bush. We kept the children's heads down as a tractor/trailer came through. We could hear voices, and someone got a glimpse of the Concerned Relatives and Congressman Ryan's entourage. Moving deeper into the jungle, Basil got turned around. The markers he had placed to help guide us were gone.

We sat down in a small clearing and gave the children more punch waiting as patiently as possible, while Basil and the other men tried to find the path out. We were so close to the front gate we could hear the guards talking. Oh, no, I thought. If we could hear them, they could hear us. We had to keep the children and ourselves still, not speaking at all. The men came back and motioned to us to move. We did, carefully, watching our footing, bending low to the ground and gliding as silently as cats.

The area opened and we came out on a road. Basil said "Port Kaituma is a couple of miles down the way. That's where the airplane is." "That's also where people from Jonestown might accompany the congressman back to the plane," I said. That's where Joe could find me. The other way was to Matthews Ridge, but it was 27 miles away. I told them, let's go that way. If I had to do it alone I would, but the rest of the group agreed. We needed to get to a phone in a safe place and call the American Embassy. We had exchanged phone numbers of relatives in the States in case some of us did not make it out. I implored them to take Jakari if Joe caught up with me. If they saw me shot dead, they needed to get my child out to safety, our story needed to be told.

As my fellow defectors set out on the longer distance, sometimes walking on the road, sometimes on the railroad track running parallel, we moved quickly. Jakari was becoming sleepy, so I tied him with a sheet to my back like papoose, and carried him as far as I could. The men took turns carrying him because we had to move fast. All the children were carried. The valium had taken affect and their legs were slower than normal.

In the distance we heard a loud rumbling noise as a train approached. Moving off the tracks, and as the train slowed, the conductor called out to ask if we needed a ride. We told him no, we were heading the direction from which he had come. He waved goodbye with a puzzled look on his face, and the train began to move forward. People on the train gathered at the windows to look at us. We probably looked like hobos, except for the children.

Feeling tired but determined we continued to move on. How many miles we had covered I don't know. I thought of my family, and wondered if they had realized I was no longer there. We had to have been on the road for maybe four or five hours now. The sun was high in the sky; it had to be around 3:00.

We came to a bridge high above a ravine and had to get on the tracks to cross. My fear of heights paralyzed me. "I can't do it." I said my voice shaking. "You have to," Sarah said. One of the brothers grabbed Jakari from me and sternly said "Go" Dropping to my hands and knees, I crawled along the tracks, scared I would fall off. My comrades kept telling me not to look down, but they didn't have to worry about that. My task was to remember to breathe. When I finally made it – my knees scratched with pebbles – I sat down for a minute. We all did. After about a ten-minute break, we picked up the pace, because we knew the train would be coming back, and we were not sure who would be on it. By now, we had certainly been missed in Jonestown and the search would have begun. We knew that what we had done was going to change our lives, but we did not know to what degree. Not in any of our minds did we expect our lives to change the way they did.

It was dusk now. We didn't know how far we had traveled or how far we had to go. We just kept moving. As it got dark, we heard the train coming back. As fast as we could, we ran to hide, but the train was faster. The train stopped. I waited for the shots to ring out. Kill the Defectors! That's all I could think would happen. The conductor stuck his head out and asked if we wanted a ride. The women said nothing. The men said yes. We climbed on board and sat down. The men were discussing who to approach on the train to ask where we might find a phone in Matthews Ridge. The scoped out a man who looked like he might be friendly and told him we were trying to get to a phone to call the American Embassy. The man said sure, he would take us to a phone. *I hope we can trust him,* I thought.

Matthews Ridge was small, with little houses scattered across a little glen and some hills in an indiscernible pattern. We followed our guide up a road and approached a building that appeared to be a police station. As we drew closer, several men emerged with guns drawn on us. "Halt, put your hands up," a voice commanded. This can't be good, I thought. Somehow they got word from Jonestown that we escaped. Well I thought, at least we tried. We did as we were told, keeping the children at our sides. One officer led us into the police station and began a search for weapons. They took my knife and various weapons from the others, an ice pick, knives and machete.

The captain introduced himself and asked us what we were doing. We told him we had escaped from Jonestown and wanted to call the American Embassy. He asked us if we knew about the shootings at Port Kaituma. "What shootings?" we asked. The captain didn't have the whole story, but he'd received a report that people had been shot at the airstrip. The conductor told the captain that he'd seen us a number of miles away from the airstrip earlier in the day, so that it could not have been us. That man saved us.

The captain took our names and ages, asked us why we wanted to leave Jonestown, then he got on the phone. As he was dialing he stated "We heard it was a concentration camp." Someone would be there to take our statement and get us to Georgetown, he said after he hung up. He led us to some cots where the officers slept and asked us if we were hungry. We were fine, we said, but the children needed to eat.

We talked about what could have happened, who could have been shot at Port Kaituma, what it might mean for our friends and families in Jonestown. Not once did anyone bring up the idea during this time that our loved ones were being murdered and committing suicide. Either it did not enter our heads or we refused to think about the possibility; it was too much to comprehend. Finally, the four men in our party told the women and children to get some rest, that they would stand guard over us. I lay with Jakari, praying that what I'd heard was not true, that people had not been shot at Port Kaituma. Later, in the early morning darkness, I was awakened by the sound of heavy aircraft overhead. They sounded like huge helicopters. We could only assume it was the Guyana Defense Force going to Port Kaituma.

The next morning, the captain came to us and said he'd received a report that 500 people in Jonestown had run into the jungle, but that 500 were dead. We began to cry. That was what I was feeling earlier in Jonestown…eminent death. Chills went up and down my spine. I prayed my family had escaped. And still, the word "suicide" didn't come up at this time. We stayed there for another agonizing day, worrying, imaging the worst – which would never compare to the worst that had transpired. After someone from the American Embassy came and took our statement, we were flown on a Guyanese military plane to Georgetown and taken to an old abandoned school while the world decided what to do with us.

We met others who had been at the airstrip and who told us what happened. I asked if anyone had seen my family. The only one they'd seen was Joe, who'd searched for me on the tractor/trailer, desperate to find us. I half expected him to walk in at any time and finish what he'd regard as his purpose.

A woman from the State Department arrived to brief us and to get information from us, including our next of kin. The State Department would fly us home for a flat fee of $1,100, she told us, and if we signed an agreement to pay that amount, we would get our passports back. I was enraged and I told her so. "We are U.S. citizens" I snapped. "Taxpayers who put money into the U.S., and we have to pay you back?" Someone told me to be quiet, but I was livid. How dare they? As far as I was concerned, if they had been doing their job, this would not have gotten as far as it did. Nevertheless, we all signed the paper. And even though I believe most of us never intended to travel outside the U.S. again – so we wouldn't need our passports again – we did not want to burden our families.

We were moved to the Park Hotel in Georgetown and given rooms. I removed those tennis shoes I used in our escape and exposed my feet, rotten with athlete's foot. Someone donated a pair of sandals, which I wore. Sarah also gave me a couple of T-shirts. Jakari's clothes were washed by hand and hung out to dry. It seemed I was the only one with nothing but my clothes on my back. I had not wanted to take a chance on carrying anything out of Jonestown for fear of calling unwanted attention to myself.

We were allowed to call home, but since most of my family was now presumed dead, I started with Joe's parents. His mother was upset with me when I said that Joe was one of the gunmen. That was what the survivors at the airstrip had told me, I said, even as I reassured her that he'd been forced to do it. I then called my grandparents. My grandmother had almost died thinking that none of us had survived. Reverend Cooke was there and he was crying too, giving praises to God for keeping us safe. It was an emotional phone call.

The hardest call of all came next. "Dad?" I said timidly. His voice shook in reply. "Where is your brother?" I tried to encourage him. "Dad, they said 500 ran into the jungle, and I know he's out there, trying to find his way back." I fought back the tears, thinking that if I said it enough it would come true. At that point we still did not know what to think. He asked me why I didn't get him out. I could hear the accusation in his voice and the regret that I and not my brother had survived. Crying, I told him I was going to go back and get them, but that I hadn't been able to move a whole family. The coolness in his tone made me realize he hated me. I felt fatherless when I hung up the phone.

Stanley Clayton and Odell Rhodes, two young black men who'd survived the carnage that day, described what they had seen. I cried when they told me my sister went down fighting. Of course she did. When I saw Mike Prokes – whom the Jonestown leadership entrusted that day with suitcases of money – I asked him why he did not get my sister out. They were having a relationship. Hadn't he cared enough about her to save her too? He walked away crying, but that didn't mitigate my hatred for him at that moment. Four months later, Mike Prokes would shoot himself to death following a press conference.

The hotel lobby was filled with reporters. It was in the hotel bar area where I met one of them, a reporter named Tim Cahill, who worked for *Rolling Stone* Magazine. He was very nice, and we sat and talked over drinks. Someone offered me a cigarette, which I took. Tim Cahill and I spent a lot of time together talking about Jonestown. He seemed to be as gentle in his questioning and compassionate as to what we may be going through. He was the only reporter I spoke with. He asked me about my plans upon my return to the States then gave me his phone number with assurances that he would do what he could do when I got back. I thanked him.

We stayed at the hotel for two weeks. We were getting bored and ready to go home. Reporters were everywhere, but I did not want an interview. I knew to stay under the radar even then. When they finally told us we would be leaving, Odell had gone to a store and bought me and Jakari an outfit. It was an incredible act of kindness. We were still looking after each other. Mine was the typical Guyanese wear, a white gauze pantsuit and a pair of sandals, Jakari's a pair of pants and shirt.

As we headed for the airport, we saw Temple members we had not seen, who'd been staying at different hotels. One of the brothers asked me to go to Chicago with him. I told him I was going to New Jersey to be with Joe's parents, but asked to keep in touch. None of us wanted to let go of each other, because even then we knew the pain of the tragedy would bind us together for a lifetime.

A complication arose when we arrived at the airport: the male survivors would not be allowed to board the aircraft without sky marshals. Only the women and children were allowed to leave. Everyone was still suspicious and unclear on who had been involved in what. Rumors of hit squads made up of former Temple members flashed everywhere we turned. We all hugged each other. As we boarded the plane, I still had hope that my family was alive. This was a way of keeping my sanity I realized later. To accept this loss in one great moment would have sent me over the edge. I did not accept – could not even think – that they were dead. It was two weeks later, and I was still numb.

My mom – Inez Wagner

Michelle and Leslie

Michelle, High School Graduation

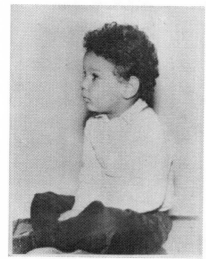

Mark at 4 years old

Mark, 16 years old in Jonestown

Don, Dawynelle and Michelle Fitch

Dawynelle Fitch

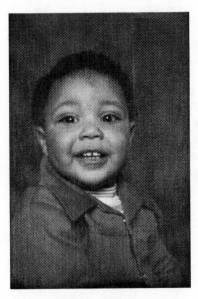

Daron Davis

Michelle with Dawnyelle-Before Jonestown

Joe, Jakari
and Leslie
– Before
Jonestown
1975

Joe, Jakari and
Leslie in Guyana

Leslie and Jakari –US 1979

It was dark as we approached JFK, and fear enveloped me as I looked down at all the lights. What was I going to do here in a system of government characterized by injustice that we had left? How would I fit in? My plan for leaving Jonestown was to return and get my family out. Now I was alone... how would I survive? Even though I was out of Jonestown, I still did not believe that I saw the age of 21. The future did not mean anything. When I allowed myself to think of the death squads, I anticipated being picked off before my feet hit the ground. I was a traitor, I had escaped. We had survived when most had not, and what remained were sorrow, pain and guilt. Later on through the years, I would feel the true effect of this experience.

The plane taxied to a stop at the gate, but as we gathered our meager possessions, an announcement came over the intercom system: "All those from Jonestown, Guyana, stay on the plane. Do not disembark." Oh my God, I thought. Now we really were sitting targets. The other passengers looked at us with suspicion and curiosity. We did as we were told, and the plane soon emptied of other passengers. Men in suits boarded the plane and identified themselves as FBI. They sectioned off two to each of us and began asking us questions. They wanted my name, place of birth, place of residence, parents' name, nearest relative and age. Some of the questions they asked me were strange. Why did they want to know about the pawn shop in Redwood Valley? Most of the questions and the reason for them were so incomprehensible that I answered that I had no knowledge of them. After an hour, we were allowed to leave the plane, but only to board a bus. The first week of December 1978 was much different in New York than it had been in Guyana. My little gauze outfit I had and Jakari's thin outfit was insufficient for the snow coming down. I asked one of the bodyguards if my mother-in-law could take my son right away and keep him warm. Mama and Pops Freeland soon arrived at the bus. They were crying and so was I. I was relieved when they left with Jakari for their home in New Jersey.

The Guyana survivors were driven to a hangar where about 25 Winnebago's were parked. We were fingerprinted and photographed as if we were criminals. We protested our treatment, but since this was an international incident involving the murder of a U.S. Congressman

– the first time in U.S. history – and since the facts of what happened were not clear, we were all considered as suspects in a crime.

As each of our names was called, we were escorted to one of the Winnebago's. Inside were three men from the Federal Bureau of Investigation, the State Department, and the Department of the Treasury. None of them admitted to being CIA, but my Temple education on the machinations of U.S. government – especially in its relationship with African Americans – didn't let me believe that for a second.

They interrogated me for hours – who I was, how I got in the Temple, what I knew about Jonestown, what happened on November 18th. Did I see guns? How many? Who had them? They asked about a couple of people that disappeared. When I was finally allowed to leave, the night had passed into day. The FBI agent drove me to New Jersey and he asked me what I was going to do now. I said I did not know that either. He told me his wife worked at a broadcasting station, and she might be able to find me employment. I thanked him, but the idea of me working had not even registered yet. When we pulled up to my in-laws house, I saw smoke coming from the chimney. It was a nice comfortable place which I had not seen since Jakari was a few months old.

My son was asleep when I went in. My in-laws had many questions and I tried to answer them all. Joe's mother was still upset that I had said Joe was one of the gunmen. I told her I had reported only what the people at the airstrip had said. If he had been, he may not have known what he was doing. He was different towards the end, and he may have been drugged. I finally said I needed to sleep for awhile. I asked to call my grandparents. The call was just as emotional as it had been the first time. They put me in the room with Jakari. I held my baby and dozed off.

A number of reporters called the house while I was asleep, but I did not want to speak to anyone. I ate the dinner Mama had prepared and changed into some clothes she gave me. Again my in-laws had questions, and again I told them what I could. Jonestown had started in glory and ended in hell. I also told them my own belief that the people had not killed themselves.

When reporters showed up at the house again the next day – vowing to stay until I talked with them – I relented and said that I would answer only a few questions. I put on a coat and stepped outside into the cold. They were rude and cruel, and after a moment, I left them standing on the doorstep. They could freeze out there if they wanted. Later, the FBI agent who'd dropped me off returned with another agent with *their* questions, and for them, I had no choice. I think they were trying to see how consistent my story was with what I had said during the previous session.

We celebrated Christmas at my in-laws house. People came from all around to donate clothes. It was a true example of charity. Mama and I talked a lot – where I would go, what I would do – but I still had no idea of what I wanted. I could barely accept the fact that my entire family had been lost. My father and I spoke, but I could still hear the pain in his voice. My grandparents begged me to come home, but reports of Temple death squads were still fresh in my mind, and I told them I was safer in New Jersey.

For about a week after, I read the newspapers – there was a picture of Mama carrying Jakari through the airport – and continued to stay underground. There was no contact with anyone except Sarah and Basil. Eventually, I willed myself to begin job hunting. How I do not know. Mama had told me she would send me to college and said she could watch over Jakari. When I think back on that opportunity, I am sad in some ways. The offer was generous, but I was not ready to accept it. I had made a promise to myself that Jakari would never be taken away from me again.

I traveled into New York City to sign up with a couple of employment agencies. I had to lie on my resume, saying I had been out of the country with my husband and we were in the middle of a divorce. Looking back, I realize I was in total denial. Everything was buried. People deal with grief differently, and the way I dealt with it was not to deal with it. I feared that if I returned to Jonestown in my mind, I might disappear and never come back.

My grandparents in Sacramento, California pleaded with me to come home. They needed to see me. My grandpa placed bars all over the windows and doors. He had provided protection for us, and promised that I would be okay.

Knowing how much they had lost, I finally made the decision to return to California to the safe haven of my grandparents. Lord knows that the fear that engulfed me was tremendous, but I also knew that God had watched over me thus far. If I could make it out of Jonestown, I could make it anywhere. My sister's boyfriend flew from California to take us back; he was our own personal security. My heart had to forgive him for his abuse of Michelle, the abuse that impelled her to go to Jonestown, where she'd died. In order for me to go on, I could not judge him or anyone else who grieved. We all had lost so much. With tearful goodbyes to my in-laws, I took my son's hand and boarded the plane, heading for a place once protected, now unsure. As we watched New Jersey fall away beneath us, I thought about my future. I'd passed my twenty-second birthday while we were in New Jersey, but it had not felt like a celebration. I no longer feared death, yet in some ways welcomed it. That way the pain would stop. I took a deep breath and sighed. Surely, God would continue to protect us.

What I couldn't imagine was that what would soon come my way would test my faith, my strength, my resilience as much as Jonestown had. I had faced it once. I would have to face it again.

New challenges lay over the horizon.

PART TWO

Chapter 11:
Returning to
Where it Began

As we disembarked from the plane in San Francisco, the look I tried to achieve was one of anonymity: a woman with a young son in the company of her sister's boyfriend. That was all. Wearing my big hat and shades I doubted anyone would recognize me, much less associate me with an international tragedy from a few weeks before. I walked quickly to the baggage claim area, while Clark went to get the car. Despite my studied nonchalance, I tensed, waiting for the burning that occurs when you are shot. At least that is what I was told a gunshot felt like: a burning sensation. *Please God,* I silently prayed, *we have come this far. Carry me a little further.* As we walked through the airport, I surreptitiously glanced at faces for anyone who looked familiar. *Why did I come back here?* I asked myself. *You came where you are most loved,* my other self answered. I deliberately slowed my gait, so my son's little legs could keep up. In my heart, I knew that God had not let me come this far, only to let it to end now. There was another plan, I knew deep in my heart, there was another plan and one day I would know what it was.

I recognized Clark's car as one I'd seen in Michelle's photographs, a long black Lincoln Continental. A sad feeling engulfed me as I pictured her driving and riding in this big fine car. There were no reporters, thank goodness. No one knew I was returning except my in-laws in New Jersey, Grandma and Grandpa, and Reverend and Mrs. Cooke. My arrival was not announced. I had hoped to slip back into California quietly and unnoticed, and so far, my plan was holding.

Clark and I rode to his townhouse in silence. Jakari was a little tired, ready to take a nice hot bath and to stretch his little body out on a bed. The flight had been four hours long, time enough for any kid to get restless. There was no way I could have allowed him to roam up and down the aisles. I hadn't known if anyone else was on the plane, if the government's omniscience included my presence on this flight, if they put something in my food the night I arrived in New Jersey that entered my blood stream, acting as a tracking system. Who knew what they were capable of? One thing I knew for sure, they could find me if they wanted to. *I am thinking way too much,* I told myself.

After 30 minutes, we pulled up into a nice complex. I felt strange as Clark unlocked the front door. This was where my sister used to live. It did not feel good. Clark offered to cook something while I got Jakari cleaned up. So far, my son Jakari was really behaving himself, considering how new all this was to him. He had to feel my emotional dishevel. I did not cry in front of him. Instead, we laughed as I splashed water on him. He loved his baths. Afterwards, we went downstairs to the dining room, where Clark had laid out a feast. I really didn't have much to say.

After dinner, we watched a little TV until Jakari fell asleep in my arms. I took him upstairs and lay with him for awhile. Then I went back downstairs to talk to Clark. He asked me how I felt. Tired, I told him. Tired, confused, and messed up. He said to give it time that it would get better. *I don't think so, how could it get better, I am lost.* My energy was not in the conversation, and I excused myself and retreated to my son, my only comfort.

The next day I woke to the smell of bacon, toast and coffee. Jakari turned over to me and kissed me. I loved my baby so much. Holding him made me feel alive. We got out of bed and I held his hand while we made our way to the smells emerging from the kitchen. As I had my first cup of coffee, I noticed the apartment showed no signs of my sister or their child Daron. *Everyone has to deal with this differently,* I thought. *His pain was there but hidden just as he had hidden all signs of their existence. We all had so much pain, how would any of us move on?* That feeling of desperation hit me, and my eyes began to tear up. Blinking hard to keep them from spilling over, I put my head in my son's neck, smelling him, taking in life. I understood.

"When you're ready, we can head to Sacramento," Clark said. "Everyone is anxious to see you." I lit a cigarette, delaying the moment of departure. *Will this numbness ever go away?* I wondered. It would just sweep over me without warning, and take me to the space I need not go. But the moment was here. I took my son upstairs to get ready for another emotional day.

I could feel my anxiety, even before we got in the car. I hadn't spoken to my father since Jonestown. He hated me, so why try? I had to push that back also, because I knew I was already overwhelmed with pain and guilt. Again we drove in silence. I knew I would not be very good company for a while. I fought back the tears because I was scared if I let myself go, I would never stop crying. So, I was quiet, thinking, holding my son. Clark was sensitive enough to sense not to force conversation.

We finally crossed over the Davis causeway that my sister and I were so proud of. Grandpa worked construction when we lived with them and he'd helped build the causeway. "This is the bridge grandpa built," we would remind each other on our way either going to or coming from our grandparents' house. Sacramento's skyline interrupted the flat horizon. Not a big city with lots of high-rises, but still recognizable. I gazed about looking for any changes, but there were none I could see. *Same small town,* I thought.

When we turned the corner at their home on 40th Avenue, I noticed a few cars in front and prayed the house wasn't full. The screen door opened, and my grandpa came out. Tears immediately welled up in my eyes, and I got out of the car, running to him with Jakari in my arms. I held on to him so tight, scared to let go. He hugged me, patting my head. "It will be all right, girl," he said, his voice was shaking with emotion. His arms tightened around me. This is one place I always found comfort, in the center of my grandpa's arms. "Thank you Jesus," my grandmother cried from behind him. "I prayed for one, and the Lord brought me two! Hallelujah, hallelujah." She grabbed us, and held me close. "Thank you Jesus, thank you Jesus, thank you Jesus," she whispered over and over. Her face was wet with her tears and mine. Some of my favorite people stood to hug me: Reverend W.P. Cooke, Mrs. Cooke, and other Deacons and Deaconess. They were praying for me, they said, and I thanked them. Prayer is what I needed to be able to adjust.

They did not press me, but I know they wanted to hear my story. So with a cup of coffee and a slice my grandpa's famous Chess Pie, I began the story. Through tears and laughter, I described what I had endured for a year and a half.

My grandmother said she had prayed, "I kept asking for one, but the Lord graced me with two." I understood what she had gone through, the same agonizing wait that I did, not knowing if any of our family had survived. My mother was her only child; I was now her only grandchild, and Jakari her only great-grandchild. They wanted to keep Jakari and for me to go back to the Bay Area and stay with Clark until I could get enough rest. They knew I was not in any shape to take care of my son, and I knew that he was in the best hands possible. Jakari had been traumatized also, and they wanted to give him a lot of love and one-on-one care. A stable place where I would always find refuge. Grandpa had kept his word; he had installed bars around the house for our protection. But there was more.

I stayed for two weeks and relished in the love of my grandparents and my son. Every day I slept in not knowing how exhausted I really was. Not wanting to leave the house, church members would stop by and bring food; wanting a glance of the survivor, the miracle. Because I believe my grandpa was especially proud of me and as he said "your bravery" he wanted me to tell the story to his fellow friends in Christ. So I did, over and over and over. It felt as if people just wanted to know about Jim and about Jonestown. Sharing as much as I could, and loving my grandparents so much, I wanted to appease them. They deserved everything…because they loved me and mine.

When it was time for me to leave, and for what I did not know…it was not as if I had a life now. Honestly, I did not have any idea about what I was going to do. When I thought back about trying to go to work immediately after arriving in New Jersey, I realized how much I was in denial. A hospital would have been better… for what I kept inside would eventually come out years later.

Before I left, grandpa called me into his room. He went to his closet, reached up to the shelf above the ganging clothes and handed me a pearl handled gun. "This is a .22 caliber," he said. "Keep this on you at all times. Sleep with it under your pillow; carry it in your purse. Use it if you have to. Aim for the heart or the head." The gun in my hand made me feel a little safer, but also did not let me forget that danger still existed for me. A newspaper had published a list of survivors, and listed me as being from Sacramento. The media was not sensitive to our concerns. "No one knows you have this, understand?" he added. "Yes" I whispered and wrapped my arms around his neck. "I love you so much, Grandpa." He said in that tone "Girl, I love you too."

I kissed my son, who was engrossed in the toys they'd bought him. He waved and hugged me. "Bye mommy," he said. Although I did not want to leave him, I knew it was best for right now. Clark had came back to pick me up and we made the long drive back to Foster City without Jakari. He tried to engage me in conversation, but I was talked out. The music he played on the radio was our only accompaniment.

This was the just the beginning of living a life underground, weaving stories about who I was and where I came from. Clark worked at night and I just stayed alone, watching TV with the volume turned low, listening for unusual sounds. I could not sleep upstairs, so I slept on the couch, close to the door. I laid around, eating a lot. Reading kept my mind occupied for a while, but I was not accustomed to doing nothing. The gun was with me always, and even Clark did not know I had it.

The days were just as bad as the nights. Guilt would enter my heart, and I'd start crying again. *Why did I have to live? My brother should have survived, he was the precious one. He was the sweet one.* Most days I felt as if I were sinking in a dark hole, not knowing what lay ahead. Trying not to think of what happened that day. I spoke to my child every day, never thinking about how the long distance bill was adding up.

As I began to get used to my new life, I began to wonder how Clark was doing. After all, he had lost my sister and a son, Daron. He cooked for me when he got home from work, and on weekends, he took me out to clubs. *If nothing else works,* I thought, *the club always does.* It felt strange though, to be partying so soon afterward, as if nothing had happened. It was then that I realized it was easier for people to forget than to remember, because memories cut deep into your core. Everyone was really trying to get me back to a normal place, but what I really felt I needed was a bullet to my head. How could I go on?

I continued to live burying the feeling of emptiness, existing in that townhouse in Foster City.

One day after living at Clark's home for about two months I told him I wanted to go to Sacramento for awhile to see my son and grandparents. He agreed. Then I told him I wanted to go by Greyhound. "Are you sure?" he asked "I can drive you." But it was time for me to do something on my own, even if it was only climbing onto a bus.

My grandpa met me at the station in Sacramento. He asked how I was, and I tried saying "Okay," but that wasn't true. I was only going through the motions of living. As soon as we arrived at the house and I saw my son though, I felt better. This was the youngest survivor of Jonestown. I was watching a miracle, and I thanked God every day. Somehow I knew it would get better, but I had no idea how long it would take.

After I was there for about a week, my grandmother told me she had set up a blind date for me. I did not want to go on a date, and I told her so, especially when she gave me so few details. It was with her friend's son, whose father owned a club on Stockton Boulevard where Joe and I used to go when we visited my grandparents. Worst of all, the man knew all about me. I know she was trying to make me have a normal life, but I was not interested in dates. "It's already set up." She persisted, sounding disappointed, and I relented. Later that afternoon, we gathered up Jakari and went shopping for something to wear. I had not had any money since I got back from Jonestown. Everyone was taking care of me. I had a purse, but nothing in it by way of money.

The fact is everyone was doing everything for me. I noticed that night when she cooked dinner. Everyone was feeding me. And everyone knew not to put rice on my plate. The sight of it made me sick to my stomach.

Friday came before I was ready, and increasingly, I dreaded the blind date. When the doorbell rang, my grandpa admitted a tall young man, with a mouth full of teeth. They introduced him and he studied me with interest. *Not my type*, I thought. *This was going to be a long night.* I kissed everyone and hugged my child, giving my grandmother a look only a woman would understand. She smiled coyly and sent us out the door. Grandpa told the young man to be careful. *Did you tell him he may be in danger? That I had a target on my back?* I wanted to ask.

He opened the door to the Cadillac for me. I knew he was pleased with my appearance. *A little trophy,* I thought. We pulled up in the parking lot of his father's club, he opened my car door, and we headed towards the entrance. The club was small and the dance floor was already crowded. I decided to make a real effort to enjoy myself. People greeted him like he was a celebrity. He finally asked me to dance. On the dance floor, I let the music take me somewhere else. I tried to look at him and smile, but it was hard. I did not want to be there.

As I swung around, I came face-to-face with a fine dude. He was Latin and gorgeous. The electricity moved from his body to mine. We kept our secret dance going for the duration of the music. As my date and I left the dance floor, I turned one last time and he tilted his head. I knew exactly what that meant. When I got back to the table, I grabbed my purse and excused myself to the bathroom. He was there. "You are beautiful," he told me. "You too," I said. He asked about my partner, and I told him it was a blind date that my grandparents set me up with. "I don't live here," I continued, "I live in Foster City." "What?" he said. "I live in Hayward." His name was David. Hayward was right across the bridge from Foster City.

I could barely contain myself. I felt alive talking to him. I gave him my number, and he promised to call, then leaned forward and kissed me on the cheek. After that, I was ready to go home and dream about him. My date had noticed I was gone for a while and had a little attitude when I got back to the table. *He will get over it,* I thought. After a couple more dances, I told him I was ready to go. He was a little disappointed, but took me home anyway. I kissed him on the cheek and told him I had a good time. I just didn't say the good time was with someone else.

When I awoke the next morning, I felt as if I had something to look forward to. It was almost time for me to go back to Foster City. My grandparents were disappointed that I did not want to go to church. I explained to them that I was not ready for all those people coming up to me to talk. They tried to understand, but I know it was difficult. I stayed home and made homemade rolls which were our family secret. Every Sunday there was a big dinner. They always invited someone over; I guess that was their way of easing me back into the world. I tolerated it because I loved them. As much as I wanted to retreat to my bedroom, I forced myself to endure the questions. After all, it was for them.

The day I got ready to leave, I kissed and hugged my son – it seemed I was doing a lot of that lately – and boarded the bus. Grandma packed me a lunch, a shoe box with two biscuits and two chicken wings, just as she had when I was a kid. Clark picked me up at the other end of the bus trip and told me that some guy kept calling me. When I told him it was someone I met in Sacramento, he warned me to be careful, because I didn't know who this guy was. I detected something in his voice, but I couldn't pinpoint it.

I couldn't wait to get the call from my new friend, and I didn't have to wait long. The phone rang later that night, and Clark answered. It was for me. Trying not to sound too excited, I picked up the phone. It was him. We talked for a good hour, mostly about him. Thank goodness he did not ask about me. I wasn't ready to share that secret with anyone.

He started calling almost every day, and I looked forward to them. After about a month, he finally asked me out. All of a sudden, it seemed important for me to ask Clark. "Listen," I said, "can you call me back in about ten minutes?" "Sure," he replied, but his voice sounded a little weird. After I hung up, I went to Clark. It seemed like the thing to do, because, after all, he'd been taking care of me. He grilled me about my caller, who he was, what he did for a living, then concluded "I don't think it is a good idea." "I'm bored," I told him. "What, we don't do enough together?" "I am not my sister," I replied.

That was the wrong thing to say. He walked over to me as if he was going to slap me, but I stood up to him. "Don't you dare," I told him. He stopped and recovered. "Sorry," he said. "You're right, you need a life too." The fact was we were both depending on each other too much. When the phone rang, I answered and told my friend that I would go out with him. I almost said, "I can go out with you." But that would sound like I'd been controlled. If he only knew...

He was as handsome as I remembered. We went to a local restaurant and talked for about three hours. He drove me home, and leaned into me for a kiss. I turned my head and it landed on my cheek. I wasn't ready for that yet either.

Shortly afterward, Clark told me he had a friend coming up from L.A. When the "someone" turned out to be a pretty woman, I was not happy. How in the hell could he find someone this soon after Michelle? How could he replace my sister that fast? He introduced me, and I glared with fury. I hated that woman right away and I hated him. *How long had he been seeing this skank*, I wondered. *Probably the entire time he was with my sister.* Clark took the two of us out, but I had nothing to say to her. They danced, laughed and talked.

The worst part of it was she apparently wasn't there for one date. It seemed like she was there forever, including being with me at home while Clark worked nights. Every day after he left, I went upstairs to my bedroom and closed the door. I wanted nothing to do with her. I know I treated her badly.

When she finally left, I decided enough was enough. Grandma had told me that mom's old boyfriend wanted to talk to me, and I called him. I remembered he had a construction business. He took very good care of my mother. He was a big man, tall and kind of fat. He came over the next day, to take me out to eat and clothes shopping. My wardrobe was improving. He asked me if I liked living with Clark, and I admitted that I did not. He then offered me a place to live and a job. "Let me ask my grandparents," I said. This need to ask others for permission to do things was getting to be a habit. "Why do you have to ask them? Aren't you grown?" "I have to ask my grandparents," I repeated. *What is wrong with everyone*, I wondered? I had to consult my grandparents; they knew what was best for me right now. Even though I was 21 years old, they had to be asked.

That night, I called Grandpa, who said he would have to talk to John to get some things clear. He would let me know. In the meantime, Clark was going to visit the skank in Los Angeles, and I was stuck without any transportation. And in the other meantime, my friend and I were still talking every day, but when he began giving off sexual innuendos I told him I wasn't ready. I had just lost my husband, I told him. He knew that already, so he did not press the point. Of course I told him he had died in a car accident.

My grandpa called back a few days later and said it was okay to go with John. Clark was still in Los Angeles, and I thought it would be a good time to leave while he was gone. I wrote him a long note thanking him and explaining that I was going move into an apartment and work for John. I made sure I had his number on me, in case I needed to call him.

After I finished packing, John picked me up and took me to a motel in Daly City with individual bungalows. He must have noticed the look on my face and answered my silent question. "The apartment will be ready in a couple of weeks. You'll stay here for now." I had a strange feeling, but I immediately ignored it as unfounded paranoia. Certainly my grandpa would not tell me to go if he felt I would not be safe. We entered the Spanish-style bungalow. It was dim but had a small kitchen and a TV. The refrigerator was already stocked. John gave me a business card and told me to call if I needed anything. And then he asked if I remembered David. Who could forget David? David was an Italian straight out of New York and he'd adored my sister and been her boyfriend for awhile. "David will keep an eye out for you," John said. I didn't like where this was heading. He then handed me a hundred dollar bill, adding, "In case you want something else."

I peeked through the thin curtains after the door closed behind him and watched him pull off in the truck. It felt strange to be alone. I did not like it. The place was noisy. How could I hear if someone was trying to get in? I kept my gun close to me. I wondered why Grandpa did not arrange for me to talk to someone. Maybe I was really okay, even though I felt really confused. *I need to pray more*, I told myself. *God has got you, Leslie, don't every forget that. Yes, God has you*, the other voice said to me. *He has you in this weird place, with these strange people. Stop making me doubt God*, I told the other voice. *There's a reason I'm here. What is it then? The other voice interjected. Stop listening to that. God has you, remember?*

The first night, the bed ended up a mess, as I tossed and turned. I woke up feeling so disconnected and the feeling of hopelessness would take over. I felt as if I were deep in a hole, with no way to get out.

I had not really grieved. I willed myself not to cry, nor to think too much. In the back of my mind, I still waited for word that my family had been found deep in the jungle, maybe in Venezuela. Hope was still there when I prayed hard enough. But there was so much I still would not let myself accept.

David showed up that morning. He looked the same as I remembered. I also remembered he had been a heroin addict, and it had aged him more than his young years. The signs showed in the deep lines in his face. His age was not what showed in his face. "You look good, Leslie," he said by way of renewing our acquaintance. *Why is he telling me that how can I look good, I have been through hell and right now I feel like I'm going a little deeper.* "Thanks" I replied, forcing a smile. *Was he supposed to be my bodyguard or what?* I thought. I already wanted him to leave. He was making me uncomfortable. I asked what he was doing now. He was working for John, as I would be. After a few minutes, we left the bungalow to go buy a pack of cigarettes. The smell of early morning filled my nostrils. The sky was almost clear, small clouds replacing the fog that Daly City usually produces. The white four-door station wagon was parked in front of the motel. The store was within walking distance – only four blocks away – but I hadn't been sure if I should go out alone.

I don't know if my discomfort showed, but he left soon after he returned me to my bungalow. As much as I dreaded solitude, I had dreaded his presence even more. I spent the entire day in front of the TV bored out of my mind.

John stopped by later that evening and asked if I wanted him to drop me off at a club. Sure, I said, and he told me to get dressed, that he would be back in an half an hour. I showered and put on some clothes Clark had bought. John was true to his word: Within 30 minutes, I heard the knock on the door and a key in the lock. *Why does he have a key?* I panicked. *I did not know he had a key.* "You ready?" he asked. "You look nice," he continued. *He should stop telling me that*, I thought. *I need to calm down*, I added.

John dropped me off at a club in the financial district off of Broadway. He told me not to stay out too late and to catch a cab home. The moment I walked in, the music put me in another place. It had only been four months, and I was trying to find a normal life, whatever that meant. I found a table and ordered a Hennessy, straight up with water back. After the waitress left, a man came up and asked me to dance. As we entered the dance floor, I felt like part of me was there and the other part somewhere else. Trying to push back that feeling, I danced harder, smiling at my dance partner. He walked me to my table and asked if he could sit down. I really did not want to talk, but I told him yes. He asked me my name. I lied. Where did I live? I lied. What did I do? I lied. His questions were harmless, but they seemed like an interrogation. And I answered them all with lies. It felt a little rough, so I made a mental note to at least keep my story straight.

At about 1:00 a.m. I was ready to go home. I asked the waitress to call me a cab, since I'd had too many drinks. The guy I had been talking to offered to take me home, but I graciously told him no. He walked me outside and waited with me for the cab. When the cab pulled up, the driver called out a name. I stood there. My companion said, "Hey, that's you." Hell, if I lied, I'd certainly have to remember what I said. As I settled into the cab, the man asked me for my phone number. I lied, rattling off some random digits.

The alcohol had one benefit: I slept hard. As the sun shone through the curtains the next morning, I felt more rested. John showed up later on and asked me how my night went. I told him okay. I could go out as much as I wanted, he said, and I took his advice and went out at least another three times that week. He kept putting money in my purse, and I began to get more comfortable with him.

Then one day, with no build-up, he demanded to know where the gold was hidden. Just as quickly as I had felt comfortable, the feeling melted like ice in a glass of hot water. What the hell was he talking about? "What gold?" I asked. "The gold everyone said was in Jonestown," he insisted. "You know where the gold is, don't you?" I wondered if he were crazy. How would I know where the gold is? He even had a plan! "We can go to Jonestown, and get it. The government will allow us in!" My danger radar was on high mode, but I did not trust my feelings enough to know that this feeling was real, and I shrugged it off. "Never mind," he softly assured me. "We'll talk about it later." He left a short time later.

I should have left too. I lingered, trying to understand why John believed I knew where there was gold. A knock on the door jarred me from these deep thoughts. It was David. He told me John was angry, that I had been going out too much and had brought a man back to the motel. I hadn't, but even if I did, why would he be upset? What business was it of his? Then he really shocked me. "Leslie, he said "I have to beat you up! He's taking care of you, and you have to obey his rules." *What is he talking about?* The voice inside me screamed. *What rules? No one told me about any rules.* "I'll tell you what I'll do," David said reasonably. "Let me put a couple of bruises on you so he thinks I did it." I asked where. I couldn't believe, I was negotiating a beating, but I asked. "On your arms, you can cover those," he said, and before I could say another word, he hit me hard on my upper arm. I yelled. He hit me again. He was enjoying this, I thought. The bruises began to form right away. My light skin tone made sure of that. He apologized, and when John showed up shortly afterwards, he hugged me and, offering own apology, repeated that he was sorry it had to happen like this. "Your apartment will be ready tomorrow," he added, as though that would compensate for what had just happened. Instead I was even more confused. I wondered if I should tell my grandparents, but decided against it. I didn't want them to worry anymore about me.

When the two of them finally left, I retrieved the gun from underneath the pillow and placed it on the nightstand. I fixed a drink and then another until I felt like I could go to sleep. My arm really hurt, so I put some ice on it. Finally I drifted off to sleep.

The next day, they returned and picked me up. I was already packed, because I had not taken the clothes out of the suitcases John had bought me, and we bundled into a station wagon and left the motel. I realized I still hadn't called Clark to let him know what was going on or that I was okay. My grandparents had told me he was worried about me with John. Hell, *I* was worried about me with John.

The apartment was in a building with a security door. We walked up a flight of stairs, and he stopped outside a door, unlocking it. The place was already furnished – quite attractively, too – and I told him so. After all, he had paid my mother's rent in her high-rise apartment in San Francisco. He was taking care of his dead girlfriend's daughter. That was all there was to it.

The refrigerator was well-stocked too. Everyone made sure I had food. Already I could feel that I had put on some pounds, but I didn't care.

He pointed out the phone to me. "You will answer it and take messages for me," he said. "This will be your job." When they left, he handed me set of two keys. "I'm leaving the station wagon with you, so you'll have transportation. The other is the door key." I already knew he had one for himself, but the car was more important, and I was excited about that. Going to the Department of Motor Vehicles was done right away with Clarke, as I had no formal identification. I was able to get my name as Leslie Fortier…the beginning of my identity change. As soon as they left, I called my grandparents and told them about the apartment and the car, everything except the beating. When I spoke to Jakari, he asked when I was coming home. I didn't know, I told him. I didn't know what I was doing, I added to myself. Everyone has planned what I am doing.

Nevertheless, as I settled into my new place, I felt like things were improving. I found a small club in the town of Cotati, not far from the apartment, and frequented it about three times a week. Having a car allowed me to do more clubbing. One night I met a very tall, lean and handsome brother who danced very well with me. Soon Scott and I were meeting every week to dance. I loved the way he moved on the dance floor. The relationship was strictly platonic, and he never came on to me. We would talk for hours on the phone, and finally, thinking I had a true friend, I shared my secret with him. We would drive up to Coit Tower in San Francisco some nights, turn the radio on low, and while taking in the spectacular view of the city, talk way past midnight. He told me about his mother who'd passed and his two younger siblings. He worked hard and he was a very good listener.

The phone in my apartment rarely rang during the day. After about a month, I called Keith, my old church buddy, who was staying in Oakland with Allison. In the course of our conversation, he mentioned that Matthew, my first boyfriend, had asked about me, and I told Keith to give him my number. Matthew called, and we talked for more than two hours. He was living in Los Angeles, he said, and had a good job. Then he asked if I wanted to come and see him and – when I said yes – promised to make the arrangements, including paying for the airline ticket. John stopped by later, as he did almost every day, and I told him I was going to Los Angeles to visit my aunt and uncle, who wanted to have a fundraiser to help me get on my feet. I had become an accomplished and comfortable liar. John had no reason not to believe I was going to see relatives, and gave me the time off.

The day finally arrived, and John drove me to the airport. The plane ride was smooth. When I disembarked, Matthew was there at the gate. He had not changed a bit. We hugged and headed out to his little convertible sports car in the parking lot. I could tell he was proud of himself. We began to talk as if the years since our last meeting were mere days. He took me out to eat, and we had drinks. By the time we got to his apartment on Gramercy Place in Hollywood, I was feeling pretty good. I asked if I could take a shower. "You don't have to ask me to take a shower," he said. Smiling, I headed for the bathroom. The long hot shower felt good. The next step would be a lovemaking session, and with him I knew I was ready. When I stepped from the shower, he was already undressed and lying across the bed. He had put on a Minnie Ripperton tape, nice and low. I took off my towel and went to lie next to him. But he stopped me, got up, and went to the corner of the room. He pulled up some carpet and removed a piece of paper. "Have you ever tried coke?" he asked as he headed back to the bed. Wow, he sure did change, I thought. I hadn't had coke since Carlos left that package for me. I played the innocent, and said that I hadn't. He pulled out a hundred dollar bill from his wallet and rolled it up. Disappearing again for another minute, he came back with a plate. Putting some of the powder on the plate, he put the bill to his nose and bent over the powder. After two quick hits, he turned to me. I recognized the look from Carlos. His face had lit up, even his eyes. He gave me the bill and told me what to do. My head opened up. I felt good. In fact, it was better than before. My world looked brighter.

It is amazing how you never forget your first. He had been my first and it felt natural to be with him, and I knew that Joe would approve. After all, he'd known Matthew from the Temple and stolen me from him. Now Matthew had me back.

The next day, we went to see the Eartha Kitt musical *Timbuktu*. I had never been to a musical, and it was fantastic. She was incredible, with her beautiful outfits and her throaty voice. I truly enjoyed it. Afterwards, we went to a restaurant, and then headed back to the apartment for more of the same as the night before. At some point, I managed to find time to call my son in Sacramento. My grandparents remembered Matthew and said they were glad I was having a good time.

The next evening, he introduced me to some people he wanted me to meet, a nice attractive, Caucasian couple. We ate at their house and played backgammon. When we left, Matthew said that they'd liked me. "I liked them, too," I answered. "No," he insisted, "they really like you." I laughed. "Me too." But I hadn't gotten it yet. "They want to swing with you," Matthew said. "He wants me to have his girlfriend and he wants to have you." "As in, sleep with?" I said, shocked. "No, I don't think so." Matthew asked me to think about it – "I owe him a favor," he explained – but the ride going back took longer than it did coming. I was quiet, feeling weird. If he cared about me, how could he want me to have sex with someone else? I tried to rationalize it: people in the church had sex with people all the time for the cause, and maybe his cause was just as important. The stress of the evening didn't leave my body until he got out his package, and this time when we made love, I was the aggressor.

He came to me the next day as I packed, and asked if I had thought about the question he asked. I told him I was sorry but that I couldn't do it. "Well, you must not love me," he said. This time as we drove, he was the one who was quiet. "Give me a little time," I told him when we arrived at the airport. "Maybe I will change my mind." I was scared he would not want to see me again. He kissed me deep and hard and watched me board the plane.

Life reverted to routine back in Daly City. I went to L.A. on some weekends, but more often to Sacramento. Jakari was doing well with his great-grandparents. He was fat and happy and spoiled. Every time he saw me, I had a gift for him. It eased my guilt. Matthew and I saw each other regularly, but after I decided I was not going to "swing" with his friends, he stopped calling. In the meantime, John was beginning to give me sexual hints. It was making me uncomfortable, but I ignored them as the actions of a typical man. At 22, I was old enough to have known better.

One evening when John stopped by, he told me it was time for him to get what was due to him. I was genuinely baffled, so he laid it out for me. "Did you think I was paying for all of this and that you would not have to eventually pay for anything?" "I am your girlfriend's daughter," I reminded him. "I thought you were doing it for that reason." But that wasn't it.

I had been grateful to John. He had done a lot for me. But he was my mother's boyfriend, and he was probably 25 years my senior. I asked him to give me more time. He left looking like a sick puppy.

I called Keith and Allison the next morning, and told them I needed to leave, because John wanted me to sleep with him. When they picked me up, I took only what belonged to me. I told my grandparents the same story I gave my friends.

Allison's apartment was nice, she always had good taste. Keith and I slept on the floor, surrounding by what looked like a greenhouse. Allison had beautiful big plants which gave the apartment a homey feeling.

Feeling stable enough to look for a job, I ventured out to an agency. I wanted to get back into the hospitality industry, but there were no openings. Finally, I interviewed with Bateman, Eichler, Hill & Richards, a stock brokerage firm located on the 25th floor of the Bank of America building. My new job paid $850 a month, which I thought was pretty good. I rode into work with Allison, but since she was working two jobs, I caught the bus home. I stayed at that apartment for about two months. With nowhere else to go, I called my father and asked him if I could stay with him. The plan was to work and create a stable environment so that I could bring Jakari home to me. I did not bring my child out to be raised by someone else. Still there was no fooling myself that I had healed from the tragedy. It had not yet been a year.

I called my father and asked him if I could stay with him. He agreed, but I heard the reluctance in his voice. I guess he felt it was the least he could do. Although we talked about what happened, he never brought up the belief that I should have gotten my brother out. I know my father was in as much pain as anyone else affected by the deaths. He loved my brother so much. They spent a lot of time together. I felt guilty about it anyway. I wanted to ask why he let Mom bring Mark over, but – respecting our mutual silence on my brother – I felt it wasn't appropriate. Whatever he thought he could have done, it was too late to change. I never wanted him to feel the way he made me feel.

Dad's apartment was right on Union Street, a ten-minute bus ride away from my job. I was secretary to three stock brokers, and I loved it. The work was interesting and both my supervisor and the manager of the office were very friendly. Learning the job was no problem. When the receptionist went to lunch and breaks, I sat in as her relief. We were still using typewriters. The switchboard was the old-fashioned PBX kind.

The only time I did not like was lunch time, when people talked about their personal lives. Someone asked me about my family, and I told them they were killed in a car accident. They were sympathetic, and even though I regretted making them sad with my lie, I also knew it would keep them quiet. Besides, it was better than telling them I had been in Jonestown, Guyana. They would surely find a reason to get rid of me if they knew.

Once again, I tied to establish a routine. I went to work and went home afterwards. I rarely traveled to Oakland to see my friends there. Every other weekend I went to see Jakari, who was thriving with his great grandparents. He was surrounded by men who took him fishing, and other activities. Every time I would visit there would be guilt. Yet I still felt I was not worthy of him. I had lost contact with Scott, which bothered me.

I found myself extremely attracted to one of my bosses, R.A. He flirted with me and I flirted back. He was at least twenty years older than me, but it didn't matter. One night he appeared at the bus stop, and we bantered a bit before he asked if I were hungry. I said I was. "Do you like Italian?" he asked. "Of course," I responded. "Okay, it's settled, Italian." We boarded a different bus than the one we took home, and when we got off in North Beach and walked the block to a restaurant, he took my hand.

The walls of the restaurant were covered with beautiful artwork. I felt as if I had walked into a location in Tuscany. The tables were adorned with white linen tablecloths and burgundy napkins. The maitre d' seated us at a small table in the corner. Never had I been in a restaurant like this, and I asked if he would order for me. He suggested cannelloni – veal and chicken wrapped in a light pasta shell – which sounded wonderful. The waiter brought wine to the table and poured only a tablespoon or so in the glass. My boss swished it around while holding it up to the light. He took only a sip, letting it move around his mouth. "Excellent," he proclaimed. Wow, I thought. I was learning how to eat in fine restaurants.

The cannelloni was delicious; the salad that preceded it was fine. We talked a lot. Later, as we stepped out of the restaurant, he invited me to his house for dinner. We talked about keeping our friendship out of the work place. He called me a cab to take me home. I thought about him and the wonderful evening I had had. His age was not a factor. He was thoughtful, a real man and a gentlemen. Although he was much older than me, I believe that he was like a father figure to me and I felt safe around him.

One night, I woke up in the night, screaming, "Hide the children in the jungle." The nightmare startled him. He held me close, comforting me, drying my tears. The next morning I went home early.

Working together was difficult, hiding our relationship. I never told him what the nightmare was about.

* * * * *

My father and I were traveling down Van Ness Avenue, when I happened to glance over at a movie theatre. "Stop the car, Dad," I blurted. I think I scared him. I would see him at the house, hopped out of the car and walked quickly to the line in front of the theatre. "Scott?" I said to the tall, lean, handsome man as I tapped him on the shoulder. His face lit up. The movie forgotten, we began walking towards Union Street. My heart filled with joy. We talked about everything that happened since we'd last seen each other. Arriving home, I introduced my father to Scott, and the four of us – Dad was dating the woman downstairs – sat in the living room talking. I cooked and Scott helped, and we all ate together. When Dad went to bed, so did we.

We were inseparable after that night. I broke it off with my boss who was not happy. One day, Dad told me that Scott could not move in. It amazes me now that I had no qualms about him staying with me at my Dad's house. I realize that those small manners were not taught in the church. But it was my father's house, and I abided by his wishes. We were not taught morals or sexual etiquette. Peoples Temple had its own.

I took Scott to Sacramento to meet Grandma and Grandpa, and of course, Jakari. They all loved him. We started going there every other weekend when Scott could get off from his job in a small clothing store in the Fillmore District. Sometimes on the weekends, I stayed at his place he shared with another friend. He taught me how to make stuffed Cornish hens and introduced me to a traditional Filipino dish called lumpia. As time went on, I realized I had fallen in love with him. I missed my son and wanted him with me. When I asked my dad if Jakari could come and stay he said no. It was then that I told him, if you don't accept him, you don't accept me. It was time to get my own place.

Grandpa had other grandchildren by his son. Grandpa was not my blood grandpa but through marrying my grandmother he got us. It never mattered to me one way or another. He was my grandpa. One of his other granddaughter's husband owned an apartment building on E. 13th Avenue in Oakland. He had a vacancy and said I could have it. It had two bedrooms and one bath, and – on a clear day – a view of both the Bay and Golden Gate bridges. There were red carpeting and built-in bookcases in the living room and dining area. It was perfect.

About that time, I finally received my social security checks, and the first one, retroactive to the time of Joe's death, was over $3000. I put $500 down on a car, and Grandpa co-signed the note for the balance. Scott and I went to pick out furniture for our new apartment. We were finally going have our own place. A couple of months later, we began planning our wedding and a honeymoon in the Pocono Mountains, in Pennsylvania. We finally moved in and the next weekend Grandma and Grandpa brought my son to me.

Jakari's room was furnished with a custom bed with drawers underneath. Scott and I fixed it up as we were excited to have him home. Again, I felt as if my life were coming back together. When my grandparents arrived with Jakari, I took him upstairs and showed him his new room. He was excited. My grandparents stayed the weekend and we had a great time playing dominoes, with Grandma cooking up a storm.

The arrival of Mothers Day caught me off guard. I woke up very depressed. Scott went to work that morning. I went next door and asked my neighbor to keep Jakari so he could play with her children and I could have some time alone. Folding towels always relaxed me, so I sat in front of the linen closet in the small hallway with the .22 caliber gun on the floor next to me. Everything in my life was working, but I felt so sad. As I sat there folding towels, tears began to flow – uncontrollably.

The flood gates opened and I could not stop thinking about my mother. The lightness in her laugh, her brown eyes full of love and a passion for life. A woman I could share everything with and who never judged. Inez Jeanette Wagner. The sobs rocked my core. I missed my mother so much. A sinking feeling overtook me, and I began to put the gun to my temple. But what if I missed? What would happen if I couldn't do this right? Would I end up as a vegetable? And what about Jakari? He had already suffered the loss of one parent – and more tears flowed. For several hours, I kept picking up the gun and studying it. By the time Scott called, I was hysterical. He told me he would be home as quickly as he could get there.

I was emotionally distraught when he arrived an hour later. He ran me a bath, helping me undress and helping me in the tub. As he washed my back, I realized how much I loved him. He put me to bed and gave me a massage. I rested well that night.

This was the man who introduced me to Angela Bofill, Chuck Mangione, Herb Alpert, Al Jarreau and a host of others. He took me to my first Berkeley Jazz Festival. This was the man who would witness me break down in the middle of a major grocery chain store crying because the lines were so long. He was so patient with me. Even though I was making more money, my money was our money and he never abused that. But somewhere deep inside I believed I didn't deserve any thing that was good.

Jakari was enrolled in Montessori in Oakland and did well for a while. He still had a bad temper and would throw tantrums. The teachers could not deal with it, so they asked me to remove him. Another school took him in the Montclair area of Oakland. He did better there but still had tantrums. I had read somewhere that coffee helped children that were hyper, and began to give him a cup every morning. It helped for a while. Jakari was a loving child. Once as I lay on the couch he would put a blanket over me and kiss me "you are my sleeping beauty." I hugged him until I almost cried.

Post traumatic stress and survivor's guilt do not contribute towards a successful good life. Even though Scott made me as happy as he could, I was beginning to exhibit self-destructive behavior that would affect our relationship and our future. I began going out clubbing without him. He would stay home with Jakari while I went out.

One night would change everything. Dancing like crazy at a club in San Francisco, I turned to see a man who would knock me to my knees. He stood there smiling at me. After the music stopped, he reached for my hand and helped me off the stage dance floor. I was sweating and out of breath. "You want to get some air?" he asked. Scott vanished from my mind. The man introduced himself as Nicholas and we sat outside and talked for an hour, then we left the club in my car. As we headed across the Bay Bridge, it was hard to concentrate on the road. We finally arrived at his apartment.

I awoke at four in the morning and rushed home. Scott was waiting up for me. One look at me and he knew what had happened. "Why are you doing this to us?" he asked. "What am I doing?" I retorted.

Things became worse, and he finally moved out. I felt empty. I missed Scott, but my new man was full of ideas and the same dreams that I had finally begun to have.

Chapter 12
The 1980's.

The first time Nicholas slapped me was when he came home after going AWOL. He didn't explain what AWOL was, but after the slap, I wasn't asking any confrontational questions. He apologized and said it would never happen again. But it did. It kept happening until I finally broke up with him.

Jakari needed a lot of attention, so I stayed home more than I used to, going out maybe once every other week. Being with my son was enough for me.

I took a job as a secretary in the Laundry and Valet department at the St. Francis Hotel in San Francisco, because there were no other jobs available at the hotel. I knew that once I was hired, I would be able to move into a department I really wanted. My dress did not change; silk blouses, Bandolino pumps, and my Louis Vuitton satchel. My hair was pulled back in a bun, giving me a sophisticated and professional appearance. Every time another job came open in the hotel, I would ask for a transfer, but my boss would tell me to be patient. Finally, when the director of HR said that the controller Terry Neils had a position open in his department, I seized the opportunity. My salary went from $900 a month to $1,300. With rent only $250 and my car payment $64, I kept my expenses under $500 per month. The money was coming in. We just weren't saving any.

Nicholas and I got back together, but he was not working. He had deserted his station – that's what AWOL meant – and the military was looking for him. So I was the one supporting the family. Then we lost the apartment. It belonged to my cousin, but we'd had a disagreement when I pulled up the hideous red carpet with an ugly stain in the center. I sent Jakari back to Sacramento, because his temper was out of control, and Grandpa thought he would be better off with the stability that he and Grandma could provide. Nicholas and I lived in a hotel while I looked for a new apartment. With no savings, the search was difficult.

The solution occurred to me soon after Jakari's departure: we should *all* move to Sacramento. It would be a fresh start for all of us, and Nicholas wouldn't have to look over his shoulder all the time the way he did in the Bay Area. We found a brand new duplex right down the street from my grandparents, emptied everything out of storage, and moved into our new place. Jakari had his own room and we were happy. I even found a vanpool running to San Francisco, so I could keep my job. It worked for quite a while. We began to build a nice life.

Things changed when Nicholas began disappearing on me, the same way he'd disappeared from the military. He left one day in my car and with a vague assurance he would be back. I did not see him for a week. I finally called his dad's house and learned that he was at the hospital. But it wasn't Nicholas who needed medical attention. Nicholas's previous woman Denise was having his baby. It shouldn't have come as a surprise. When I asked him one time if he had a child out there, he denied it. It wasn't a lie yet: the child had not been born. He finally decided to come home, but I kicked him out. It was back to just Jakari and me.

On my own once again, I decided to relocate to the East Coast to attend one of the top notch secretary schools in the nation. Graduates of their programs landed positions with CEO's of major companies and even the White House. Speaking to my in-laws in New Jersey they welcomed me and Jakari to stay with them while I went to school.

One phone call would set me on another course; the one from Nicholas. When my grandmother handed me the phone, I could see from her expression that she was not happy. His voice on the other end sent my heart skipping and he asked me to drive to Berkeley to see him. Weak and still in love, I planned the trip. The following weekend as soon as I saw him, the old feelings emerged right away. We talked for hours and made a decision to get back together. Sharing the news with my grandma and grandpa would not be easy. They did not accept it and asked me not to go.

Not yet giving up on him, I went and found a hotel while we looked for an apartment. My job at the St. Francis was still intact. Money was not a problem; I was receiving my blood money from the Jonestown tragedy soon.

We found an apartment and moved in within a couple of days. I still had my car but Nicholas wanted another one, so he found a convertible El Dorado. Money meant nothing in the church and unfortunately that was my attitude. He continued not to work and I kept commuting to the Bay Area. We finally went to Reno to get married. My spirit told me not to go through with it and as I sat in front of the minister in a small chapel, my mind was somewhere else, not able to hear his words, I had to repeatedly ask him to repeat the vows.

Returning to Oakland as a married woman, the feeling of elation was not there. My husband was still jealous and this did not diminish with my pregnancy. We were supposed to live happily ever after, but he increasingly seemed agitated and angry. I continued to work in San Francisco and tried to convince Nicholas to turn himself in. He would not.

My daughter was born in 1983 after a beautiful delivery, but things did not improve with Nicholas. One day, when she was about two months old, he came home, found the .22 caliber pistol my grandpa had once given me and set it on the coffee table. His ranting and raving was without cause. I told him to keep his voice down, but that made him even madder. He lurched forward me and grabbed me by the throat.

I survived that night, but I was numb. As devastated as I was, I packed the kids up for the babysitter and school. When I turned the key in the lock I knew it would be the last time. When I dropped my daughter off at daycare, I shared with the sitter the trouble I was having. I did not plan to return to the apartment once I left work that evening. It was the last time we lived in that apartment as husband and wife. That night I knew one day it would be life or death; his or mine.

As I had so often in the past, I returned to my grandparents for safety and solace. It was my home. My grandpa was the most consistent presence in my life, strong and wise. This was the man who told me when I was 15 that if I wanted to smoke, to get it from him; that if I wanted to try reefer, to tell him first. You could talk to him about anything without him judging you. My mother had done the same. Learning from them, I've raised my children in the same manner.

My grandparents tried to make life better, but underneath the hurt, brokenness and disillusionment, I still loved my husband. Yet, I could not understand his treatment of me. But I would beat myself up pretty well, too. I would never be happy, I told myself. I didn't *deserve* to be happy. How could I ever be happy when so many others had died? Resolving myself to misery, I focused on my beautiful children.

Commuting every day to San Francisco began to wear on me with my baby girl, and Jakari. I started looking for a job in Sacramento, and then – when those efforts failed – I enrolled in Sacramento Community College. School was great. One of my classes was dance, a love I had had as a child in San Francisco and most recently in Oakland, where I took jazz dance twice a week. I worked at a nightclub for more cash. I was starting life afresh. I was home with the kids four nights a week and – most importantly – home when Jakari arrived after school, just as my mother had done with us. And Grandma and Grandpa were happy to have us home.

Jakari had begun to show his talent. One day he brought a picture in he had drawn. "Who did this?" I asked. It was an exact replica of the Dr. Martin Luther King.

I called to Grandpa to see what he had drawn. He was surprised "Boy, you did this?" "Yes" Jakari replied. It was then that I knew I had a child with a God given talent. I bought him a pad, charcoals and a introduction to art book. He began to draw constantly. He was nine years old.

Stephanie, my cousin through marriage, and I became very good friends. She was one of the most beautiful people I had ever met, but her husband was controlling and used to hit her as my ex-husband had beaten me. Deeper than her love for him, though, was her religious belief that divorce was a sin. "Not when he is kicking your ass," I told her more than once. She was slowly beginning to love herself enough to plan an exodus. I kept a suitcase in the trunk of my car, and one by one, she would bring items for me to put inside.

Two weeks before Christmas we went to San Francisco for a day of shopping and stopped at a restaurant at the Berkeley Marina on the way home. We talked and laughed. A gentleman approached our table. He just wanted to say hello and offer us a drink, he said, because we were having such a good time. He looked familiar but I couldn't place him until he gave his name. Conrad. He'd dated my friend Elaine, a couple of years back. When I mentioned her name and the time they came to pick me up in Oakland to take me to the city, he remembered me.

We asked him to join us. He was a delight, with a worldliness that appealed to me. Exchanging phone numbers, he told me to call him collect after I arrived back in Sacramento. Stephanie and I talked about him all the way back home. I had not been attracted to anyone since I left my daughter's father.

Our first telephone conversation lasted an hour. He invited me to the Bay Area, and said he would pay my expenses to get there. We planned to see each other in two weeks.

The relationship blossomed. We saw each other at least every other weekend, and I would stay for a minimum of three days. We went to concerts and dinner. He brought me back around to me. I finally started putting back the pieces that my abusive ex-husband had destroyed, and with that came my self-esteem.

Everything was looking up. School was good, the children were good and my grandparents were fine. My only concern was that Grandma's eyesight had worsened. She could no longer drive, do basic chores around the house, or even cook meals. Grandpa and I ran the house. But the children were in a stable and loving environment, and that was all that mattered.

* * * * *

We reversed direction one weekend, in more ways than one. Instead of me going to the Bay Area, Conrad came to Sacramento one Saturday several months after we started dating. We went to a restaurant in Old Sacramento, but even as we ordered our lunch, I noticed his pensive look. "What is it?" I asked. Taking a deep breath, he said "I'm getting married." *Well, this is the strangest proposal I ever had,* I thought, immediately followed by, *Oh my goodness my grandparents would be so happy, because they really like him,* but even before he continued, I had the sense something was wrong. "To Mary," he finished. It took ever ounce of my strength to maintain my composure. I knew who the woman was. She had shown up at his house one day, banging on the door, yelling that she knew I was in there. I believe his youngest son had told her about me. I had gone into another room while he'd dealt with her. Or so he told me. Slowly, I rose from the table, willing my legs not to collapse, picked up my purse and stumbled out of the restaurant. I was already inside a cab, when he came out of the restaurant. My world had collapsed again. Love was not for me. This time I would bury it very deep inside of me, and if it took a painkiller to numb myself, so be it.

One day soon afterwards, I went into a nail shop to get my nails done. The manicurist and I hit it off immediately. She was Filipino and black. She asked me had I ever smoked coke. I hadn't. Would I like to try? I would. She asked if Friday night was good. It was. She asked if I had kids. I did. "Bring them along," she said. "They can play with my kids." She sounded excited. Why wouldn't she be? I had just agreed to everything she asked.

On the appointed Friday, I left my daughter in care of my grandparents – she was too young to go along to a cocaine party – and took Jakari to her house. She had prepared snacks for the kids, and we left them alone with an admonition to be good – "do as we say, not as we do" – and headed for her bedroom. She closed and locked the door. She pulled out a spoon, baking soda and a lighter from a box, and then presented a clear little baggie with white powder in it. It made me think of my L.A. and my international fling. She mixed everything together and lit a flame underneath the spoon. The mixture began to boil. She stirred in a couple of drops of water and suddenly, there was a big hard rock. "Wow," I exclaimed. A glass pipe emerged from her collection of magic, and she offered to go first, to demonstrate how it was done. She put a piece of the rock on the pipe, moved the lighter around underneath, and when the substance began to melt, took a slow, long drag. A bead of sweat popped on her forehead. When she gave the pipe to me, her voice was a little shaky, almost as if she were nervous. With her help, I inhaled deeply and immediately felt the rush. *Good God*, I thought, *this is great*. We went back and forth for a good hour. I had no thoughts of any ex-boyfriend, no thoughts of 918 dead people, and no thoughts of anything. When it was finally all gone, we sat around talking.

My high crashed prematurely, when she began to pick at the floor, looking for remnants she might have dropped. Watching her crawl on her hands and knees made me feel uncomfortable, and I told her I was going to leave. But the little setback didn't stop me from agreeing to do some more the following week. I had found a cool friend and an effective way to lose myself.

The next week turned into six months of serious crack addiction. An addict's single goal is to get high. That is the mission. Your social circles shrink to only addict's because everyone else's priorities are not the same as yours. They want to live and you want to die. In a dangerous world, they have to trust someone, and they can only trust each other. My children were kept dressed and clean and my daily life was always the same. It was the after bed time that was different.

At the same time, I met another man who was 45. I was 28. His name was Anthony. He was a regular at the bar I used to work at and the first thing he said to me was "I will get you anything you want." It scared me because he was a manly man. Dressed well, nice jewelry and he looked very experienced. Our relationship continued and even though I knew he had another woman it did not matter.

My new drug buddy Elena and I decided to get a place together. My addiction was monitored, because I still did not know how to cook the cocaine. It saved me for a while. My new boyfriend Anthony co-signed for the apartment and kept a key. We moved into our new townhouse in Greenhaven and settled in. The kids had adjusted to her two boys and we had a little family. My daughter slept with me. She was about a year old now. The boys had the master bedroom, because it was the largest. Greenhaven is a nice area in Sacramento. Jakari could play outside with me not having to worry too much about him. I felt safe there.

The drugs moved up my list of what was important. My household budget now included the monthly item of $300 for cocaine. Needing more money for my habit, I dropped out of school and found a job with an independent insurance broker. He was very cool. Even as we planned on building the business to one of the top companies, I was smoking coke every night once the kids were put to bed. Jonestown began to become a distant memory.

One weekend our usual connection did not show up. The dude who came instead, and who became our steady supplier, was gorgeous. His name was Chad. One night he was at the same club I was. We danced and ended up going to his place. He gave me a packet of coke. I snorted some and put the rest away. This relationship would change my life once again.

I was still seeing my boyfriend, but my connection and I hooked up about once a week. One day at his house, he asked if I wanted to make some money. I thought he'd want me to start dealing, so when he told me what it was instead, I felt relief. I shouldn't have. All I had to do was let someone deposit a check into my checking account and when I was instructed, I would withdraw the funds in small increments. My payment would be $2,500.00. I thought about it but for only a second, my mind was on getting a free package. I couldn't be connected to the deposited check, because it would have none of my fingerprints on it. It sounded like a foolproof plan, so I agreed, and all in the same breath asked for credit for a gram of cocaine. He smiled and assured me he could get it back during this deal. I thought about the money and got excited. A lump of $2,500.00 could buy a lot of clothes, and enough cocaine to last me for awhile.

Elena was home when I arrived after my meeting, but I was not going to tell her anything about what my connection and I were doing. And of course, I did not offer to share my cocaine with her. After the kids went to bed, I told her I was going to bed. Instead I went into the closet, closed the door, prepared my painkiller, and got high. The next thing I knew it was three o'clock in the morning, and my drugged state kept real sleep in abeyance. When the alarm clock went off at six o'clock I had barely dozed off. *I have to stop doing this shit on a work night,* I told myself. Dragging, I woke the children and readied them to leave. My daughter went to my grandparents, and Jakari went to the elementary school around the corner.

Driving to work across town was a challenge. Feeling half dead, I stopped and bought a cup of coffee. I was okay once I arrived at work, and since my boss was in and out a lot, I was able to steal away to the bathroom and take a nap. I survived the day, weary but unscathed.

About three days later, my connection called to tell me to withdrawn $5,000. I called in sick the next day and went to the bank at about 10:00 a.m. Wanting to look like I had money; I wore a silk dress my boyfriend had bought me, nice shoes and the faithful original Louis Vuitton purse. I filled out a withdrawal slip and handed it to the bank teller. She looked me over and asked me why I wanted so much cash. "Not that it is really any of your business," I began in my very professional white voice, "but it is my down payment on my new BMW." I was very haughty, secure in what I was about to do. The teller was unperturbed. "We usually need advance notification for a withdrawal this size." "Listen, they are waiting for this money. The car has been shipped from out of state and they want to get rid of it." She said she needed to ask her supervisor, and returned a moment later to let me know it would take about twenty minutes. I thanked her for her help and took a seat in the reception area.

My cool exterior was just that: a front. Inside, I was scared. Watching the bank door for the police officer I expected to walk in, I replayed the script my connection had given me. "You can always say you were dating a guy with a Porsche who lived out of town. One day he told you he was going to put some money in your account for a new car, but you did not believe him. While you were checking your balance, you were surprised he had actually done it. If they ask for a name, just tell them that you think he may be married, because he always initiated the calls. Then just make up a name." "You make me sound like a call girl," I'd told him. "Want to make even more money?" he joked.

Twenty minutes seemed like hours, but finally the teller motioned me back to her window. As she counted out the one-hundred dollar bills, I tried not to act too excited. She handed me the money, then told me to count it, just to make sure. After I thanked her, I split the stack in half, placing one stack on one side of a private bank in my bra and the other on the other side. I drove the mile to my connection's apartment and knocked on his door. He was as excited as I was. Upstairs in his bedroom, I pulled the money out, throwing it in the air and singing, "Money, money, money, money." He joined in my little song and dance. "We are gonna be rich, baby, you are too good at this."

When I prepared to leave a while later, he gave me $800. I asked about the rest, but he cautioned me to take it in small amounts and keep $1,000 in the bank. *This was not the plan,* I thought. *Is there no honesty amongst thieves?* I asked for a thousand instead of $800.

They needed me to get the rest of the money, and I was not going to be used. But he demurred. He had to split the withdrawal with two other people, he growled, trying to look mean. "I don't care, I want my thousand now."

I knew – and I knew he knew – he did not have a choice but to keep me happy. There was $15,000 sitting in my account, and I was the only one who could withdraw it. He huffed and muttered under his breath, but he gave me the entire grand. And an eight ball, three hundred dollar worth of cocaine. Happy, I went to pick up my daughter and then home to wait for my son to get out of school. It was Friday night, and I had the whole weekend to get high. I thought to share some of it with my roommate, but not to tell her how much I had.

I had to find a place to hide the money, because I knew she rummaged through my room periodically. I remembered one of my past boyfriend's secret hiding place. I went to the far side of my bed, moved it, and used a razor blade to cut and lift the carpet against the wall. I lined the money in small rows so there would be no bulge. There, I said to myself, she'll never think to look there.

I treated everyone to Chinese delivery that night. We ate before the TV and, and after my roommate and I put the kids together, I told her I had a surprise. We got high the entire night.

That Sunday my connection picked me up to go shopping. I gathered up Nicci and Jakari and spent a nice junk of change on them and myself. My boyfriend Anthony, had no idea about the drug use. But others were beginning to notice something. Once when I was at my grandparents, my cousin asked what was wrong with my hair. "It looks so dry and dead." I knew then that the abuse was beginning to show. That day I went out and bought a wig.

The next time I got the word to make another withdrawal; I called the bank in advance and asked for ten thousand dollars. The teller's advice made it much easier. It was ready for me when I went to pick it up. They counted it out and I recounted it, and then walked out. Crime does pay, I thought. My connection gave me $500 when I delivered it. We had to keep some money in the bank, he said. They needed me, I reflected, and didn't think they would try to mess me over. It was, of course, a mistake on my part.

I was getting high almost daily now. I was thin, but still did not look like a drug user. I dressed nicely, and kept the children looking good. The only real difference was that I began to get sick a lot. Once I caught a cold and it sent me to bed for three days. Finally, when my drug use robbed me of my interest in sex – when the only thing that made me feel good was hitting the pipe – my boyfriend figured it out and confronted me with a direct, unavoidable question. I couldn't deny it. He called a cocaine hotline, which many cities had at the time. Cocaine was rampant and smoking cocaine was the method of choice. Once the counselor came on the line, he closed my bedroom door and sat on the edge of the bed. Crying, I poured out my addiction to the counselor, and by the time I hung up the phone, I had promised my boyfriend and myself I was going to get clean. He stayed with me, giving me medicine and just being there when I woke. After four days of not having any drugs, I thought I could kick it. I also thought I could kick my job with my connection.

But I had one more scheduled pickup, one more withdrawal for the remainder of the money from the bank. I'd called in advance as before, and when I got there, I left the children in the car, as I was going to be just a minute. I walked up to the teller with my newfound confidence and handed her the deposit slip. She punched in my account and told me it would be a moment before they had the cash. She was good, but I still heard an internal warning signal. My confidence – my cockiness – let me ignore it. A few minutes later, I felt a tap on my shoulder. Two police officers stood behind me and said "Miss can you come with us" quietly escorting me to an office. They had been trying to reach me, they said, because a stolen check had been deposited into my account. I went into the story my connection and I had scripted. It did not work. "We need to take you downtown to answer some questions." I couldn't, I replied, I had two children in the car. "You'll have to call someone."

The only someone I could think of was my partner in crime; Chad. When I first explained the situation to him on the phone, he thought I was lying to him, but when he realized I was serious, he told me not to say a word, that he would take care of my kids. "It will be okay," he promised, but his voiced was panicked.

My children never saw me put in the back of the police car. I thanked the officer for that. The ride to the police station was easier than I had a right to expect it would be, but I was still frightened, and thought only about my grandparents and my children. Once we arrived at the station, I was stripped search. They allowed me to keep my wig but took out the hair pins. They fingerprinted me, took a mug shot and placed me in a holding cell. About three hours later I was told I could make a phone call. Again, I called my connection, who told me he was arranging bail. "Keep the same story!" he told me. His voice was drowning in the same fear I was feeling. I asked him to take the children to my grandparents, and to let them know I was okay, but not to say anything yet, that I needed to tell them. *How in the hell did you end up here,* I thought as the officer led me back to my cell. *You have really messed up.*

My name was called about four hours later, and I gathered my personal effects at the desk. Chad waited until we got out of earshot of the jail before asked what had happened. Even after I explained everything, he told me not to worry. When he dropped me off at my grandparents' house, we hugged and I walked to the front door.

I hugged my kids, but the answers to their questions would have to wait. Years. Forever, if I had anything to say about it. But I had to tell my grandparents. Once the children were in bed, we went to the kitchen, the center of most family activities, from meals, to prayer, to pick up sticks and dominoes. "I was arrested today," I said bluntly. The look on my grandpa's face was enough to bring me to tears. He slapped his knee, leaned over, and asked why. "I got hooked on cocaine, and someone put a check in my account. It was stolen." Grandma called out for Jesus and let the tears flow. Grandpa just said he knew something was wrong. I apologized to them both for the disappointment I'd caused them. I think – and hope – they understood.

I went to work on Monday to resign. The majority of my boss' business was with the Sheriff's Department, and I did not want to jeopardize his dreams. After a couple of days I was called downtown to speak with investigators, who told me my future included a five-year term in a state prison for Grand Theft, unless I cooperated. They had poked holes in my story and let the drugs come pouring through. Cocaine was rampant in Sacramento. Gangs were fighting over drug territory and it was now an epidemic. And I was part of it. I told them about my connection without using his name. I had not heard from him, and from what I pieced together, I gathered he was pretty much trying to forget my existence. He was going to leave me hanging.

There was no way I could do five years away from my family, so I agreed to cooperate. The detectives told me they could put a wire on me and set up a buy with my connection. They talked about offering me witness protection, but living in a strange city without any support was not an option. The fact was, I didn't see many options, but believed my cooperation with the police would help.

The day I was arrested was actually another day of Grace. It literally saved my life. I was still functional when I received that blessing. At some point the addiction would have completely taken over and I would've been dead. I knew it then. I know it now. That's why I agreed to the plan.

I called Chad from an investigator's office. I told him I was going remain silent, I said, but I needed to get really high to get through this. "You owe me," I said over his protests. He finally agreed, and we set up a time and place for my purchase.

The bust would go down in two days. It seemed like an eternity. When the day finally arrived, I went to the detectives' office. Someone put the wire on me so skillfully; it felt like it wasn't even there. Trying to get my head together and smoking cigarette after cigarette, I was relieved when we were finally ready to go. As dusk fell, I got in my car, and they in theirs. I was surprised at how some of the cops looked: a homeless dude, a biker, a hippy. These guys could be anywhere, I thought. I arrived at the destination – a Victorian on P Street – but there was no parking. The building was not familiar to me. I found a space around the corner, got out and walked a block to the stairs of the building. Chad wasn't there. And suddenly he was. A guy on a bike with a baseball cap pulled up next to me, got off and walked up to me. "You're setting me up!" he growled. "Man, get real, let's go, I need a hit," I insisted. But now that I was with him, my urge to cooperate was threatened by my feeling of betrayal.

We entered an apartment in the building. The group at the living room table consisted of three men and a woman. A large caliber weapon was openly exposed on the table. My connection came over and put his hands around my waist. "What are you doing?" I giggled as I pushed him away. "Man, control yourself." The woman at the table was glaring at me. She had two big corn rows in her hair and cheap gold jewelry. Finally they gave me the dope. As I left, I told my connection I would call him later so we could get together. I started breathing again when I rounded the corner to my car.

Opening my car door, I realized I had to use the bathroom and – hoping the wire was still active – said "Hey, you guys, I have to pee." They heard me. So did Chad, who'd followed me out of the building. Witness protection was now my only option.

I received the first post-wire call from my Chad a couple of days later. Trying to sound normal, I asked him how he was. He was having none of it. "I knew you were setting me up, I knew it." My tone changed too. "Leave me alone," I told him bitterly. "You left me hanging." I began to get phone calls in the middle of the night with silence at the other end. Sometimes headlights would appear through my bedroom window, but no one would get out of the car. I began to get scared.

Finally I accepted a call from Chad and agreed to see him, as long as it was in front of my grandparents' house in broad daylight. He told me he had an attorney but he was looking at some serious time. I told him I was too, and that at least he had money for a lawyer. All I had was a public defender. He asked me not to testify against him, but that was impossible. He told me the other people at the house on P Street were so pissed, they wanted me dead. *What a surprise, I would want me dead too.*

I finally hatched a plan. I wouldn't testify, but he had to agree to several things: payment of $2500; a promise that my kids and grandparents would be all right; the end of the phone calls; and no harassment from the folks in the house. Most people would have said I was crazy to even think of such a deal, but we were both caught up in the craziness. I knew I would end up with jail time after backing out of my testimony, but I didn't think it would matter once I got out. I was young and my appearance would never in and of itself warrant a background check at a job, nor would it be obvious that I had a record. I knew not to apply for work at places that ran fingerprints. As a young black man, he would not be able to get past a background check so easily. Who would have it the easier? Me, of course. The thought of living without my grandparents was also a factor. Living underground was already a way of life for me, but I did not want to go any deeper. That was my reasoning.

I was sentenced to four months at the Consumes Correctional Facility about thirty minutes from my grandparents' house. The experience saved my life. I didn't think it would be difficult, but only because the church had taught me to be able to function in any situation. I kissed my grandparents and children goodbye and turned myself in.

Although the dorm was noisy, I was so tired from six months of no sleep and too many drugs, I couldn't stay awake. I had no withdrawals at all. Drugs were readily available inside, but I did not take part. Jail itself became my "Get out of jail" card to have a new life, and I seized the opportunity. The hardest part was seeing my daughter and my grandparents. Jakari had gone to stay with Joe's parents, who unfortunately told him I was in jail. It was unnecessary, and I resented them for that. After about a month, I was transferred to a facility for prisoners convicted of DUI's. I was assigned to the kitchen. We had pool tables, a large TV in the rec room and a volleyball court. We had plenty of activity and relaxing time.

Most of the women I met in jail were there because of men and drugs. I learned that either you do your time, learning from your mistakes, or you learn how to be a better criminal. An older Caucasian woman once asked me if I would be interested in making lots of money working for her when I got out. "What is your game?" I asked. As though she was telling me she was a nurse or a teacher she said, "I run an S&M house." I declined the offer.

One of the most interesting people I met was a woman who'd been appointed to her state position by Governor Jerry Brown. She left her position and began living a fabulous life in the Caribbean until it all came crushing down. Arrested and extradited back to the States, she was convicted for misappropriation of government funds. Even though the misappropriation was a seemingly small amount of $2500, the government decided to make an example of her, and it did.

By the time I was released, I was anxious to begin another life. I decided to go to Beauty College and learn to be a manicurist. The nail business was good then: $50 for a full set of artificial nails and for a pedicure. I attended with one of my jail mates – she studied hair and

I nails – and became state-licensed upon completion of the course. I landed a lucrative job in an upscale nail shop, but I burned out after a while. I returned to being an administrative assistant, securing a job at the California Trial Lawyers Association. After about five months, I moved out of my grandparents' house into my own apartment closer to the job. The children loved it, a big swimming pool, playground, and tennis courts.

One Friday night, a depression came over me that I could not shake. For the first time in several years I actually felt suicidal, but I did not understand why. Anthony and I were still dating and I wrote him a letter and stuck it in his truck window at his workplace. I shared with him my state of mind with an explanation and a thank you for being there. What I could not deny was that the weight on me was overbearing and heavy. When I awoke with the same feeling the next morning, I gathered the children and went to visit my grandparents. If anything could make me feel better, it was being around them. This visit turned out to be an exception.

My grandpa was in the living room watching one of his favorites – baseball – and my daughter and Jakari sat in his lap to join him. I went into the kitchen to fix my kids some hot dogs. When Grandma walked in a couple of minutes later, she started in on me. "What, you don't have any food at your house?" she asked. I loved my grandmother but sometimes she was just mean. I knew she was having a difficult time, especially in comparison to her husband, who at 83, still had the gait and energy of a 40-year-old. "Grandma, please don't start," I pleaded "I came over here because I was feeling a little down. Cheering up is what I need." "Well, don't go doing them drugs again." *That's right,* I bitterly told myself. *This is just what I needed.* Rather than get into it with her, though, I retrieved my children from my grandpa's loving grasp and took them home.

The next morning, a banging woke me up from a finally sound sleep. Opening it stood Anthony, "Oh, my god, I just got your letter! My son had the truck and I just got it back. What is wrong?" he asked. I shared with him the way I was feeling and he pulled out his money clip saying, "Get dressed, go buy some breakfast food and let's eat." He was just that way – money took care of everything. When my daughter and I returned from the store, I felt no better. The feeling was still nagging me and I thought to call my grandparents from a payphone – I did not follow my spirit- it was around 10:00 a.m. As I was cooking breakfast, there was another knock on the door. Anthony went to answer it. 'Leslie" he called. With a puzzled look on my face, I put down the spatula and headed towards the door asking him to watch the food. There stood two of my grandparents' neighbors crying. "What happened? Grandma?" They shook their heads. That left only one alternative. The next thing I remember I was heading for the balcony, preparing to jump. They grabbed me and pulled me back in. "No, no, not him," I screamed, "not him."

The neighbors took Nicci and Jakari with them. As my boyfriend drove me to the house I had come to love so much, the house that had been my refuge, I recalled a conversation my grandpa and I had a few weeks earlier. "I hope your grandmother goes first," he'd said. Shocked, I asked why. "No one will want to take care of her." "I'd take care of her, Grandpa," I'd assured him, but he answered with silence.

A crowd of relatives, friends, and neighbors had gathered outside the house. I found my grandmother inside, sitting on the couch crying. "Your grandpa's gone," she moaned. "Lord, my husband is gone." Someone took my arm and led me off the couch. "Leslie, your grandpa is dead." My legs gave out, and I fell to the floor, balled up like a baby. And then the final news came. "Your grandpa shot himself, baby." I couldn't – wouldn't – believe it, and clambering to my feet, stepped into his bedroom off the kitchen. But it was true: the bed had been stripped of its sheets, but the mattress was dark with a huge, ugly bloodstain.

All the pain from the death of my family and friends roared back. I felt like I couldn't take anymore. I was 30 years old and felt like a hundred. This man who was never too far from me, who patched me back together when I was falling apart, who helped me raise my children as he had raised my sister and me, who was always my source of wisdom and strength, was gone, and by his own hand. It was unbearable. I couldn't get through this one, I thought, there is no way I can make it through this one. I went into the room where the children stayed when we visited – and where they were now – and gathered them close to me. "Grandpa is in heaven now." We cried together, for a long time.

It was the coroner who told me what happened, what he learned from the blood splatter. That Sunday morning, he explained, my grandpa took the .22 caliber from his closet, lay on the bed, placed it close to his heart and pulled the trigger. Although seriously wounded, he realized the bullet from the small caliber gun wasn't going to kill him. So he got up from the bed, returned to the closet, retrieved the .38, laid back on the bed, and placing the barrel directly over his heart, pulled the trigger a second time. My grandpa could have survived if he hadn't had the second gun, the coroner said. We could have made up a story saying he shot himself by accident. He did not have to die, but for some reason he wanted to. For some reason he was tired. I asked if it were possible that he was shot by someone else, but the coroner said there was no doubt. This man was so kind and patient with me. He told me that suicide was the number one cause of death among the elderly. Still, I could not grasp that this man would attempt to take his own life, and then knowing he could have survived, made sure the next shot would be fatal. It was just too much.

And so, the life of Spurgeon John Smith ended in September of 1987.

My boyfriend bought me a dress to wear for the funeral. My children were not allowed to go. The memory of their grandpa the last day they saw him – watching baseball, playing with them in the living room, making them laugh – was what I wanted etched in their minds. I could not help Grandma. I had promised my grandpa that I would be strong for her, but that day my strength had evaporated. Looking at my grandpa in that casket was so painful. When I went up to kiss his forehead, it was over for me. The soft, pliable chocolate skin was reduced to stone. The fog that had enveloped me since his death dissipated, and I tried to climb into the casket. My boyfriend's arms encircled me, pulled me out and I was carried out of the church. My heart felt again as if it had broken into a thousand tiny pieces, never to be put back together. I just wanted to die. Death is the only way to escape pain. Death is the only way not to feel anymore.

My boyfriend finally got me to a place of calmness. He walked me out of the church lounge and into his car. This man was always there for me and as I looked back on my life, I realize he really loved me.

We went to the cemetery – my undignified exit from the church meant we were ahead of everyone else – and I saw the pile of dirt with the canopy. I didn't think I could stay, but my boyfriend insisted that

I try. I lasted ten minutes into the gravesite service. I could not watch my grandpa placed in the cold earth.

A week later I moved back into the house, and after about three weeks I went back to work. I needed the time to spend with the children and my grandmother. I was on autopilot, while acceptance of his death hovered overhead, waiting to take root in my soul.

The day I finally went to work, I stopped on the way at the church on 11ᵗʰ and K Streets. Getting on my knees, I talked to my grandpa and begged God to forgive him, crying every day. I returned again to the church, and again. Every morning and at lunch time, I was there. This beautiful cathedral is where I found refuge in God. My faith had been minimal, and I knew it would have to be renewed for me to go on without Grandpa. My co-workers and boss were wonderful, allowing me the time I needed and not invading that quiet space I would escape to.

One of Grandma's old friends from the church took care of her during the day. The children were okay, except Jakari began to exhibit behavior that was not positive. We spent a lot of time talking, as I tried to help him grieve.

I had to strip my life of distractions and diversions, and one casualty was my relationship with my boyfriend. One of the toughest decisions was breaking up with him. He'd been good to me, but there was a love triangle I didn't need to deal with now. I was the head of my household, and I wanted no mistakes, no drama, and no problems.

After a few months, Althea, one of my dearest girlfriends, got me out of the house to attend a social function. I agreed in order for her to stop bothering me. We went to a resort hotel in West Sacramento for a wine tasting. It was there that I met the man who would become my husband, Thomas Cathey.

We hit it off as if we had known each other for years. He was kind and had no hidden agendas. The weekend after we met, we barbequed at our house. Jakari decided to be honest and told him we were from Jonestown, Guyana. What an ice breaker. But it didn't drive him away. On the contrary, after that evening, we were inseparable. Grandma liked him and so did my daughter. He gave me my third and last child. The delivery was beautiful, with jazz playing in the background. When they handed me my son, I held him close and my heart was almost whole again. It took me three days to name him. Demetrius Spurgeon John. I used to think he was the reincarnation of my grandpa because of his sweet spirit. He is that way still.

Thomas and I began having problems after Demetrius was born and we ended the relationship. About the same time, a teacher at Jakari's Jr. High school began speaking to me about Jakari and his behavior. She recommended I have him professionally tested. Using the referral she gave me and a couple of hundred dollars, I scheduled an appointment for him. The consultation took about four hours. The results were surprising. Jakari had tested out at a freshman level of college in all areas. They commented that my son was extremely intelligent and his behavior was partly due to the fact that he was not challenged enough. So, working with the sister at the school, he became somewhat evened out without medication.

My relationship with her introduced me to orthodox Islam. I studied enough to know, it was not a religion, but a lifestyle – and concomitant lifestyle – I could embrace. My first experience in a Masjid was in Sacramento. My Shahada (declaration of Faith) was taken during Ramadan at the home of a sister who was a writer for the *Sacramento Bee*. When I walked in the home, I was immediately welcomed and felt right at home. Their guests, who met at sundown to break the fast, were from all backgrounds. I did not talk about my new faith, but it had nestled in my heart.

Chapter 13:
1990's

The decade of the 1990's allowed me to begin to reconnect with family and friends from my past. One of my first was with my sister Michelle's boyfriend and father of her son Clarke. He stopped working for Western Airlines and was with Delta, and I tracked him down that way. Clarke was saddened to learn of the death of my grandpa. He had remarried and had three children. I was happy for him. He invited us to come to Atlanta, but I wasn't quite ready for that yet. What happened in the past had been forgiven.

One day in the paper I saw an advertisement for a Physic Faire. Although I had found Islam, a force pulled me there. Jakari was really having a lot of difficulty, and I hoped to find something to help him. Not knowing what I was seeking, I walked into the room and noticed a woman at a table draped in color fabric. Dr. Brenda Love greeted me by saying that my aura was so bright. I was unaware of what an aura was, as she could see from my expression, so she invited me to sit down while she explained what the colors meant. She lit a candle and, taking both of my hands in hers, said a prayer. "Your son is hanging around with a blue-eyed blond-haired white boy." I gasped my amazement of her knowledge. "He's in trouble," she continued. "There's marijuana involved." "Yes," I admitted, "I believe he is smoking weed." Jakari's temper was non yielding. Throughout his life, his difficult behavior made him angry and violent. This was part of his upbringing. Growing up around violence and trauma it would take an affect. His grandmother in New Jersey and I both had him taken to doctors. They wanted to put him on Ritalin, but we both refused. So we dealt with his personality. Years later I would wonder if this was the right choice. She continued to reveal personal information, things no one else would have known except for someone that possessed a gift. But then she paused. "There is a place rich in greenery. Do you know where this is?" she asked me. I didn't. "You will be moving there," she added. I wondered if she meant Atlanta, but since I had no idea what it looked like, it didn't mean anything. I left feeling renewed, and when I told some of my friends about Dr. Love, they wanted to meet her too. She started doing readings at my house. This continued for a couple of months. She touched everyone she talked to, leaving them overwhelmed with tears, joy, surprise, bewilderment. It made me think about all of the secrets I had. One day I would be released from secrets.

I decided to move to Atlanta in March 1990. After Grandma agreed to it, we put her home up for sale and left in June. During that time, I connected long distance to the Masjid on Fayetteville Road in Atlanta. It helped me with a lot of things, including a referral to a realtor.

We stayed at my brother-in-law's for about two weeks. He and his family lived in Rex, Georgia, near the airport, so I had yet to see Atlanta. He worked at night and his wife did not work. She was sweet and welcoming, and we became close. The children had fun. Grandma was visiting her sister's in Oklahoma City, and was scheduled to come when I got settled.

Despite their warm hospitality, the time came when I was ready for my own place. My Muslim real estate agents helped me find a nice three-bedroom home on a cul-de-sac in Decatur. The home was empty and ready to be rented. They also took us to Jumah that Friday. I was amazed by the number of Muslims at this Masjid. The one I visited in Sacramento was so much smaller. As with the prayer area in other Masjid, the men sat in the front and the women in back. Many people think this offensive to women, but it is not. It is to protect the men from paying attention to the women's backside instead of the Imam in front while making prayer. What I found in Islam was holding women in the highest esteem. After all it was Muhammad's wife, Kadijah, who pushed him to the mountain to receive instructions from Allah (God) and hence the Quran. Whatever abuse takes place against women is cultural, not Quran.

After Jumah ended, I waited at the bottom of the stairs for my host and hostess to take us back to my brother-in-law's. It was there that I saw a regal young woman descend the staircase in this incredible outfit. Her headpiece standing tall, she looked like royalty. We introduced ourselves – Bilquis was from Harlem, New York – and we hit it off right away. She promised to make me some outfits, and with an incentive like that, I promised I would visit her after I got a car. I saw her every Jumah, and when I finally got a car, I kept my word. So did she, her designs and outfits made me look like a queen.

Life suddenly got busy. We moved into the Decatur house, I arranged for our furniture to be shipped from California, Grandma came, and I bought a car. The children, Nicci and Jakari both were enrolled in the Clara Muhammad School, where they wore uniforms, took their lessons and recited their prayers in Arabic. I finally felt as if I belonged somewhere and I was happy. Queen Bilquis and I became very close friends. She put my European clothes aside and made all of my outfits. Men would show me so much respect, it felt great. She also taught me more about Islam. Drinking and partying had not crossed my mind since I converted. Finally I felt at peace.

But with my first drink, I started once again down a path I thought I was through with. Moving from that home to another, I began partying again. Everyone kept saying that whatever you did was between you and Allah. So I thought, I could outweigh my bad with good and strived hard to create that balance.

Grandma had fallen and broken her hip. I had to place her in a convalescent home for about a year. I had not found a job yet, but I wasn't worried about money. After all, I had the proceeds from the house in Sacramento and Social Security from Joe. I never really needed an excuse to go into the nightlife, but when I had a nervous breakdown, I delved even more deeply. Eventually, the death of my grandpa reached me, and I finally grieved. Jakari continued in school, yet his temper still got the best of him. He moved away from me at 17 staying with friends of the family. After getting expelled for hitting a teacher, he worked at a Muslim brothers' Baskin and Robbins. Since school was no longer an option and I could not force him to go, he opened and closed the store. Most nights I would pick him up and take him to the apartment. Eventually his two best friends and he worked hard enough to get an apartment. Jakari always kept a job and had no problem walking two or three miles to get to one. He had the same traits that his father did.

He knew how to save money and take care of himself. We remained close, but there was always a tension between us. I contributed that partly to my not being there all the time and when I was I would spoil him out of guilt. Still he became the type of man who would give you the shirt off of his back…just like Joe. Although Jakari would come by and visit often, we never got along. I believed he had a love hate relationship with me. He adored his younger brother and would take him to the mall and hang out.

I gave up Islam and decided that I would try to develop a personal relationship with God because I was so very cynical about anything organized and felt like a hypocrite.

Now I needed a job. I applied at Grady Hospital in the Patient Education department. I was hired as the desktop publisher for the program funded through a grant for Violence Prevention. Violence involving youth was considered a national epidemic, and I believed my work was important. Certainly it gave me a sense of pride. My depression began to lift and I felt as if I had a handle on things.

Jakari put his God given talent to work and assisted me with the newsletter that health educators distributed to children at the schools they visited. His artwork graced both the covers and interior pages.

My salary was $7.50 an hour, my rent was high, and money was very tight. The daughter of my real estate friend was struggling too, so we decided we could share her house and help each other out. One night while I was out partying, I fell and broke my ankle. I would end up staying at the hospital for ten days awaiting surgery. I called my roommate and her parents and told them what happened. My roommate kept my daughter and her parents watched over my son. Jakari was living with friends. The patient next to me was handcuffed to her bed. Finally gathering up the nerve to ask her what happened she told me. "Stabbing my children's father," she said. 'Oh, did he die?" I asked. "No, dammit." She laughed, and I giggled knowing exactly what she meant. As we got to know each other we would jimmy her bed close enough to the bathroom where she could smoke. I would jump on one leg and a crutch and we would smoke in the bathroom. This woman had grown up in one of the worst projects in Atlanta. Her mother was a hardcore crack addict and her biggest concern was her mother selling her children for crack. My eyes welled up, knowing the devastation crack can cause. My heart ached for her and I thanked God I got clean. Men and drugs: you find one; you will usually find the other somewhere close by.

While I was still in the hospital, my roommate's parents visited me and told me that things had fallen apart at the house in my absence. Jakari had gone over there one day and found his stereo system broken. Apparently my roommate allowed her sister to play with it and broke the turntable. The worse news came the day I was finally released from the hospital. I'd been kicked out of my roommate's house. When Jakari picked me up, he had a pair of his pants and shirt for me to wear, and my car. As we pulled up before the house, I was shocked to see that she had packed all of my things and placed them on the front porch. It was a blessing that I was on crutches, because with my temper and temptation to rampage, I think I would have ended up in jail. We got a hotel room and I called Queen Bilquis in New York. She told me to call a mutual friend who invited us to her home. God was watching over us.

Things often happen in threes, and following my surgery and summary eviction, the third thing happened. Jakari and a friend had taken the car somewhere, and it had broken down. So there I was, on crutches, with no apartment, with no car. However what I did have was a little bit of Faith. But right about then, it seemed pretty little.

I couldn't shake my overwhelming sense of failure. I thought about throwing myself under the wheels of a semi on the interstate. Life was almost unbearable. I had already fallen twice on the crutches. As God intervenes, the phone rang, and as God has surrounded us with angels, they many times are people we interact with every day. "As-Alam-Alaikum," I was greeted by the only voice that I knew from Harlem, New York. "I am not doing well right now," I told Queen Bilquis, and mentioned something about throwing myself into a truck's path. "Nah, you don't want to do that," she replied. "You must turn it over to Allah, Allah is the best planner."

I also turned it over to my Muslim friends. One found a brother to take me to work and drop the kids at school. Majima, my friend from California, picked me up one Saturday and we went apartment hunting. We found a place the first day: it was on a major bus line and was within my price range. I moved in exactly one week later.

Jakari got two of his friends to help us move. Having my own place again was heaven. I thanked God for that. But my faith had faltered when it came to Islam, and I rarely attended the Masjid. The children were happy. I enrolled my daughter in public school and found childcare for my son with a wonderful couple named Dee and Ulysses. Their curriculum included teaching these toddlers, not just African American history, but African history. I was impressed as my child was in a loving environment.

In the meantime, I had met a man named Dean who opened my world in another way. He was a convicted felon and had had a tough life. I admired his strength. After getting out of prison, and with no support from his mother, he worked and attended school to obtain his degree. The love he had for his children moved me more than what he had overcome. They were the center of his life. He introduced me to black scholars like Dr. John Henrik Clarke, Dr. Yosef ben-Jochanan, Dr. Frances Cress Welsing and others. Our relaxation time consisted of listening to tapes, reading and discussing history. We worked together on a newsletter which we passed out on the corners of downtown Atlanta. Our relationship lasted three years and it was another loss for me when it ended. Dean made me dig deep into the resources I had internally and he reminded me constantly that I was strong. Knowing him had a great impact on my mind.

Chapter 14:
Is It Over Yet?

Feeling homesick for California, and wanting an easier life, I gathered up my grandmother and my children, resigned from Grady Hospital and headed back west. We arrived in California with about $2,200, enough for the first and last months' rent on an apartment. Jakari stayed in Atlanta.

A friend of mine in Georgia had prayed upon a stone and advised me of this before I left: "If you panic, nothing will come. You must give everything over to the Universe and it will all work out. Times will be hard, but you cannot panic, if you do nothing will come." Another test of my faith.

She was right. Things were tough at first. It took a month or so for Grandma's Social Security to kick in, and since she now needed fulltime care, I wanted to be able to stay home. We slept on the floor with Grandma on a mattress. My cousin brought us $20 a week in groceries. In fact, every time I needed money, it would appear. Thanking God and having renewed faith, I found an apartment in Greenhaven for my family. Walking the children to school every day and coming home to tend to my grandmother made me feel worthy again. She was my mother's mother, the last of a generation. Finally bedridden after a series of mini-strokes, she needed someone to bathe her, wash her hair and read scripture to her. Sometimes I would crawl into her hospital bed and hold her, crying. Grateful that I had the opportunity to care for her and offer her love, the children also bore witness that this is how you take care of your elderly.

Ten months later my grandmother would pass. All my income disappeared the next month. Not having enough money, we were evicted and I moved in with a friend I'd known from my previous years in Sacramento. She helped me in other ways, too.

My belief was that other people had the problems, not me. My friend disagreed, telling me that I needed to learn how to accept help. My refusal to do so was false pride. "You can't give to everyone else, and not allow them the blessings of giving to you," she would tell me. Years later, I would come to that understanding myself.

The attorneys from Atlanta handling my broken ankle case called to tell me I needed to get back to Georgia in four days. I contacted an old friend who offered me a place to stay and a promise of transportation once I got there. We boarded the ever so faithful Greyhound bus and headed back to Atlanta. Again we were on the road. After my grandmother's death and my diminishing enthusiasm for Sacramento, I had contemplated moving north to Seattle, but here I was on the way back to Atlanta.

My lawsuit yielded me a total of $500. The place where I had broken my leg had filed bankruptcy. I let the attorneys have the wrath of my anger.

Expectation of riches in Atlanta had not worked out, and I needed to work. I got a waitress job at the Omega Phi Psi house in the Cascade area, where my tips averaged about $150 a night. The management recognized my talent and my hustle, and moved me to bartend in the private room. Its patrons paid a whopping annual fee to have access to that room. My tips increased, and I felt like I was okay. I also worked as a nail tech at a day spa called LaBelle Peau. It was a beautiful environment. All natural, no artificial nails there, the job gave me satisfaction and helped to pay the bills. When the owner took off for Paris, forgetting to pay us before she left, I quit.

Getting depressed again, I applied for welfare and stayed home. My roommate was an aspiring entrepreneur, but when my daughter told me that she felt uncomfortable around him, we moved into the In Town Suites near Cleveland Avenue. I took the children to school and stayed home, although I continued to look for work.

One day, I was frying bacon and the stove caught on fire. The entire building was evacuated. Even though the manager said she was distressed when she found out the fire originated in my place, one of the house rules was, a fire meant eviction. And that meant I had to move. I called a couple of friends whom I had helped at one time and asked for shelter but I was turned down. One of the tenants helped me pack my things and another friend brought me almost three hundred dollars. The hotel around the corner flashed vacancy.

Although it looked a little seedy, like the hotels in the Tenderloin in San Francisco, or Times Square in New York City, I needed a place for the children to sleep. The gentlemen waited outside while I walked in the lobby. I paid for a week and we made our way to our room. People were openly smoking crack in the corridors. For the first time in a very long while, I was scared. Holding my children's hand tightly and with the gentlemen behind us, we found our room. The walls were covered with carpet from the 60's. It smelled moldy and humid. The friend told me to be careful, not to open the door for anyone.

I tried to joke with the children about this fancy room, and their little spirits lifted. *My children have a really screwed up mom* was the thought I didn't voice. I put a chair underneath the doorknob and we went to bed. While they slept, I stayed up, praying and asking God to help me out of this one. I was suddenly very tired.

The next morning I had to make a phone call and told the children to lock the door after me. The corridors were empty. The walking dead were resting after an evening of staying up all night getting high. All I met were ghostly memories of my own life. I found a phone booth and called a homeless hotline. The woman on the other end of the phone gave me an address on Moreland Avenue. I returned to the hotel lobby, explained to the clerk that I had a new place, and asked to have my money back. The woman must have heard this before, because – with understanding and compassion – she counted out the remainder of my money. *Angels come in all forms*, I thought. When I told my children of the change in plans – and where we were going – my daughter hugged me and said it was okay. I realized that all the love I needed was right there. I vowed that they would always be safe.

The address on Moreland Avenue turned out to be a church. As we walked through the doors, my daughter, one of the strongest children I had ever known, suddenly broke down crying. The workers were friendly enough, but there was no denying it: the place looked just like a shelter from television or movies. The room was large enough to sleep fifty women and children. I felt both disheartened and ashamed, and told my children, no one can know where we are. That was a mistake, as my daughter should have been able to talk about this traumatic situation with whoever could help her. My own false pride was going to damage my children if I didn't look out.

We weren't there long. I got a temp job at Kaiser, and even though my children were going to the same school they had been attending for years, there would be times during the day I couldn't be with them. I called the homeless hotline again and asked to be relocated. The operator gave me the address for another place off of Cascade; an old renovated firehouse which she said was clean and comfortable. It was beyond her authority – she wasn't supposed to let me go anywhere else for 90 days – and she must have heard my line about having a job too many times, but she did it, and I appreciated it. *Angels come in all forms. And Gods protection and Grace is ever constant.* I took my children to the second shelter. It did look like a firehouse, even though there was no sign saying what it was – just a number on the outside with a driveway large enough for fire trucks to park – it was exactly as the homeless shelter worker had described it, a safe haven for those single mothers who had fallen upon hard times. The worker on duty asked the children if they were hungry and took them off towards the kitchen while my intake worker took my information and gave me the house rules. "You must have a job within 72 hours. You will be assigned chores." There were others. They were all reasonable.

Our room had two beds and a dresser. There were high ceilings with children's colorful artwork, probably from previous occupants, and it had a warm feeling to it. We were allowed to have our own TV and radio, whatever we needed to make it our home. We could stay there for up to six months.

My job then was to find employment right away. I called an agency that had my resume and gave them my new phone number. I asked if they had any work, and 72 hours later, they'd set up an interview for me at a company called Industrial Risk Insurers.

On the way to the interview, I stopped by the Kroger's across the street to have taps put on one of my shoes. Poverty can show in the condition of your shoes. I hated to hear women wearing shoes with the metal coming through, tapping loudly on concrete, but there I was. As long as I was in the store – and since it was so close to the shelter – I asked to fill out a job application. A woman reviewed it right away and told me that, even though they could not pay me what I was used to making, they did have an opening. I accepted on the spot and agreed to come in the next morning for training. I wanted to hug her. I felt the presence again of God and my faith.

With a job in my hip pocket, I went to the scheduled interview at Industrial Risk Insurers. I was asked if I knew how to do formulas in Lotus. I knew that Lotus was a spreadsheet program, and even though I had never used it, I told the interviewer of course. When I left I thought I had the job.

That night I felt a load had been lifted. The stress began to leave my body, and as I watched my children adjust to their new environment, I felt good. I felt even better after my scheduled training at Kroger's. It was not going to be hard work, and that Kroger polo shirt meant security.

And then things got even better. The second job came through, and it paid $27,000 a year. Screaming for joy, I found the children playing in the backyard and told them I found an office job. As young as they were they knew what that meant. We would be okay. I went to Kroger's, found the manager, and thanked her for the opportunity. "Honey, I am so glad for you," she said. "Good luck and keep praying." She couldn't know that I would never stop praying.

The weekend was good for us. The children and I rode the bus to Five Points, where I bought them hamburgers, ice cream and some trinket or other they wanted. Things appeared somewhat normal.

I showed up early at work the following Monday. I did not want to be late the first day on the job. Industrial Risk Insurers was located at 191 Peachtree Street, one of the most prestigious buildings in Atlanta. Cascade House had allowed me to hit the clothes closet and I picked out five outfits. When I walked through the front doors of the luxurious office, I felt right at home. People greeted me warmly, both as I waited in the reception area and during my tour of the office. It was a comfortable and inviting place. IRI was a high risk insurance company, and even though I did not quite understand what that was, I was glad to be a part of it, happy and scared at the same time. I would be working with six engineers, providing secretarial support. Located on the 11th floor, the office had a beautiful view.

As I left for home at the end of the day, I stopped off at a bookstore and picked up the book *The Seven Spiritual Laws of Success* written by Deepak Chopra. The description of the book sounded exactly like what I needed. What I could not know was how that book would be the beginning of a new awakening inside of me. I started reading the book on the way home, and was engrossed. I could not wait to finish it.

The children were happy to see me. They'd been well looked after. All of the women in the shelter got along and would watch each other's children when we needed to. It reminded me of Peoples Temple, people pulling together to help each other out. Churches from the area brought in dinner every night, and we had access to the kitchen whenever we wanted, so we never went hungry. The only real schedule was in washing our clothes. With four other families there, we needed to have laundry days assigned.

We'd been there for about four weeks, when a group of women from a sorority showed up one Sunday evening to bring us dinner. Dinner was okay. The flash of a camera that unexpectedly blinded me was not. Someone was taking pictures. I buttonholed the woman who led the group and told her I had not given permission nor sign a release for anyone to take my picture. Her expression told me she thought she was better than me. "We do it all the time," she said haughtily. I asked what the photos were used for. "We put them in our quarterly magazine," she answered, daring me to continue. So I did.

"Everyone here has a right to their privacy," I told her. "And whether or not anyone else cares that their faces of them and their children are printed in your magazine, I do care. Please refrain from taking a photo of me. I appreciate what you are doing to assist us, but giving is rewarded when silence is maintained. We are all here because of life circumstances. Those circumstances do not give you the right to exploit us."

She was livid. If red could have shown through her chocolate-colored skin, she would have surely been a beet. She stomped her way to the worker on duty, and they disappeared into another room. With them gone, I turned to my sisters in the shelter to make my case. The church did teach us to stand up for our principles. "Ladies, do you want your pictures displayed across the pages of a magazine?" "Hell no," one of the mothers said. "Well, they don't have the right to take our photos without our permission," I told her.

Nothing came of it the rest of the day, but sometime in the middle of the night, one of the workers went through the shelter, knocking on doors and asking the mothers to come downstairs. I had a flashback of a White Night.

As we sat down, the worker began that an "incident" had occurred today. "One of you approached the head of the sorority, and told her that they could not take photos of you. She was quite upset and they may not come back again. I shouldn't have to tell you, but it is not anyone's place to give direction to any of the volunteers."

I was furious. She had roused the entire household to talk to one person. It felt more like Jonestown with each passing moment. I couldn't let it go on. "Listen, I was the one that spoke to the woman," I said. "We are not on display here. Neither you nor this facility has carte blanche to treat us whatever way you like." I doubted that worker even knew what carte blanche was. Knowing that I was risking the possibility of being kicked out, still I could not stand around and let them do what they wanted to us. I'd had enough of that. Some of the mothers nodded their heads, and a couple murmured their agreement. "Some of us are hiding from abusive situations," I continued, "protecting their children, life threatening situations, and damn it, we deserve our privacy." The worker was so angry, she could barely respond. "We will deal with this later when the Director arrives." "Yes, by all means, and I will speak with her too." I was so pissed I could barely talk.

The next morning, I got my wish. The Director called me into her office. "You put on quite a show last night, from what I was told." It seemed like she was trying to hold back a smile. I explained what happened until she finally spoke. "You were right." She asked how I had found myself in a shelter. "We have never had anyone like you grace us. You sound like a college graduate." Tears welled in my eyes, as I thought on how my life could have been different. Her statement humbled me, and as hard as I tried to blink the tears away, I was unsuccessful. "Thank you," I gulped. "You were trying a coup d'état," she laughed, and then waved away my protest. "I am glad you did. It was inappropriate and I will counsel the staff on this." She then asked how I was doing at Cascade House. "Working and getting back on my feet"

I said. and that I wanted my own place. She told me about a program called Transitional housing, where a group of single mothers shared a house and each paid a percentage of her salary. I could take classes in parenting, lifestyle changes and finances. No one could stay longer than a year, but in the meantime, it provides a home environment. I said I thought it sounded great, to which she replied that she'd known I'd say that, and so she'd already put in for the transfer. I would leave the next day.

I had no idea what the house was going to look like and I didn't care. We loaded a van with our meager belongings, and drove the twenty minutes to a huge Victorian near Fulton County Stadium, where the Atlanta Braves baseball team played. With its huge front porch, the house reminded me of San Francisco Victorians. It was surrounded by trees. The children looked as happy as I felt.

A worker named Chantal greeted us and showed me the house. There were only three families, so I had a choice of a bedroom. The large living room had chairs, a couch, and a television. There were hardwood floors throughout. I chose a downstairs room with two double beds and a bathroom. As I completed forms on emergency contact information, job location, and children's school, she gave me the house rules. It was not as structured as Cascade House, she began. There was a curfew, but it would be up to us to keep it. The staff did not stay there at night, but, she warned, if I wanted to risk being put out, break the rules. Everyone had communal chores, and each mother had a week that she was responsible for the meals. This meant the planning, shopping for food and cooking.

It reminded me of the commune I lived in San Francisco. I was used to that life. These types of adjustments weren't hard, rather the adjustment of living on my own that I found difficult.

Gathering some cleaning supplies I cleaned the room, and finally it smelled fresh. Later that evening we met the other children and their mothers. The group was friendly, and we enjoyed getting to know each other. We all had our stories of how we arrived there. Monday morning, I enrolled the children back in school and my new life began.

We were living in that house when the Braves were in the hunt for the World Series crown, and came up with a brilliant idea to charge for parking in the vacant lot next to the house along the street. We posted two moms at the entrance of each side of the lot and charged $5 a car to park. For the price – already cheap – we told them we would also keep an eye on their vehicles. They paid. We made about $200 over the period of the home games. This became our Friday night pizza party money. With music on the boom box, we would have dance parties, eat pizza and enjoy ourselves.

I continued to find strength from *The Spiritual Laws of Success.* As I followed the rules laid out in the book, I meditated daily, and being very grateful, spending all my time with the other mothers and my children, everything felt in order. During the days I was at work and not getting caught up in any office politics. The year was slowly winding down and each of my roommates began to find their way out of the house.

Christmas was upon us. One of the workers named Lucy told me a group of employees who worked for the State wanted to adopt a family for Christmas, and she had proposed ours. She told me to have the children write down what they wanted. They tackled the job with enthusiasm, and their lists were long: bicycles, boom box, clothes, train set. When I gave them to Lucy, she asked where mine was. I told her I don't need anything, except the assurance that my kids would have a great Christmas.

It snowed in Atlanta that year. It was freezing. Although the kids had winter coats, all I could afford was a little jacket with a lightweight lining. Freezing as I stood on that corner in the mornings, I willed myself to go on. *Stop complaining, you wimp, you walked 27 miles through the jungle, you can deal with this.* But it was hard. The people at work noticed my thin jacket, and two co-workers offered to buy me a coat. *Angels come in all forms.* My false pride got in the way and I refused the offers.

Answering a knock on Christmas Eve, I opened the door to find three women and two men telling me they we were their adopted family. I thanked them for their generosity, but I didn't yet know how generous they truly were. The men kept going back outside, lugging in more and more gifts. It looked like enough presents for five children. The children could not believe their good fortune. I invited them to stay for coffee, tea, and conversation. Knowing they wanted to ask how I ended up there, but too polite to, I helped by explaining my situation.

I thanked them profusely, but I could tell that they took pleasure in bringing so much joy to children. They hugged the children as they left, and my kids hugged back. They began to jump up and down as soon as our angels left. "Mom, can we open one?" they shouted. I pointed out that they could see the two bikes with big bows on them. "Yeah, but can we open one?" they insisted. My daughter opened a set of *Babysitters Club* books, and beamed her delight. My son opened a handheld game. "I want you to realize that they did not have to do this for us. You must always remember to be giving. Someone is always in need." They nodded in understanding.

Before my year was up at Transition House, I found an apartment off of Cleveland Avenue. With tearful goodbyes, and exchanging phone numbers with Lucy and Chantal, we moved in.

It was not in the best area, but it was affordable and close to public transportation. We went to a warehouse which had been set up to give furniture to people in my situation. The children found matching twin beds and dressers. I found a kitchen table, a bed, and a couch. By the next day our place was furnished. We even had another member of the family, a cat my son had found.

Even as I had struggled, and after I started to work, my children did well. I did not like my daughter's junior high – it was violent and unsafe – but she maintained her place on the principal's list the entire time we were going through our transition. My son was on the honor roll. I was so proud of them. One day, my daughter put her arms around my neck and said in her innocence and truth "Mom, you used to not be a good mom, but you are a great mom now." Tears filled my eyes, and I hugged her tightly and whispered my thank you. That moment changed me again. The most important thing as parents is to keep our children safe, well-loved and protected. It made me really understand I could never risk losing them through drug addiction or anything else.

Our life was very good. We spent many weekends at the Atlanta SciTrek a hands-on science museum. We attended free concerts in Piedmont Park, where my children saw the legendary jazz drummer Max Roach. Packing a lunch and blanket, we would lie out for hours listening to all types of music.

A friend of mine at work – also a single parent with three children – and I decided to cut some costs by sharing an apartment. The six of us moved to a nice complex in Tucker, but when the landlord said thee were too many people in the apartment, my friend found a house in Conyers. We also shared a car, commuting to work together.

For a number of years, I did not receive any child support, but managed to raise my children alone. My son's father finally decided to do the right thing, and the money he sent was a blessing. He and I started communicating again. We discussed getting back together to raise one child together. In February 1997, he invited us to California. Taking two weeks off from work, I flew to California. We resumed our old connection as if we had never been apart. He proposed a week later, and I accepted. We were all excited about the new life we would begin. I would bring my two younger kids out, but Jakari would stay in Atlanta.

We moved to California in June 1997. Thomas and I planned to marry in a backyard wedding that August, but every time I began planning it, it became overwhelming. By the third month, I was ready to have everything shipped back to Atlanta, then realized I needed to give it a little more time. We purchased a home and married in 2000, three years after the original date.

Life was good. My job at Molina Healthcare proved to be very rewarding. Many times people would sit in the conference room and a conversation would somehow turn to churches, cults and of course Jonestown. Still I could not say a word. However, my way of having them think about the stereotypes portrayed was "Well they said people really wanted to live love, regardless of race. Do you think that was crazy?" Still I never knew how to interject that I was a survivor. I mean really, what you say "Oh, by the way, I survived that day." But most of all I did not want the attention of it all.

What prompted me to go into real estate was the sale of our first home. I realized that the broker was not as forthcoming as he should have been. Uneducated, we bought the house without a home inspection, yet when we listed it for sale many people would drive in the cute quiet cul-de-sac, take the number down from the sign and drive away. I asked my husband, why so many people drive by but no one had called to see the house. About two weeks later our broker called and said someone wanted to see the house in twenty minutes? I asked him who was his real estate agent and he said "I am." Then it clicked.

He was not showing the house to anyone he did not represent. It left a very bad taste in my mouth. I had worked in his office on Saturdays sometimes to get to know the business, but the more I was around him, the more I knew that he was not as he appeared. Yet, he talked me into applying for my license, even with a record. 'Just be honest and explain what happened" he said. He never did know about Jonestown. So, I moved again on faith and signed up for my real estate course. It was tough as a foreign language. As I went to class and studied I thought there would never be a time when I understood what I was reading and could take an exam of 150 questions out of 1500. Most days it was overwhelming, but my husband and family were supportive. Nicci was attending college in New York and as always she encouraged me to keep pushing. I did. I ate, drank and slept it, doing exactly what the teacher and owner of Accredited Real Estate School told us to do after we left the three week class. Determined to pass it the first time, I heeded his advice to the letter. Trying not to listen to the negative voice tell me *you have a record, they won't allow you to get your license,* I pushed forward. When I finally got the date for the exam and stepped my studying up a notch.

The day finally arrived. As I sat down nervous, I prayed that if this was God intended I would get my license. In forty five minutes I was walking out of the door, done. Twenty four hours later I called the automated line and got the news that I had passed. One thing out of the way. I went and got fingerprinted and waited again for the investigator to call. A month passed and then another. No word. Well, no news is good news I thought and the next day an envelope arrived. *Darn I thought, a letter telling me that I could not have my license.* When I opened the envelope there it was. I was now a Licensed California real estate agent. I thought about my summary of my crime that accompanied my application and thought the honesty and the years that had passed had softened someone's heart. *Another angel.*

Real estate allowed me the honor of handing a client the keys to their first home. The satisfaction was enormous. All the while, I remained working at Molina Healthcare and real estate afforded my daughter an education in New York City; paying most months for her apartment and then the dorm. I wanted her to have such a better life than I was able to offer her before.

Our youngest son Demetrius played Little League and attended Dusty Baker overnight baseball camp for a week every summer. Jakari came out to California in June 2002. He and my husband became good friends, which pleased me. When Jakari was younger they had gotten into it and both harbored what I thought was ill will. His relocation back to California I knew would be the end of my marriage. Not that it was not already in trouble. They connected like white on rice, and developed a relationship. Jakari has had major challenges in his life. His God given talent was his art. He made a major attempt to change his life around.

Chapter 15:
Peace at Last

Still, my soul had not reached a level of peace. There was a deep yearning for more meaning for me. It pleased me to be able to help support my family and provide for my children. The material things were in place, but still my soul cried out. *There is more for you to do.* I thought. Although my husband had many good points; a hard worker, talented in anything he decided to do, he would not join me in my search for a deeper meaning of life, of faith. I wanted my partner to know God, to be led by God. It did not mean joining a church, but it meant leading the family in a spiritual setting. I craved that in a relationship. My grandpa was one of the most devoted men to God I had ever met - yet somewhere he faltered. Yet, his example in my life is what I wanted in a husband. I was hoping that eventually we could both start the journey, yet that was not the case. My life consisted of living well, but not being well. In March of 2007 we discussed again (too many times to remember) divorce. This time I knew the time was right as did he. He filed for divorce, and two months later, I moved out of our house. I wrote long letters to my children, and a month later, when they drove me the airport for my cross-country flight, I handed them their letters and thanked them for loving me. With tears still glistening on my cheeks, and theirs I boarded the plane and left for Atlanta.

The move was seamless. It was my confirmation that I was moving in divine order, yet I was still unclear as to the mission. Separating myself from my small family was difficult, but the mission was bigger than even them. For the first time in my life I would be alone, and it was frightening, yet necessary. The purpose was to complete this manuscript, to tell my story. It had taken me seven years to remove my veil of secrecy and hopefully to be an inspiration to those whose lives have consisted of too many low blows and setbacks.

Atlanta has proven to be a spiritual move for me. Reconnecting with someone I knew ten years before – we began a journey of discovery. Chatfield introduced me to Adama, who opened up the world I needed to enter. The universe continues to bless me and – through lifestyle changes such as embracing Veganism – my spiritual center opened up and I could complete this story. My very soul began recalling situations that I had buried a long time ago. It allowed me dig deep to discover another me. Along the way, I have also the purpose of what life can be if we decide to let it be.

The title may be disturbing to some. However when Peter Moyes, someone that helped me in the beginning stages and Louise Jones (may she rest in peace) sat with me for two months, weeding through the first stages of this book, Peter realized that my faith is what carried me through. My entire life has been moved by spirit: spirit of self, spirits of my ancestors, and spirits of my living family. God cast angels upon me, providing protection. The thousands of prayer warriors who fell to their knees praying for us have also allowed me to love. With an understanding that universal love can manifest itself in each and every one of us, it has been worth the journey. It took years to hear in my heart what I heard with my ears, that God is Love. I realized that my gift is to love. We all can – and must – take this journey of forgiveness so we can look at each other as an extension of self, to relate to each other center to center instead of surface to surface. We are moving towards a different reality. Will you be ready?

I have no regrets. As each one tried to emerge, a larger self-awareness awoke that this is bigger than me. The drug use which made me understand the masking of pain, my jail time which allowed me to hear the stories of others, and experience of death which made me appreciate life, have combined to make me a Slave to Faith.

As a cosmic citizen, I find in our world as a place where we have just elected a man of color who believes in Universal love to lead our country. I find camaraderie with millions of people who want a different world, a different country and different existence. How I wish my ancestors, my brother, my mother and all those who passed could witness this. This is what the Peoples Temple Disciples of Christ was supposed to stand for: an awakening of spirit for people to embrace each other to begin to view each other as citizens of the world, not just Americans; neither black, nor white, nor Latin, nor Asian, but brothers and sisters. We all share that common thread of belief that each of us can be anything we want; we can mold our lives even through the worst of adversity. We grasp that with each problem is an opportunity to solve it and grow.

Now the question that is always asked. Could Jonestown happen again? Of course. Many seek refuge from the storm, seek outward instead of inward. We create our heaven and our hell. Which will you choose?

On November 18, 1997 I awoke early in the morning from a deep sleep, turned on the bedside lamp, pulled my laptop closer to me, and willed myself to write. After I completed the first part of this manuscript, I clicked on the link to the website, http://jonestown.sdsu. edu/, and began to write remembrances of those lost. I had noticed that even though entire families were lost in Jonestown, all that was displayed were their pictures. Nothing was said about them. No memories. No stories. No trace for any descendants who might have escaped. Through tears and laughter I pulled up names and began to write what I remembered about each of them.

There was one more thing to do: to listen to the final tape of November 18, 1978. I had tried re-living that day many times, but it had been too difficult. My heart ached for the voices on the tape, as I heard the ambivalence and the confusion and the fear and the anger and – ultimately – the acceptance of those about to die. I listened to Christine Miller plead with Jim to give them a choice. Finally, it sank in. My God, I thought. What would have happened had everyone *lived?* A Congressman and four newsmen were dead on a jungle airstrip thousands of miles from the U.S. This was an international incident. The adults surely would have been extradited and imprisoned in a Federal facility or – worse – tried in Guyana and imprisoned in a Guyanese prison. Our babies, our children, our adolescents would have been separated from their parents and put in our nation's already-overwhelmed foster care system.

Were the people of Jonestown given a choice? No, they were not. Their fates were held in the hand of an egotistical madman, whose inner circle had the opportunity to stop the madness. I've often been asked, what would have happened if I'd been there. I answer without hesitation, "I could not have been able to bear the thought of living." Did the residents think it was another test? Eyewitnesses say that the children were the first to be poisoned. Some parents – my sister among them – fought for their children's lives, while others acquiesced. But after the deaths of their children – the death of their futures – parents no longer had reason to live. The vision makes me fall to my knees in tears, for 30 years later, I still grieve. There are circumstances that I pray will come to light before I leave this world. How were the reports from the media so skewed? The body count changing every day? Living in Jonestown and knowing the compound like the back of my own hand, nine hundred bodies could not be hidden from anyone's sight at any view. Impossible. The space between the front of the pavilion was huge and would be the first thing you saw upon entering the camp. Also, the areas to the pavilion were paths, narrow paths. The reports were conflicting throughout. It will be a blessing to finally know all of the truth.

So as you contemplate what you have read, I ask that you read the names of those listed on the following pages, allowing their names to come forward from your lips, speaking them aloud to acknowledge that they were here. The list is courtesy of http://jonestown.sdsu.edu/, which I thank for compiling this list and maintaining a comprehensive website.

I am living their love, not their death.

Thank you, thank you. May the Universe continue to bless each and every one of you. Peace, Blessings and most of all Universal Love.

Leslie

ADDISON, Stephen Michael 5/4/44 Missouri (Santa Rosa, California 95401)

ALBUDY, Ida Marie 8/26/06 Missouri (San Francisco, California 94115)

Amos, Liane, see HARRIS, Liane

Amos, Linda, see AMOS, Sharon

*AMOS, Martin Laurence 4/19/68 California

*AMOS, Sharon (AKA Amos, Linda; Harris, Linda Sharon) 7/4/36 California (Redwood Valley, California 95476)

*AMOS, Wayborn Christa 3/7/67 California

ANDERSON, Jerome Dwayne 10/30/60 California (San Francisco, California 94115)

ANDERSON, Marice St. Martin 7/22/62 California (San Francisco, California 94115)

ANDERSON, Marcus Anthony 7/29/63 Mother (Richardell Smith Anderson, aka Richardell Perkins) and siblings (Jerome Dwayne Anderson, Marice St. Martin Anderson, and Tommy Lee Anderson)

ANDERSON, Orelia 6/8/10 Louisiana (Los Angeles, California 90006)

ANDERSON, Samuel Moses 4/12/11 Mississippi (Oakland, California 94604)

ANDERSON, Tommy Lee 12/25/59 California (San Francisco, California 94115)

Armstrong, Oreen, see POPLIN, Oreen

Arnold, Birdie, see ARNOLD, Luberta

ARNOLD, Luberta (AKA Arnold, Birdie) 2/27/07 Texas (Los Angeles, California 90003)

ARTERBERRY, Linda Theresa (AKA Pierce, Linda) 12/6/48 California (San Francisco, California 94115)

ARTERBERRY, Ricardo D. 1/15/68 Mother (Linda Theresa Arterberry)

ARTERBERRY, Traytease Lanette 4/6/71 Mother (Linda Theresa Arterberry)

Atkins, Lydia, see MORGAN, Lydia

ATKINS, Ruth 3/4/04 Texas (San Francisco, California 94113)

BACK, Daniel J.

BACKMAN, Viola Elaine 3/23/50 South Carolina (San Francisco, California)

BAILEY, Geraldine Harriet 3/23/12 Oklahoma (San Francisco, California 94121)

BAILEY, Mary Jane 9/6/15 Arkansas (Los Angeles, California 90006)

BAISY, James Samuel, Jr.1/15/65 Mother (Shirley Mae Wilson, aka Shirley Mae Baisy)

Baisey, Jerry, see WILSON, Jerry

BAISY, JonDeshi 9/27/71 Mother (Shirley Mae Wilson, aka Shirley Mae Baisy)

BAISY, Kecia 6/10/66 Mother (Shirley Mae Wilson, aka Shirley Mae Baisy)

Baisey, Shirley May, see WILSON, Shirley Mae

BAKER, Shawn Valgen 4/21/65

BAISY, Siburi Jamal 6/28/69 Mother (Shirley Mae Wilson, aka Shirley Mae Baisy)

Baisy, Trinidette (see Trinidette CORNNER)

BAKER, Jair Alexander 5/23/59

BAKER, Tarik Earl 10/29/61 California (Pomona, California 91766)

BALDWIN, Mary Be 4/8/26 Alabama

BARGEMAN, Rory La Vate 6/21/61 Florida

BARGEMAN, Terence Vair 11/3/62 Texas

BARRETT, Ben Franklyn 11/18/34 Texas (Ukiah, California 95482)

BARRETT, Becky Ann 3/8/74 Parents (Cathy Ann and Ben Franklyn Barrett)

BARRETT, Cathy Ann (AKA Stahl, Cathy Ann) 3/30/53 Indiana (Ukiah, California 95482)

BARRON, Jack Darlington 11/9/21 Delaware (Redwood Valley, California)

BATES, Christine Ella Mae 3/22/05 Texas (Ukiah, California 95480)

BEAL, Geneva Mattie 9/4/40 (Peoples Temple records list birthyear as 1920) Mississippi (San Francisco, California)

BEAM, Eleanor Marie 3/5/61 Indiana (San Francisco, California 94115)

BEAM, Jack Lovell 11/25/23 Kentucky (Ukiah, California 95482)

Beam, Joe, see HELLE, Joseph Leo III

BEAM, Rheaviana Wilson 8/15/24 Kentucky (San Francisco, California 94117)

BECK, Daniel James 5/15/66 California (Redwood Valley, California)

BEIKMAN, Rebecca May 11/29/40 Indiana (Redwood Valley, California 95470)

BELL, Alfred 3/12/09 Arkansas (San Francisco, California)

BELL, Beatrice Claudine 2/3/55 Arkansas (San Francisco, California)

BELL, Carlos Lee, Jr. 11/8/64 Mother (Richardell Smith Anderson, aka Richardell Perkins) and siblings (Jerome Dwayne Anderson, Marice St. Martin Anderson, and Tommy Lee Anderson)

BELL, Elsie Ingraham 6/11/1918 Arkansas (San Francisco, California)

BELLE, Ethel Mathilda 4/13/1890 (Peoples Temple records list birthday as 4/7/1892)

BENTON, Lena Mae Camp (AKA Benton, Lena Mary Camp) 11/24/09 (Peoples Temple records list birthdate as 2/2/10) Texas (Los Angeles, California 90006)

Benton, Lena Mary Camp, see BENTON, Lena Mae Camp

BERKLEY, Yolanda 7/22/73 Mother (Wanda Souder) and grandmother (Martha Souder)

BERRY, Dana Danielle (Mother is Carnella Truss)

BERRY, Daniel Bernard 2/24/75 Mother (Beatrice Claudine Bell)

BERRYMAN, Ronnie Dewayne 2/26/52 California (Los Angeles, California 90006)

BIRKLEY, Julia 7/25/09 Alabama (Los Angeles, California 90611)

BISHOP, James Arthur (AKA Jones, James Arthur) 11/25/64 California (San Francisco, California 94107)

BISHOP, Stephanie Lynn aka Stephanie Jones aka Stephanie Brown 12/20/63 Guardian (Marceline Jones)

BLACK, Mary Emma Love Lewis

BLACKWELL, Odell 1/13/10 North Carolina (Los Angeles, California 90003)

BLAIR, Ernestine Hines 8/9/17 Arkansas (Los Angeles, California 90037)

BOGUE, Marilee Faith 3/31/59 California

BORDENAVE, Selika Glordine 7/10/18 Mississippi

BOUQUET, Claudia Jo (AKA Norris, Claudia Jo) 5/1/56 California

BOUQUET, Pierre Brian 7/20/53 California (Burlingame, California)

Boutte, Corlis, see CONLEY, Corlis Denise

BOUTTE, Mark Anthony 4/14/57 California (San Francisco, California)

BOWER, Donald Robert 2/3/27 California (Oakland, California)

BOWERS, Christine Shannon (AKA Talley, Christine) 6/22/57 California

BOWIE, Kenneth Bernard 4/20/60 Louisiana (Redwood Valley, California)

Bowie, Willie Lee, see GRAHAM, Willie

BOWMAN, Anthony 2/7/64 California (Los Angeles, California 90002)

BOWMAN, Delores 9/23/49 California (Los Angeles, California 90002)

BOWMAN, Edna Mae

BOWMAN, Patricia Ann 9/1/57 Louisiana (Los Angeles, California 90002)

BOWSER, Regina Michelle 4/1/63 Mother (Viola Duncan Forks)

BRADSHAW, Pamela Gail (AKA Moton, Pamela) 8/17/56 New York

Brady, Dorothy, see WORLEY, Dorothy Lee

BRADY, Georgiann Patricia 12/23/65 Mother (Michaeleen Patrica Brady), sister (Michele Margaret Brady) and guardian (Maureen Cynthia Fitch aka Maureen Talley)

BRADY, Michaeleen Patricia 5/14/43 California (San Francisco, California 94121)

BRADY, Michele Margaret 12/2/66

BRANDON, Najahjuanda Jherenelle aka Najah Darnes 9/21/70 Numerous members of Darnes family

BREIDENBACH, Lois Fontaine 5/29/28 Oklahoma (Redwood Valley, California 95470)

BREIDENBACH, Melanie Lee 9/14/60 California (Redwood Valley, California 95470)

BREIDENBACH, Wesley Karl 9/15/59 California

BREWER, Dorothy Ann 10/24/38 Texas (San Francisco, California)

BREWSTER, Kimberly Louise 8/25/55 California (San Francisco, California 94102)

BRIDGEWATER, Miller 2/11/08 Texas (Palo Alto, California 94306)

Briggs, Donna Louise (see Donna Louise LACY)

BRIGHT, Juanita Jean 12/8/67 Mother (Ruby J. Bright)

BRIGHT, Lawrence George 10/18/65 Mother (Ruby J. Bright)

BRIGHT, Ruby Jean 2/12/47 Missouri (San Francisco, California 94115)

BROWN, Jocelyn 4/10/58 California

Brown, Johnny Moss, Jr., see JONES, Johnny

BROWN, Joyce Marie (AKA Polk, Joyce) 2/8/60 Indiana (San Francisco, California 94107)

BROWN, Luella Holmes 6/1/19 Louisiana (Redwood Valley, California)

**BROWN, Robert

BROWN, Ruletta 12/26/53 California

Brown, Stephanie (see Stephanie Lynn BISHOP)

BRYANT, Lucioes (Peoples Temple records spell name "Lucious"), 6/23/25 (Peoples Temple records list birthyear as 1927), Arkansas (Los Angeles, California 90011)

BRYANT, Princeola 10/12/12 Arkansas (Los Angeles, California 90018)

BUCKLEY, Christopher Calvin 5/28/66

BUCKLEY, Dorothy Helen 8/17/61 Mississippi (San Francisco, California 94107)

BUCKLEY, Frances Elizabeth 11/18/64 California (San Francisco, California 94107)

BUCKLEY, Loreatha (Peoples Temple records list name as Loreitha) 7/16/57 Indiana (Ukiah, California)

Buckley, Luna M., see BUCKLEY, Minnie Luna

BUCKLEY, Minnie Luna Mae (AKA Buckley, Luna M.) 5/6/41 Mississippi (Ukiah, California 95482)

BUCKLEY, Odessa 11/30/62 California (San Francisco, California 94107)

BURGINES, Rosie Lee 11/7/53 Arkansas (Los Angeles, California 90007)

BUSH, William Paul Sean 11/4/64 California (Ukiah, California 95482)

CAIN, Ruthie M. 9/30/40 Mississippi (Los Angeles, California)

Camp, Lena, see BENTON, Lena Mae Camp

CAMPBELL, Ronald Ray, Jr. 5/27/72 Mother (Rochelle Halkman)

CANADA, Mary Francis 1/20/01 Louisiana (Pittsburg, California)

CANNON, Henry Frank, Jr. 11/10/60 Mother (Thelma Mattie Cannon, aka Thelma Doris Mattie Ross)

CANNON, Thelma Doris Mattie 7/29/30 Texas (San Francisco, California 94121)

CANNON, Vities Rochele aka Vita Cannon 11/3/62 Mother (Thelma Mattie Cannon, aka Thelma Doris Mattie Ross)

CAREY, Jeffery James 12/12/50 Michigan (Redwood Valley, California 95482)

CARR, Karen Yvette 7/18/63 California (San Francisco, California 94102)

CARROLL, Ada Marie

CARROLL, Mildred Ada (AKA Mercer, Mildred) 2/19/99 Virginia (San Francisco, California 94109)

CARROLL, Ruby Jewell 6/10/37 Texas

Carter, Gloria, see RODRIGUEZ, Gloria Maria

CARTER, Terry 10/3/54 Montana (San Francisco, California)

CARTER, Kaywana Mae 4/4/77 (Peoples Temple records list birthdate as 5/10/77) (Georgetown, Guyana)

CARTER, Malcolm J. 8/10/77 (Georgetown, Guyana)

CARTMELL, Patricia A. 7/31/29 Ohio (San Francisco, California)

CARTMELL, Patricia Pauline 7/3/54 Ohio (San Francisco, California)

CARTMELL, Walter Clayton 5/15/28 Kentucky (Redwood Valley, California 95470)

Casanova, Angel, see SCHEID, Angelique Marie

Casanova, Don, see SCHEID, Donald Eugene Jr.

CASTILLO, Mary Frances 1/7/20 Maryland (Los Angeles, California 90006)

CASTILLO, William Richard 2/19/44 Texas (Los Angeles, California 90006)

CATNEY, Georgia Mae 10/26/17 Arkansas (Redwood Valley, California 94061)

CHACON, Stephanie Katrina 5/27/60 California (Berkeley, California 94703)

CHAIKIN, David Lee 1/21/63 California (Redwood Valley, California 95470)

CHAIKIN, Eugene B. 12/18/32 California

CHAIKIN, Gail Stephanie 2/26/61 California

CHAIKIN, Phyllis 5/6/39 California (Redwood Valley, California 95470)

CHAMBLISS, Jossie Evelyn 6/30/02 (Peoples Temple records list birthdate as 3/6/02) Virginia (San Francisco, California)

CHAVIS, Loretta Diane 4/1/55 California (Los Angeles, California 90007)

CHRISTIAN, Robert Louis 9/10/47 Louisiana

CHRISTIAN, Robert Louis, 2nd 11/9/70 Parents (Vernetta Carolyn and Robert Louis Christian)

CHRISTIAN, Tina Rayette 9/1/69 Parents (Vernetta Carolyn and Robert Louis Christian)

CHRISTIAN, Vernetta Carolyn 12/25/44 Texas (San Francisco, California 94117)

Clancey, MaryLou, see CLANCEY, Mary Louise

CLANCEY, Mary Louise (AKA Clancey, MaryLou) 4/16/54 California

CLARK, Joicy E. 10/28/11 Texas (San Francisco, California 94115)

CLARKE, Leola L. 7/29/1911 (Peoples Temple records list birthdate as 7/9/09)

CLAY, Nancy 5/26/09 Texas (San Francisco, California 94115)

CLIPPS, Ida Mae 12/4/17 Texas (San Francisco, California 94117)

Coachman, Alma, see COLEY, Alma

COBB, Brenda Carole 9/4/63 Indiana

COBB, Christine

Cobb, Elois Christine, see YOUNG, Elois Christine

COBB, Joel Raymond 2/2/65 Indiana

Cobb, Sandra Yvette, see JONES, Sandy

COBB, Sharon Rose 8/31/48 Ohio (Redwood Valley, California 95470)

COBB-BROWN, Ava

COLE, Arlander 12/22/06 Mississippi

COLE, Arvella 9/28/06 Mississippi (San Francisco, California)

COLE, Clarence Elmer III (AKA Klingman, Clarence; Jackson, Clarence) 8/11/63 California (Ukiah, California 95482)

COLE, Matthew Todd aka Todd Klingman 11/12/67 Mother (Martha Ellen Klingman) and siblings (Clarence Elmer Cole III aka Clarence Klingman, and William Arnold Cole aka William Klingman)

COLE, William Arnold (AKA Klingman, William) 1/13/65

COLEMAN, Mary 7/23/94 Texas (San Francisco, California)

COLEMAN, Ruth Virgina (Peoples Temple records say name is "Colman") 1/3/20 Mississippi (Los Angeles, California 90003)

COLEY, Alma (AKA Coachman, Alma; Thomas, Alma) 3/10/24 Louisiana (San Francisco, California)

COLLINS, Susie Lee 7/20/00 Texas (Los Angeles, California 90011)

CONEDY, Inez Stricklin 3/5/09 Arkansas (Palo Alto, California 94306)

CONLEY, Corlis Denise (AKA Boutte, Corlis) 3/12/59 California

COOK, Bertha Pearl 12/12/12 Alabama (Los Angeles, California 90006)

COOK, Mary Ella 1/26/14 Missouri (Los Angeles, California 90006)

Coomer, Loretta, see CORDELL, Loretta Mae

CORDELL, Barbara Jeanne 8/14/38 Michigan (Redwood Valley, California 95470)

CORDELL, Candace Kay 11/7/60 Indiana (Redwood Valley, California 95470)

CORDELL, Chris Mark 9/13/57 Indiana (Redwood Valley, California 95470)

CORDELL, Cindy Lyn 12/8/59 Indiana (Redwood Valley, California 95470)

CORDELL, Edith Excell 2/6/02 Indiana (Redwood Valley, California 95470)

CORDELL, James Joseph 10/28/64 Indiana (Redwood, Valley California 95470)

Cordell, Jamie (see Jameel Regina LAWRENCE)

CORDELL, Julie Rene 7/28/61 Indiana (Redwood Valley, California 95470)

CORDELL, Loretta Mae (AKA Coomer, Loretta) 11/28/37 Indiana (Redwood Valley, California 95470)

CORDELL, Mabel 3/14/62 Nine family members, including mother (Loretta Mae Cordell)

CORDELL, Mark Nathan 6/29/59 Nine family members, including mother (Barbara Jeanne Cordell)

CORDELL, Natasha LaNa 8/17/76 Nine family members, including mother (Theresa Cordell aka Shawnterri Hall) and legal guardian (Barbara Jeanne Cordell)

CORDELL, Richard William, Jr. 9/2/64 Nine family members, including mother (Barbara Jeanne Cordell)

CORDELL, Rita Diane 9/18/62 Nine family members, including mother (Barbara Jeanne Cordell)

CORDELL, Teresa Laverne (AKA Hall, Shawnterri) 3/11/58 Georgia (San Francisco, California 94115)

COREY, Carrie Lee 1/12/34 North Carolina (San Francisco, California 94117)

COREY, Carrie R.

CORNNER, Trinidette aka Trinidette Baisy 8/5/70 Mother (Shirley Mae Wilson, aka Shirley Mae Baisy)

COTTINGHAM, Mary Maide 11/30/99 South Carolina

Crenshaw, Eddie, see HALLMON, Eddie James

Crenshaw, Francine, see MASON, Francine

CRENSHAW, Lucy 1/1/25 Mississippi (San Francisco, California)

Crenshaw, Tiquan (see Tiquan HALLMON)

CUNNINGHAM, Millie Steans 12/25/04 Texas (San Francisco, California 94117)

DANIEL, Betty L. 5/4/51 Texas (San Francisco, California 94102)

Daniels, Dorothy, see SIMPSON, Dorothy

DANIELS, Michael 6/14/64 Grandmother (Annie Mae Harris)

Darden, Mary, see JOHNSON, Mary

Darnes, Braunshaunski, see DARNES, Searcy Llewellyn

Darnes, Elondwaynion Jhontera, see DARNES, Ollie B.

Darnes, Najah (see Najahjuanda Jherenelle BRANDON)

Darnes, Najuandrienne, see DARNES, Velma Lee

DARNES, Newhuanda Rhenelle (AKA Walker, Newhuanda Rhenelle) 11/14/59 California

DARNES, Ollie B. II (AKA Darnes, Elondwaynion Jhontera) 10/29/67

DARNES, Searcy Llewellyn (AKA Darnes, Braunshaunski) 4/21/62 California (Santa Rosa, California)

DARNES, Velma Lee (AKA Darnes, Najuandrienne) 4/29/36 Louisiana (Santa Rosa, California)

DASHIELL, Hazel Frances 12/16/99 Rhode Island (San Francisco, California 94117)

DAVIS, Barbara Marie 10/3/25 Texas (Los Angeles, California 90007)

Davis, Bippy (see Margarite Yvette ROMANO)

DAVIS, Brian Andrew 7/19/62

Davis, Celeste, see VENTO, Celeste Marie

DAVIS, Cynthia Marie 12/3/49 Texas (San Francisco, California)

DAVIS, Frances Bernadette 3/14/28 California

DAVIS, Gerina Maxine 1/3/77 Mother (Margaret Davis aka Margarita Davis) and sibling (Celeste Marie Vento aka Celeste Davis) (n.b. Another Peoples Temple records says parents were Vicky and Danny Marshall, both of whom died in Jonestown)

DAVIS, Isabell Minnie 12/23/25 Mississippi

DAVIS, Johannah Danielle 9/16/74 Mother (Margaret Davis aka Margarita

Davis) and sibling (Celeste Marie Vento aka Celeste Davis)

DAVIS, Lexie Smith 9/22/09 Texas (Los Angeles, California 90018)

Davis, Margarita, see DAVIS, Margaret

DAVIS, Margaret Virginia (AKA Davis, Margarita) 1/10/50 Pennsylvania (San Francisco, California)

Davis, Renee (see Renee Sylvia ROMANO)

DAVIS, Robert Edwin 4/27/36 Washington (Ukiah, California 95482)

DAWKINS, Beatrice 8/31/18 Mississippi (Los Angeles, California 90018)

DEAN, Burger Lee 11/14/16 Arkansas (Los Angeles, California 90006)

DELAHAUSSAYE, Tammi Sherrel (Peoples Temple records spell last name "Delihaussaye" 9/28/66 Mother (Viola Duncan Forks)

DELANEY, Edith Fredonia 12/23/09 Kansas (Ukiah, California 95482)

Dennis, Carol, see McCOY, Carol Ann

DENNIS, Eddie Lee 7/4/28 Louisiana (Los Angeles, California 90001)

DENNIS, Ellihue 8/2/48 Louisiana (San Francisco,California 94103)

DENNIS, Gabriel 1968 Parents (Eddie and Orde Dennis) and brother (Ronnie Dennis)

Dennis, Leanndra (see Leanndra MCCOY)

DENNIS, Orde 10/31/32 Louisiana (Los Angeles, California 90001)

DENNIS, Ronnie 12/20/61

DE PINA, Lovie Hattie Ann 10/18/00 South Carolina (Ukiah, California 95482)

DEVERS, Darrell Audwin 12/6/55 Illinois (Los Angeles, California 90008)

DICKERSON, Roseana E. 3/26/17 Louisiana (Richmond, California 94801)

DICKSON, Bessie Lee 2/4/14 Texas (Los Angeles, California 90001)

DILLARD, Violatt Esther 9/16/27 Texas (San Francisco, California 94102)

DOMINICK, Katherine Martha (Peoples Temple records say name is "Domineck") 10/27/94 Texas (San Francisco, California 94121)

DOUGLAS, Farene 9/10/10 Texas (Los Angeles, California 90062)

DOUGLAS, Joyce Lalar 4/3/58

DOVER, Vicky Lynn (AKA Marshall, Vicky Lynn) 1/20/58 Indiana (Redwood Valley, California 95470)

DOWNS, Nena Belle 4/22/28 Texas (Los Angeles, California 90001)

DUCKETT, Exia Maria (AKA Howard, Exia Marie; Lawrence, Marie) 1/20/45 California

DUCKETT, Joanette Blugina (AKA Harrell, Joanette; Lawrence, Dee Dee) 12/31/63 California (San Francisco, California 94107

DUCKETT, Ronald Charles (AKA Lawrence, Nicky) 10/16/62 (Peoples Temple records list birthdate as 10/14/62) California (San Francisco, California 94107

DUNCAN, Corrie 11/6/06 Texas (San Francisco,California 94115)

DUNCAN, Verdella 5/20/24 Texas (San Francisco, California 94102)

DUPONT, Ellen Louise (AKA Kerns, Penny) 11/13/30 Arizona (Los Angeles, California 90006)

DYSON, Florine 12/06/90 Virginia (San Francisco, California 94109)

EDDINS, Irene 1/4/02 Arkansas (San Francisco, California 94119)

EDWARDS, Isaac, Jr. 6/9/72 Mother (Shirley Ann Edwards)

EDWARDS, James 11/28/20 Mississippi

EDWARDS, Shirley Ann 12/14/51 Mississippi (San Francisco, California 94117)

EDWARDS, Zipporah 5/27/05 Alabama (San Francisco, California 94119)

EICHLER, Erin Jahna (AKA Lawrence, Erin; LeRoy, Erin; Watkins, Erin Leroy) 3/13/60 California (Redwood Valley, California 95470)

EICHLER, Evelyn Marie 8/19/55 California (Redwood Valley, California 95470)

EICHLER, Laetitia Marie (AKA LeRoy, Tish)

EVER REJOICING (AKA Pointdexter, Amanda) 10/9/81 Virginia (Redwood Valley, California)

FAIN, Tinetra La Dese 11/8/58 California (Los Angeles, California 90008)

FAIR, Amanda 12/10/08 Oklahoma (San Francisco, California 94121)

FAIR, Sylvester Clarence 3/9/08 (San Francisco, California 94117)

FARRELL, Barbara Louise 10/5/33 Indiana (San Francisco, California 94115)

FARRIS, Marshall 8/5/07 Arkansas (San Francisco, California 94124)

FARRIS, Lore B.

FELTON, Michael Donnell 10/1/73 Mother (Viola Duncan Forks)

FIELDS, James Donald 6/4/32 New York (Northridge, California 91324)

FIELDS, Lori Beth 12/6/65 California (Northridge California 91324)

FIELDS, Mark Evan 3/22/67 Parents (Shirlee and Donald James Fields)

FIELDS, Shirlee Ann 12/15/37 Michigan (Northridge, California 91324)

FINNEY, Casey Nakyia 7/15/59 California (Los Angeles, California 90047)

FITCH, Betty Jean 6/2/55 California (San Francisco, California 94117)

FITCH, Dawnyelle 9/4/74 Father (Donald Kirk Fitch)

FITCH, Donald Kirk 4/15/46 New Hampshire

FITCH, Maureen Cynthia (AKA Talley, Maureen) 6/13/49 California (Ukiah, California 95482)

FITCH, Raymond Xavier 9/11/76 Parents (Betty Jean and Tom Fitch)

FITCH, Thomas R. 5/17/49 Massachusetts (San Francisco, California)

FLOWERS, Rebecca Ann 7/7/53 Indiana (San Francisco, California 94115)

FONZELLE, Toi 1/17/55 California (Los Angeles, California 90011)

FORD, Fannie 1/9/34 Mississippi (Los Angeles, California 90037)

FORKS, Viola Duncan 1/13/34 Texas (Berkeley, California 94703)

FORTSON, Rhonda Denise 8/26/54 Colorado (Los Angeles, California 90011)

FOSTER, Beulah 9/14/03 Mississippi (Los Angeles, California 90006)

FOUNTAIN, Betty Jewel 8/14/49 Washington (Los Angeles, California 90003)

FOUNTAIN, Robert E., Jr.

FRANKLIN, Laketta Lashun 10/7/70 Mother (Richardell Smith Anderson, aka Richardell Perkins) and siblings (Jerome Dwayne Anderson, Marice St. Martin Anderson, and Tommy Lee Anderson)

FRANKLIN, Robert Eddie Lee, Jr. 6/17/58 Missouri (Oakland, California 94608)

FROHM, Constance B. 2/9/55 Texas (Redwood Valley, California 95470)

FYE, Kimberly Ann 12/10/59 Washington (Ukiah, California 95482)

GALLIE, Bof William 10/22/73 (Redwood Valley, California 95470)

GARCIA, Cleveland Desmond 5/26/60 (Los Angeles, California)

GARCIA, Mary Helen 9/19/38 (Los Angeles, California)

GARCIA, Susan

GARDENER, John Lawrence 9/20/60 California (Ukiah, California 95482)

GEE, Hermon W. 3/27/97 Texas (Oakland, California 94606)

GEE, Mattie

GERNANDT, Eugenia 3/12/23 New Mexico (San Francisco, California)

GIBSON, Mattie 12/24/05 Arkansas (San Francisco, California 94115)

GIEG, Jason 1/21/75 Ukiah, California, Parents (Robert and Renee Gieg)

GIEG, Renee E. 6/9/55 San Francisco, California (San Francisco, California 94115)

GIEG, Robert Wendell 7/25/51 Martinez, California (San Francisco, California 94115)

GIEG, Stanley Brian 1/20/59 California (San Francisco, California 94115)

Gilbert, MN, see SMITH, Jerry

GILL, Betty Jean 7/16/60

GILL, Irma Lee 2/5/12

GODSHALK, Viola May 2/10/21 California (Redwood Valley, California)

GOODSPEED, Claude 6/13/05 Texas (Los Angeles, California 90044)

GOODSPEED, Lue Dimple 1/3/07 Texas (Los Angeles, California 90044)

GOSNEY, Mark Hartley 11/28/73 California (Redwood Valley, California 95470)

GRADY, Willie James 7/4/54 Arkansas (Los Angeles, California 90006)

GRAHAM, Willie Lee (AKA Bowie, Willie Lee) 2/9/07 Louisiana (Los Angeles, California 90001)

GREEN, Juanita 9/5/16 Oklahoma (Oakland, California 94602)

GREENE, Anitra Rochelle 1/8/61 California (Los Angeles, California 90003)

GRIFFITH, Amondo 3/10/60 California (San Francisco, California 94124)

GRIFFITH, Camella (Kamilah) 10/29/77 Parents (Gloria and Emmett Griffith)

GRIFFITH, Emmett Alexander, Jr. 7/11/58 California (San Francisco, California 94124)

Griffith, Gloria, see WARREN, Gloria Faye

GRIFFITH, Mae Kathryn 12/26/41 Texas (Los Angeles, California 90037)

GRIFFITH, Marrian Louise 9/13/62 Mother (Mary Magdaline Griffith) and siblings (Emmett Griffith, Jr. and Armondo Griffith)

GRIFFITH, Mary Magdaline 1/28/27 (San Francisco, California)

GRIGSBY, Frankie Lee 5/17/26

GRIMM, Ronald Windus 1/16/37 California (San Rafael, California 94901)

GRIMM, Sue L. 3/4/41 California (San Rafael, California 94901)

GRIMM, Tina Lynn 5/9/60 California (San Raphael, California 94901)

GRISSETTE, Youlanda aka Youlanda Smith 6/15/66 Mother (Barbara Smith)

GROOT, Pauline 5/30/50 Washington (Santa Rosa, California 95401)

Grubbs, Clark (see Clark Andrew SMITH)

GRUBBS, Gerald Richard (AKA Norton, Ken) 2/15/45 Washington (Los Angeles, California 90006)

Grubbs, Kelly (see Kelly Franklin SMITH)

GRUBBS, Lemuel Thomas, II (AKA Grubbs, Tom) 11/20/41 (Peoples Temple records say birthdate is 10/20/41) Washington (Los Angeles, California 90006)

GRUBBS, Sylvia Elaine 11/10/38 California

Grubbs, Tom, see GRUBBS, Lemuel Thomas II

GRUNNETT, Patricia Lee 11/25/41 California (Redwood Valley, California 95470)

GUIDRY, Mercedese Mavis Clare 9/6/08 Louisiana (Los Angeles, California 90006)

GURVICH, Jann Elizabeth 11/05/53 Louisiana (Berkeley, California 94702)

GUY, Brian 9/8/66 Illinois (San Francisco, California 94134)

GUY, Keith LeJon 9/12/67 Illinois (San Francisco, California 94134

GUY, Kimberly Denee 7/29/71 Illinois (San Francisco, California 94134)

GUY, Ottie Mese 6/8/44 Mississippi (San Francisco, California 94134)

GUY, Thurman III 12/2/62

HALKMAN, Rochelle Dawanna 9/30/52 Missouri (San Francisco, California 94117)

HALL, Carl Gloster 3/16/1904

HALL, Heloise Janice 12/7/11 Kansas (Los Angeles, California 90019)

Hall, Shawnterri, see CORDELL, Teresa Laverne

HALLMON, Eddie James (AKA Crenshaw, Eddie) 4/6/55 Indiana (San Francisco, California 94115)

HALLMON, Tiquan R. aka Tiquan Crenshaw 2/26/77 Parents (Francine Mason aka Francine Crenshaw and Eddie James Hallmon aka Eddie Crenshaw)

HARMS, Karen Marie 6/14/58 North Carolina (Ukiah, California)

HARPER, Artee 1/28/10 Louisiana (Los Angeles, California 90003)

Harrell, Joanette, see DUCKETT, Joanette Blugina

HARRINGTON, Ollie B. 11/7/40 Mississippi (Los Angeles, California 90003)

HARRIS, Annie Mae 1/22/04 Arkansas (Los Angeles, California 90006)

Harris, Constance Nicole, see HARRIS, Willie Maude

**HARRIS, Donald

HARRIS, Dorothy Lesheene (AKA Harris, Shajhuanna Lesheene) 1/17/61 Georgia (Ukiah, California)

Harris, John, see HOLMES, Jeff

HARRIS, Josephine 12/24/07 Mississippi (Los Angeles, California)

*HARRIS, Lian 11/27/56 California (Redwood Valley, California 95470)

Harris, Linda Sharon, see AMOS, Sharon

HARRIS, Magnolia Costella 12/11/16 Arkansas (San Francisco, California 94117)

HARRIS, Nevada 1/21/10 Texas (Los Angeles, California 90006)

Harris, Shajhuanna Lesheene, see HARRIS, Dorothy Lesheene

HARRIS, Willie Maude (AKA Harris, Constance Nicole) 11/27/32 Georgia (Ukiah, California 95482)

HAYDEN, Eyvonne Paris 9/8/59 California (San Francisco, California 94102)

HEATH, Florence 5/8/28 South Carolina (Pittsburg, California 94565)

HEATH, Michael 4/25/64 California (Pittsburg, California 94565)

HELLE, Joseph Leo III (AKA Beam, Joe) 6/6/50 California (San Francisco, California 94115)

HENDERSON, Beatrice 8/22/03 Oklahoma (San Francisco, California 94117)

HENDERSON, Charles (AKA Henderson, Chuckie) 3/8/60

Henderson, Chuckie, see HENDERSON, Charles

HENDERSON, Kenya Lakiah aka Kenya Newman 7/27/77 Mother (Darlene Newman)

Henderson, Valaray, see WRIGHT, Leomy

HENNLEY, Hassan Ali aka Hassan Smith (var. spelling Hanley) 7/28/69 Mother (Barbara Smith)

HERRING, Nena Davidson 1/15/06 Louisiana (San Francisco, California 90001)

HICKS, Anthony Allan 3/4/66 Mother (Marthea Ann Hicks)

HICKS, Marthea Ann 5/22/35 Michigan (San Francisco, California 94121)

HILL, Emma Mae 12/5/15 Texas (Los Angeles, California 90047)

HILTON, Osialee 1/4/94 Arkansas (Los Angeles, California 90001)

HINES, Mable 12/29/12 Oklahoma

HINES, Bernell Maurice (AKA Tardy, Bernell Maurice) 8/12/1914 Arkansas (San Bruno, California 94066)

HINES, Rosa Mae 9/25/08 Texas (Los Angeles, California 90006)

HOLLEY, Patricia Ann (AKA Rhea, Patricia Ann Holley; Thea, Pat) 11/18/57 Washington (San Francisco, California 94115)

HOLLIDAY, Tani Claudine-La Dese 3/17/76 Mother (Toi Fonzelle)

HOLMES, Jeff, Jr. (AKA Harris, John) 7/31/32 Tennessee

HORNE, Hazel Lark 6/20/15 Louisiana (Los Angeles, California 90011)

HOUSTON, Judy Lynn 11/9/64 California (San Francisco, California 94107)

HOUSTON, Patricia Dian 10/2/63 California (San Francisco, California 94107)

HOUSTON, Phyllis D. 3/26/44 California (Oakland, California 95482)

HOWARD, Dorris Helen 1/27/22 Louisiana

Howard, Exia Maria, see DUCKETT, Exia Maria

HOYER, Barbara F. 9/21/48 Maryland (San Francisco, California 94115)

Hunter, Denise, see PURIFOY, Denise Elaine

IJAMES, Judith Kay 12/6/49 Indiana (Calpella, California 95418)

IJAMES, Maya Lisa 9/8/69 California

INGHRAM, Alice Lorine 9/24/36 Texas (Redwood Valley, California 95670

INGHRAM, Ava Jillon 7/25/63 California (Redwood Valley, California 95670)

JACKSON, Beatrice Alberta 12/22/96 Texas (San Francisco, California 94115)

Jackson, Clarence, see COLE, Clarence Elmer

JACKSON, Corrine Mae (AKA Kice, Corrine) 3/11/45 Indiana (Redwood Valley, California 94570)

Jackson, Darrell D. Martin, see MARTIN, Darrell

JACKSON, David Bettis 12/1/92 Louisiana (Los Angeles, California)

JACKSON, Donald 7/13/44 Louisiana (San Francisco, California 94102)

JACKSON, Eileen Renee 6/2/65 California (Redwood Valley, California 95470)

JACKSON, Gladys Margarette 7/6/19 Texas (Los Angeles, California 90007)

JACKSON, Jonathan 5/7/78 Parents (Kathryn and Ralph Jackson)

JACKSON, Karen

JACKSON, Kathryn Denise 9/24/52 California (San Francisco, California 94115)

JACKSON, Leticia 2/9/70 Mother (Rosa Jackson)

JACKSON, Lourece 12/26/41 Louisiana (San Francisco, California 94112)

JACKSON, Luvenia 7/5/97 Louisiana (Los Angeles, California)

JACKSON, Paulette Karen 2/17/51 Alabama (San Francisco, California 94117)

JACKSON, Ralph Edwin 6/9/52 California (San Francisco, California)

JACKSON, Richard Stuart 5/22/73 Mother (Lourece Jackson) and brother (Darrell D. Martin Jackson aka Darrell Martin)

JACKSON, Rosa Lee 10/21/39 Tennessee (San Francisco, California 94115)

JACKSON, Thelma 8/27/36 California (San Francisco, California 94102)

JAMES, Lavana 2/26/04 Texas (Los Angeles, California 90001)

JAMES, Margaret 2/27/18 Mississippi (San Francisco, California)

JAMES, Ronald DeVal 11/1/55 California (San Francisco, California 94117)

James, Shanda Michelle, see OLIVER, Shanda

JAMES, Toni Denise 7/21/59 California (Los Angeles, California 90011)

JANARO, Darren Richard 5/1/64 California (Redwood Valley, California)

JANARO, Mauri Kay 11/20/62 California (Redwood Valley, California 95470)

Janero, Marvin, see SELLERS, Marvin Wesley

JEFFERY, Eartis 2/18/13 Texas (Los Angeles, California 90037)

JEFFERY, Margrette 9/4/13 Texas (Los Angeles, California 90037)

JERRAM, Susan Jane (AKA Noxon, Susan) 4/25/45 Indiana (San Francisco, California 94115)

JOHNSON, Berda Truss (AKA Johnson, Birdie) 4/2/92 Mississippi (Los Angeles, California 90007)

Johnson, Birdie, see JOHNSON, Berda Truss

JOHNSON, Bessie Marie 3/26/36 Arkansas (San Francisco, California 94117)

JOHNSON, Carmen Lisa 7/25/68 Mother (Bessie Marie Johnson)

JOHNSON, Clara LaNue 11/24/32 Texas (Los Angeles, California 90008)

JOHNSON, Denise 10/25/61 California (San Francisco, California)

JOHNSON, Derek Damone 2/21/70 Mother (Irra Johnson)

JOHNSON, Earl Luches Joseph 1/2/12

JOHNSON, Garry Dartez 10/5/59 Mother (Mary Johnson Rodgers)

JOHNSON, Gerald Duane 1/17/61 California (Los Angeles, California 90037)

JOHNSON, Gwendolyn Joyce 2/19/62 Mother (Clara L. Johnson)

JOHNSON, Helen 11/25/28 (Peoples Temple records say birthyear is 1928)

JOHNSON, Irra Jean 7/8/52 Louisiana (San Francisco, California 94115)

JOHNSON, James Douglas aka James Douglas Knox 6/22/62 Mother (Mary A. Johnson aka Mary Darden)

JOHNSON, Janice Arlette 5/29/60 Texas (Los Angeles, California 90008)

JOHNSON, Jessie A. 9/17/00 Arkansas (Los Angeles, California 90001)

JOHNSON, Joe, Jr. 7/12/57 Missouri (San Francisco, California)

JOHNSON, Karl

JOHNSON, Mahaley 6/5/10 Texas (Los Angeles, California 90037)

JOHNSON, Maisha Danika 12/28/76 Mother (Bessie Marie Johnson)

JOHNSON, Mary (AKA Darden, Mary) 10/20/27 West Virginia

JOHNSON, Mary Allie 2/22/47

JOHNSON, Naomi Esther 10/15/28 Illinois (San Francisco, California 94115)

JOHNSON, Richard Lee 8/3/58 WestVirginia (Daly City, California 94014)

JOHNSON, Robert 12/8/03 Mississippi (Ukiah, California 95482)

JOHNSON, Robert Keith 4/2/66 Mother (Ruby Jewell Carroll) and brother (John Lawrence Gardener)

JOHNSON, Rosa

JOHNSON, Ruby Lee 2/16/21 (Peoples Temple records say birthdate is 12/16/21) Texas (San Francisco, California 94112)

JOHNSON, Samuel Lee (AKA Thompson, Samuel Lee) 5/5/52 California

Johnson, Shawntiki, see JOHNSON, Verna Lisa

JOHNSON, Verna Lisa (AKA Johnson, Shawntiki) 11/30/58 California (San Francisco, California)

JOHNSON, Willa JoAnn 5/22/59 Texas (Los Angeles, California 90008)

JONES, Agnes Paulette 2/14/43 Indiana (San Francisco, California)

JONES, Annette Teresa 2/25/26 Illinois (Los Angeles, California 90018)

JONES, Ava Phenice 8/6/51 Indiana (San Francisco, California)

JONES, Bossie 3/5/1895

JONES, Brenda Y. 12/13/48 Texas (San Francisco, California 94107)

JONES, Chaeoke Warren 4/4/77 (Georgetown, Guyana)

JONES, Earnest 9/7/22 Mississippi

JONES, Eliza 6/25/10 Alabama (Ukiah, California 95482)

JONES, Forrest Ray 12/12/36 Kentucky

JONES, James Warren, Jr. (Rev.) 5/13/31 Indiana (Redwood Valley, California 95470)

JONES, Jessie Weana 5/3/24 Louisiana (Los Angeles, California 90001)

Jones, Jim Arthur, see BISHOP, James Arthur

JONES, Johnny (AKA Brown, Johnny Moss, Jr.) 7/19/50 Texas

JONES, Kwame Rhu Amarka 9/3/68 Mother (Annette Teresa Jones)

JONES, Larry Darnell 1/14/53 Texas (San Francisco, California 94115)

JONES, Lerna Veshaun 1/19/69 California (San Francisco, California 94107)

JONES, Lew Eric 11/23/56 Korea (Redwood Valley, California 95470)

JONES, Marceline M. 1/8/27 Indiana (Redwood Valley, California 95470)

JONES, Marchelle Jacole 2/14/78 Mother (Ava Jones)

JONES, Mary T., see CARTER, Terry

JONES, Michael Ray 6/7/61 Mother (Agnes Jones)

JONES, Monyelle Maylene 2/14/78 Parents (Sandy and Tim Jones

JONES, Nancy Mae 5/5/01 Arkansas (Pittsburg, California 94565)

JONES, Sandy (AKA Cobb, Sandra Yvette) 11/16/56 (Peoples Temple records say birthdate is 12/16/56) Indiana (San Francisco, California 94107)

Jones, Stephanie (see Stephanie Lynn BISHOP)

Jones, Terry Carter, see CARTER, Terry

JONES, Timothy Borl 6/3/59 California

JONES, Timothy Earl

JONES, Valerie Yvette 11/20/58 Texas (San Francisco, California)

JORDAN, Dessie Jones 6/1/08 Arkansas (San Francisco, California 94115)

JORDAN, Fannie Alberta 8/6/13 Louisiana (Los Angeles, California 90044)

JORDAN, Lula Elizabeth 11/25/07 Texas

JOY, Love M. 12/18/91

JURADO, Emma Jane 12/2/08 Mississippi (San Francisco, California 94117)

KATSARIS, Maria 6/9/53 Pennsylvania (Redwood Valley, California 95470)

KAY, Mary

KEATON, Rosa Lorenda Mae 2/20/07 Arkansas (Los Angeles, California 90011)

KEATON, Tommie Sheppard, Sr. 8/12/14 Texas (Los Angeles, California 90011)

KEELER, Elaine Roslyn 5/8/44 New York (San Francisco, California)

KELLER, Darell Eugene 7/21/49 Montana (Oakland, California 94609)

KELLEY, Anita Christine 3/15/50 Indiana (Ukiah, California 95482)

KELLEY, Viola B. 12/13/06 Louisiana (Redwood City, California 94063)

KEMP, Barbara Alberta 11/4/40 Alabama (Ukiah, California 95482)

KEMP, Mellonie Denise 8/13/64 Mother (Barbara Kemp)

KEMP, Rochelle Annette 4/28/68 Mother (Barbara Kemp)

KENDALL, Elfreida 10/30/09 Texas (Los Angeles, California)

KENNEDY, Emma Addie 10/28/11 Georgia (Los Angeles, California 90008)

KERNS, Carol A. 4/28/58

Kerns, Penny, see DUPONT, Ellen Louise

Kice, Corrine, see JACKSON, Corrine Mae

KICE, Robert Edward 1/4/48 California (Redwood Valley, California 95470)

KICE, Thomas David 11/18/35 Missouri (Redwood Valley, California 95470)

KICE, Thomas David, 2nd 1/14/66 Father (Thomas Kice, Sr.)

KING, Charlotte 10/26/1897 Alabama (San Francisco, California 94109)

KING, Leola 4/2/13 Louisiana (San Francisco , California 94115)

KING, Teresa Lynn 1/11/47 Texas (San Francisco California 94107)

KING, Wanda Bonita 7/14/39 Indiana (Ukiah, California 95482)

KISLINGBURY, Sharon Jean 10/16/56 California (San Francisco, California)

KLINGMAN, April Heather 4/5/73 Mother (Martha Ellen Klingman) and siblings (Clarence Elmer Cole III aka Clarence Klingman, and William Arnold Cole aka William Klingman)

Klingman, Clarence, see COLE, Clarence Elmer

KLINGMAN, Martha Ellen 5/9/46 California (Ukiah, California 95482)

Klingman, Todd (see Matthew Todd COLE)

Klingman, William, see COLE, William Arnold

Knox, James Douglas (see James Douglas JOHNSON)

Kutulas, Dan, see KUTULAS, Demosthenis

KUTULAS, Demosthenis (AKA Kutulas, Dan) 2/20/27 California (Redwood Valley, California 95470)

KUTULAS, Edith 12/8/29 California (Redwood Valley, California 95470)

LACY, Donna Louise aka Briggs, Donna Louise 11/15/62 Adoptive parent (Georgia Lee Lacy)

LACY, Georgia Lee 2/9/10 Texas (Redwood Valley, California 95470)

LACY, Tony Linton aka Tony Linton aka Tommy Oscar Linton, Jr. 2/10/64 Guardian (Georgia Lee Lacy)

LAND, Pearl 7/20/02 (Peoples Temple records say birthdate is 7/29/1902) Texas (San Francisco, California 94102)

LANG, Lossie Mae 2/16/04 Texas (San Francisco, California)

LANGSTON, Carrie Ola 2/10/23 Louisiana (Redwood Valley, California 94801)

LANGSTON, Marianita 12/10/55 California (Richmond, California 94801)

LANGSTON, Zuretti Jenicer 7/25/59 California (Richmond, California 94801)

Lawrence, Erin, see EICHLER, Erin Jahna

Lawrence, Dee Dee, see DUCKETT, Joanette Blugina

LAWRENCE, Jameel Regina aka Jamie Cordell 5/12/73 Nine family members, including mother (Loretta Mae Cordell)

Lawrence, Marie, see DUCKETT, Exia Marie

Lawrence, Nicky, see DUCKETT, Ronald Charles

LAWRENCE, Nawab 11/20/67

LAYTON, Carolyn Louise Moore 7/13/45 California (San Francisco, California)

LAYTON, Karen Lea 8/10/47 California (Ukiah, California 95482)

LEE, Daisy 12/5/56 California (San Francisco, California 94133)

LENDO, Karen Marie 10/15/60 California (San Francisco, California 94115)

LEROY, Dorsey J.

LeROY, Erin, see EICHLER, Erin Jahna

LeROY, Laetitia M. (aka Eichler, Laetitia and LeRoy, Tish) 9/14/30 Washington (San Francisco, California)

LeRoy, Tish, see LeROY, Laetitia M.

LEWIS, Adrinnie R.

LEWIS, Alecha J.

LEWIS, Barry E.

LEWIS, Doris Jane

LEWIS, Dorsey J. 10/12/39 Oklahoma (San Francisco, California 94115)

LEWIS, Freddie L., Jr.

Lewis, Karen, see SCOTT, Karen Louise

LEWIS, Karen Marie

LEWIS, Lisa M. 2/2/62 California (San Francisco, California 94115)

LEWIS, Lue Ester 4/21/30 Louisiana (Los Angeles, California 90002)

Linton, Tommy Oscar, Jr. (see Tony Linton LACY)

Linton, Tony (see Tony Linton LACY)

LIVINGSTON, Beverly Marie Geraldine 4/15/32 California (Ukiah, California 95482)

LIVINGSTON, Jerry Dwight 11/11/41 California (Ukiah, California 95482)

LOCKETT, Gordon Everette 9/23/18 Oklahoma (Oakland, California 94607)

LOGAN, Henry L.

LOOMAN, Carolyn S. 5/7/43 Ohio (San Francisco, California 94115)

LOPEZ, Vincent 2/26/63

LOVE, Heavenly 11/6/1900

LOWE, Love Life Georgia Belle (AKA Owens, Georgia) 12/2/88 Missouri (Redwood Valley, California)

LOWERY, Ruth Whiteside 4/26/21 Tennessee (Los Angeles, California 90043)

LUCAS, Lovie Jean Morton 11/16/03 Tennessee

LUCIENTES, Christine R. 1/22/52 California (Ukiah, California 95482)

LUNDQUIST, Diane 12/31/46 California (San Francisco, California 94117)

LUNDQUIST, Dov Mario 3/29/67 California (Redwood Valley, California 95470)

LYLES, Minnie Magaline 2/28/28 Texas (San Francisco, California 94109)

Macon, Diane, see McKNIGHT, Diana

MACON, Dorothy 7/17/45 Texas (Redwood Valley, California 95470)

MADDEN, Rori Lynette 5/2/73 Mother (Beatrice Claudine Bell)

MALLOY, Lillian 8/10/05 North Carolina (San Francisco, California)

MARCH, Alfred 9/10/64 Mother (Earnestine March)

MARCH, Alfreda 9/10/64 Mother (Earnestine March)

MARCH, Earnestine Thomas 6/29/30 Texas (San Francisco, California 94110)

MARSHALL, Charles 2/16/57 Texas (San Francisco, California 94132)

MARSHALL, Danny Leon 12/24/54 Texas (San Francisco, California 94132)

MARSHALL, Diana LaVerna 2/28/59 Texas (San Francisco, California 94132)

MARSHALL, Shaunte 4/11/78 Father (Charles Marshall)

Marshall, Vicky Lynn, see DOVER, Vicky Lynn

MARTIN, Darrell D. (AKA Jackson, Darrell D. Martin) 1/6/65

MASON, Irene 11/15/92 Alabama (Los Angeles, California)

MASON, Francine Renita (AKA Crenshaw, Francine) 11/21/54 California (San Francisco, California 94117)

MAYSHACK, Mary 7/20/05

McCALL, Cheryle Darnell (AKA Parker, Cheryle Darnell) 12/31/47 Texas

McCALL, Estelle Dunn 10/7/30 Texas

McCANN, Eileen Kelly 1/28/60 California (San Francisco, California 94117)

McCANN, Eukeeb J.

McCANN, Maria Louise 10/27/52 New York (San Francisco, California)

McCANN, Michael Angelo 4/6/74 Mother (Maria McCann)

McCLAIN, Allie 6/25/90 Arkansas (Los Angeles, California)

McCOY, Carol Ann (AKA Dennis, Carol) 9/9/45 Indiana (Redwood Valley, California 95470)

McCOY, Leanndra Renae aka Leanndrea Dennis 2/16/69 Mother (Carol Ann McCoy aka Carol Dennis)

McCOY, Lowell Francis 2nd 8/18/66 Mother (Carol Ann McCoy aka Carol Dennis)

McCOY, Marcenda Dyan 10/16/70 Mother (Carol Ann McCoy aka Carol Dennis)

McCOY, Patty Ann 10/6/64 Mother (Carol Ann McCoy aka Carol Dennis)

McELVANE, James N. 4/13/32 Texas (Ukiah, California 95482)

McGOWAN, Alluvine 3/13/88 Texas (San Francisco, California 94117)

McGOWAN, Annie Jane 4/6/08 Mississippi (Redwood Valley, California 95470)

McINTYRE, Joyce Faye 10/23/57 Mississippi (San Francisco, California)

McKENZIE, Clara E. (Peoples Temple records say middle initial is "L") 11/26/29

McKINNIS, Levatus V. 7/1/06 Mississippi (Berkeley, California)

McKNIGHT, Diana (AKA Macon, Diane) 9/9/56 California (Oakland, California 94607)

McKNIGHT, Earl 2/18/95 Mississippi (San Francisco, California 94117)

McKNIGHT, Raymond Anthony 6/1/75 California

McKNIGHT, Rose Marie 8/23/53 California (Oakland, California 94607)

McMURRY, Deirdre Renee 1/22/61 Germany (Berkeley, California 94703)

McMURRY, Sebastian R. C. 3/2/55 Texas (Berkeley, California)

McMURRY, Takiyah Chanée 3/12/78 Father (Theodore McMurry)

McMURRY, Theodore Devanulis 6/7/58 Washington (Oakland, California 94609)

McNEAL, Jessie B. 6/19/10 Oklahoma (Los Angeles, California 90011)

MERCER, Henry 4/3/02 Georgia (San Francisco, California 94119)

Mercer, Mildred, see CARROLL, Mildred Ada

MIDDLETON, Virginia 10/25/15 New York (San Francisco, California)

MILLER, Christine 6/4/17 (Peoples Temple records say birthyear is 1918) Texas (Los Angeles, California 90005)

MILLER, Lucy Jane 3/31/13 Alabama (San Francisco, California)

MILLER, Lucy S.

MINOR, Cassandra Yvette 10/15/56 California (Redwood Valley, California 95470)

MINOR, Cuyana Lynette 4/30/78 Mother (Cassandra Minor)

MITCHELL, Annie Lee 7/7/30 Alabama (Los Angeles, California 90011)

MITCHELL, Beverly Darlene 11/14/62 California (Los Angeles, California 90011)

MITCHELL, Callie Mae 3/25/13

MITCHELL, Lee Charles 7/24/31 Alabama (Los Angeles, California 90011)

Mitchell, Otis, see ROBINSON, Benjamin O'Neal

MITCHELL, Shirley Ann 3/9/57 California (San Francisco, California 94115)

MITCHELL, Tony Lavell 8/15/65 California (Los Angeles, California 90011)

MOORE, Ann Elizabeth 5/12/54 California (San Francisco, California)

MOORE, Betty Karen 4/26/50 California (San Francisco, California)

MOORE, Clarence Edward, Jr. 12/23/74 Mother (Linda Theresa Arterberry) and guardian (Naomi Johnson)

MOORE, Edward 8/26/15 Louisiana (Los Angeles, California 90019)

MOREHEAD, Leola Kennedy 2/26/26 Arkansas (Oakland, California 94605)

MORGAN, Lydia (AKA Atkins, Lydia) 10/4/48 California (San Diego, California 92113)

MORGAN, Marcus Emile 12/5/70

MORGAN, Oliver, Jr. 9/5/49 California (La Palma, California 90623)

MORRISON, Erris Andrew 4/13/63 Mother (Lugenia Morrison)

MORRISON, Lugenia 6/22/27 Texas (Los Angeles, California 90059)

MORRISON, Yvonne 10/12/59 California (Los Angeles, California 90059)

MORTON, Mary Nathaniel 1/24/42 South Carolina (Pittsburg, California 94565)

MOSES, Eura Lee 9/12/99 Texas (Los Angeles, California 90003)

MOTON, Danny McCarter 12/2/56 California

MOTON, Deanna Kay (AKA Wilkinson, Deanna) 10/19/50 Illinois (Los Angeles, California)

MOTON, Glen 10/11/10 South Carolina (Philadelphia, Pennsylvania 19121)

MOTON, Michael Javonnie 4/15/73 Father (Russell Moton)

Moton, Pamela, see BRADSHAW, Pamela Gail

MOTON, Russell DeAndrea 3/2/48

MOTON, Viola Mae 11/7/20 Florida (Pomona, California 91766)

MUELLER, Esther Lillian 3/30/02 Indiana (Redwood Valley, California 95470)

MULDROW, Yvette Louise 10/23/58 California (San Francisco, California 94124)

MURPHY, Mary E. 1/8/1898

MURRAY, Detra Renee aka Detra Smith 4/13/68 Mother (Barbara Smith)

MUTSCHMANN, Jane Ellen 12/27/47 Wisconsin

NAILOR, Gertrude 3/21/10 Mississippi (Pasadena, California 91103)

NEAL, Cardell 12/17/54 California

NELSON, Enola Marthenya 12/9/20 Texas (Los Angeles, California 90008)

NEWELL, Allen 7/25/64 Mother (Hazle Newell)

NEWELL, Christopher 7/10/61 Mississippi (Los Angeles, California 90002)

NEWELL, Hazle Marie 6/15/27 Mississippi (Los Angeles, California 90002)

NEWELL, Jenifer 1/13/67 Mother (Hazle Newell)

NEWELL, Karl 11/13/62 Mother (Hazle Newell)

Newell, Shirley, see ROBINSON, Shirley Ann

NEWMAN, Darlene Rudeltha 3/12/48 Texas (San Francisco, California 94117)

Newman, Kenya (see Kenya HENDERSON)

NEWMAN, Lonnie Alexander 1/11/73 Mother (Darlene Newman)

NEWMAN, Luigi Lemoyne 3/7/69 Mother (Darlene Newman)

NEWSOME, Benjamin Keith 10/28/64

NICHOLS, Ida May 7/31/00 Oklahoma (San Francisco, California 90006)

Norris, Claudia Jo, see BOUQUET, Claudia Jo

Norton, Ken, see GRUBBS, Gerald Richard

NORWOOD, Fairy Lee 1/27/30 Oklahoma (San Francisco, California 94117)

Noxon, Susan, see JERRAM, Susan Jane

O'BRYANT, Winnieann (AKA O'Bryant, Zelline) 2/2/1900 (Peoples Temple records say birthyear is 1899) Oklahoma (Redwood Valley, California)

O'Bryant, Zelline, see O'BRYANT, Winnieann

OLIVER, Bruce Howard 3/18/58 California (San Francisco California 94115)

OLIVER, Shanda Michelle (AKA James, Shanda Michelle) 4/4/59 California (San Francisco California 94117)

OLIVER, William Sheldon 12/25/59 California (San Francisco, California 94115)

OLLIE, Marle

OMAN, Edna

Owens, Georgia, see LOWE, Love Life Georgia Belle

OWENS, Jane Elizabeth 11/14/20 Arkansas (San Francisco, California 94117)

PAGE, Rhonda Rachelle 2/10/54 California (Oakland, California 94609)

PARKER, Beatrice Lucy 8/27/94 North Carolina (San Francisco, California 94109)

PARKER, Bethany Shawnee aka Shawn Walker 8/18/72 Mother (Barbara J. Walker)

Parker, Cheryle Darnell, see McCALL, Cheryle Darnell

PARKER, Gloria Victoria 2/7/70 California (Pittsburg, California)

**PARKS, Patty L. 4/29/34 Ohio (Ukiah, California 95482)

PARRIS, Lore Bee 2/28/1910

PARTAK, Thomas Joseph 7/16/46 Illinois (San Francisco, California 94117)

PATTERSON, Antonio Jemal 6/25/69 California (Redwood Valley, California 95470)

PATTERSON, Carroll Anthony 8/13/48 Texas (Los Angeles, California 90018)

PAYNEY, Lucille Estelle 9/4/99 Illinois (Ukiah, California)

PERKINS, Irvin Ray, Jr. 11/20/70 Mother (Maud Perkins)

PERKINS, Lenora Martin 4/7/13 Arkansas (Los Angeles, California)

PERKINS, Maud Ester 12/4/49 Texas (Redwood Valley, California 95470)

PERKINS, Richardell Evelyn 12/21/42 California (San Francisco, California 94115)

PERRY, Leon 8/8/17 Texas (San Francisco, California 94115)

JEFFSON, Rosa Lee 10/22/00 Arkansas (Pasadena, California)

PHILLIPS, George Edward III 3/2/70 Mother (Viola Duncan Forks)

Pierce, Linda, see ARTERBERRY, Linda

Pointdexter, Amanda, see EVER REJOICING

POLITE, Glenda Bell 8/1/57 Arkansas (San Francisco, California)

Polk, Joyce, see BROWN, Joyce Marie

PONTS, Donna Louise 1/17/63 California (Ukiah, California 95482)

PONTS, Lois Agnes 1/21/27 California (Ukiah, California 95482)

POPLIN, Oreen (AKA Armstrong, Oreen) 10/11/04 Texas (San Francisco, California)

PORTER, Marlon Walker aka Dietrich Walker 2/2074 Mother (Barbara J. Walker)

PROBY, Bessie Mae 11/23/15 Louisiana (Los Angeles, California 90007)

PROKES, Jim Jon (Kimo) 1/30/75

PUGH, Eva Hazel 11/8/1908

PUGH, James Robert 3/15/17 Iowa (Redwood Valley, California)

PURIFOY, Denise Elaine (AKA Hunter, Denise) 11/4/52 California (Ukiah, California 95482)

PURIFOY, Kathy J. 2/27/59 Indiana (San Francisco, California 94117)

PURSLEY, Cynthia 4/4/56 California (Berkeley, California 94702)

RAILBACK, Estella Mae 2/22/04 Texas (Los Angeles, California 90037)

RAMEY, Darlene 9/30/59 California (San Francisco, California 94117)

RANKIN, Robert Louis 10/19/39 Tennessee (Redwood Valley, California 95470)

REED, Willie Bell 3/8/13 Alabama (Los Angeles, California 90006)

REESE, Bertha Jones 4/18/09 Texas (Los Angeles, California 90059)

RHEA, Jerome Othello, Jr. 3/30/52 Maryland (Ukiah, California 95482)

RHEA, Asha Tabia 1/27/77 Parents (Jerome Rhea and Patricia Ann Holley aka Pat Thea aka Patricia Ann Holley Rhea)

Rhea, Patricia Ann Holley, see HOLLEY, Patricia Ann

RHODES, Isaac Jerome 7/13/71 Mother (Ruletta Brown)

RHODES, Marquess Dwight, Jr. 9/21/70 Mother (Ruletta Brown)

ROBERSON, Odenia Arthurs 3/10/05 Louisiana (Los Angeles, California 90006)

ROBERTS, Gladys 9/22/1900

ROBERTSON, Acquinetta Evans 5/16/54 Texas (Los Angeles,California 90001)

ROBINSON, Benjamin O'Neal (AKA Mitchell, Otis) 6/30/53 Georgia (Los Angeles, California)

ROBINSON, Lee Ose 5/11/19 Louisiana (San Francisco, California 94117)

ROBINSON, Shirley Ann (AKA Newell, Shirley) 12/24/55 Georgia (Los Angeles, California 90019)

**ROBINSON, Greg

ROCHELLE, Anthony E. 3/30/72 California (San Francisco, California 94102)

ROCHELLE, Jackie 4/20/56 Missouri (San Francisco, California 94102)

ROCHELLE, Tommie Charlene 11/28/50 Arkansas (San Francisco, California 94102)

RODGERS, Mary Flavia 9/16/92 Louisiana (Los Angeles, California 90003)

RODGERS, Mary Johnson 1/25/26 Louisiana (San Francisco, California 94117)

RODGERS, Ophelia 12/26/20 Alabama (Los Angeles, California 90006)

RODRIGUEZ, Gloria Maria (AKA Carter, Gloria) 3/23/52 California (Santa Barbara, California 93103)

ROLLER, Edith Frances 12/18/15 Colorado (San Francisco, California 94117)

ROLLINS, Dorothy Jean 1/10/56 California (Richmond, California 94804)

ROMANO, Margarite Yvette aka Bippy Davis 2/5/73 Mother (Margaret Davis aka Margarita Davis) and sibling (Celeste Marie Vento aka Celeste Davis)

ROMANO, Renee Sylvia aka Renee Davis 4/23/71 Mother (Margaret Davis aka Margarita Davis) and sibling (Celeste Marie Vento aka Celeste Davis)

ROSA, Santiago Alberto 12/2/54 Honduras

ROSAS, Kay 6/19/40 California (Redwood Valley, California)

ROSS, Elsie Zilpha 7/15/89 Louisiana (San Francisco, California 94117)

Ross, Thelma Doris Mattie, see CANNON, Thelma Mattie

ROZYNKO, Annie Joyce 6/2/24 New Jersey (San Francisco, California 94117)

ROZYNKO, Christian Leo 5/20/54 Washington (San Francisco, California 94117)

ROZYNKO, Michael Thomas 9/12/56 Washington (Redwood Valley, California 95470)

RUBEN, Lula 6/1/07 Louisiana (Los Angeles, California 90037)

RUGGIERO, Elizabeth 8/8/54 New York (Eagle Rock, California)

RUGGIERO, Roseann 6/12/59 California (Eagle Rock, California)

RUNNEL, Judy Ann 9/13/66 Texas (San Francisco, California 94115)

RUNNELS, Julie Ann, see RUNNELL, Judy Ann

RUSSELL, D'Andrea Moton 3/2/48

**RYAN, Leo J.

SADLER, Linda Caleice 3/9/57 Tennessee (San Francisco, California 94121)

SANDERS, Dorothy Jean 6/10/47 California (Bakersfield, California 93304)

SANDERS, Douglas 6/27/50 California (Bakersfield, California 93304)

SANDERS, Flora Bell 4/23/10 Mississippi (Ukiah, California 95482)

SANTIAGO, Alida Rosa 3/27/58 New York (San Francisco, California)

SCHACHT, Laurence Eugene 10/2/48 Texas (Redwood Valley, California 95470)

SCHEID, Angelique Marie (AKA Casanova, Angelique Marie) 10/13/65

SCHEID, Donald Eugene, Jr. (AKA Casanova, Don) 7/22/61 California (San Francisco, California 94117)

SCHROEDER, Deborah Faye 7/12/49 California (San Francisco, California 94102)

SCHROEDER, Tad 10/27/73 Mother (Deborah Schroeder)

SCOTT, Karen Louise (AKA Lewis, Karen) 10/23/59 Oklahoma (San Francisco, California)

SCOTT, Pauline 4/30/21 West Virginia (Los Angeles, California 90006)

SHARON, Rose O. 7/22/07 Virginia (San Francisco, California)

SHAVERS, Mary Louise 10/19/25 Louisiana (Ukiah, California 95482)

SHELTON, Rose Jeanette 10/21/02 Missouri (Redwood Valley, California 95470)

SIMON, Alvin Harold 1/13/45 California (Cotati, California 94928)

SIMON, Alvin Harold, Jr. 10/8/72 Parents (Alvin and Bonnie Simon)

SIMON, Anthony Joseph 7/22/54 California (Los Angeles, California 90002)

SIMON, Barbara Ann 10/11/55 California (San Francisco, California 94117)

SIMON, Bonnie Jean 3/23/49 Ohio (Cotati, California 94928)

SIMON, Crystal Michelle 7/1/74 Parents (Alvin and Bonnie Simon)

SIMON, Jerome Mark 4/17/58 California (San Francisco, California 94117)

SIMON, Jose 8/20/16 California (Middletown, California 95461)

SIMON, Marcia Ann 10/11/55 California (San Francisco, California 94117)

SIMON, Melanie Wanda 11/7/55 Louisiana (San Francisco, California 94117)

SIMON, Pauline Louise 11/6/32 Illinois (San Francisco, California 94115)

SIMON, Summer 6/29/76 Parents (Alvin and Bonnie Simon)

SIMPSON, Dorothy Georgina (AKA Daniels, Dorothy) 9/2/22 Montana (Bakersfiled, California 93304)

SIMPSON, Jewell James 12/31/21 Oklahoma (Bakersfield, California 93304)

SINES, Nancy Virginia 9/25/49 California (Redwood Valley, California 95470)

SINES, Ronald Bruce 2/18/48 California (Redwood Valley, California 95470)

SLY, Donald Edward (AKA Sly, Ujara) 3/3/36 California (Redwood Valley, California 95470)

SLY, Mark Andrew 3/30/61 California (Los Angeles, California 90020)

Sly, Ujara , see SLY, Donald Edward

SMART, Alfred Laufton 6/3/60 California (Los Angeles, California 90008)

SMART, Scott Cameron 6/11/63

SMART, Teri Lynn 9/11/64

SMITH, Barbara Ann 10/6/44 California (Ukiah, California 95482)

SMITH, Bertha Charles 9/2/02 Louisiana (Los Angeles, California 90006)

SMITH, Clark Andrew aka Clark Grubbs 1/17/67 Mother (Sylvia E. Grubbs)

SMITH, David E. 9/17/26 Colorado (Los Angeles, California 90011)

Smith, Dee Dee, see SMITH, Edrena Demetria

Smith, Detra (see Detra Renee MURRAY)

SMITH, Edrena Demetria (AKA Smith, Dee Dee) 10/4/58 California (San Francisco, California 94117)

SMITH, Gladys 1/11/46 Texas (Redwood Valley, California 95470)

Smith, Hassan (see Hassan HENNLEY)

SMITH, James Alfred 12/25/59 California (San Francisco, California 94115)

SMITH, Jeffrey Dale 2/6/71 California (Redwood Valley, California 95470)

SMITH, Jerry Gilbert (AKA Gilbert, MN) 4/17/51 California (San Francisco, California 94117)

SMITH, Karl Wayne 10/25/67

SMITH, Kelin Kirtas 3/4/65 California (Redwood Valley, California 95470)

SMITH, Kelly Franklin aka Kelly Grubbs 1/14/64 Mother (Sylvia E. Grubbs)

SMITH, Kevan Deane 5/21/61 California (Ukiah, California 95482)

SMITH, Kivin Earl 1/12/48 New Jersey (Oakland, California)

SMITH, Krista Lynn 4/28/66 California (Redwood Valley, California 95470)

SMITH, Michael Vail 7/27/69 California (Redwood Valley, California 95470)

SMITH, Oliver (Ollie) Marie (AKA Smith, Ollie; Wideman, Oliver Marie) 11/6/59 Texas (San Francisco, California)

Smith, Ollie, see SMITH, Oliver Marie

SMITH, Shirley Faye 2/3/48 Texas (Redwood Valley, California 95470)

SMITH, Stephanie Marie 11/5/64 Mother (Barbara Smith)

SMITH, Vernon (Peoples Temple records say first name is "Veron") 4/23/1914

SMITH, Winnie F. 1/11/23 Louisiana (Los Angeles, California 90062)

Smith, Youlanda (see Youlanda GRISSETTE)

SNEED, Clevyee Louise 8/14/20 (Peoples Temple records say birthdate is 8/12/20) Tennessee (Pasadena, California 91103)

SNEED, Eloise 5/18/07 Texas (Los Angeles, California 90008)

SNEED, Novella Novice 6/18/07 Texas (Redwood Valley, California 95470)

SNEED, Willie Deloie 8/1/19 Illinois (Pasadena, California 91103)

SNELL, Helen 2/28/02 Texas (San Francisco, California 94115)

SOLOMON, Dorothy Pearl (Peoples Temple records say last name is "Solamon") 9/19/40 Georgia (Redwood Valley, California 95470)

SOLOMON, Dorrus Henry (Peoples Temple records say last name is "Solamon") 12/23/56 Georgia (Redwood Valley, California)

SOLOMON, Syria Lesheena (AKA Solomon, Tiny) 9/29/59 New Jersey (Ukiah, California 95482)

Solomon, Tiny, see SOLOMON, Syria Lesheena

SOUDER, Delicia Jeanette 4/14/72 Mother (Wanda Souder) and grandmother (Martha Souder)

SOUDER, Martha Mae 3/5/16 Arkansas (Los Angeles, California 90002)

SOUDER, Wanda Kay 12/17/53 California (San Francisco, California)

STAHL, Alfred Richmond 7/24/11 Kentucky (Ukiah, California 95482)

STAHL, Bonnie Lynn 10/20/70 California (Ukiah, California 95482)

STAHL, Carol Ann 10/28/38 California (Ukiah, California 95482)

Stahl, Cathy Ann, see BARRETT, Cathy Ann

STALLING, Lula Mae 9/23/24 Oklahoma (Los Angeles, California 90006)

STANLEY, YoVonne Renee 5/20/75 Mother (Jackie Rochelle)

STATEN, Abraham Lincoln 4/10/12 Virginia (Los Angeles, California 90037)

STATEN, Ameal 1/9/1903 (Peoples Temple records say birthdate is 1/7/03)

STEVENSON, Francis Lee 7/30/16 Indiana (San Francisco, California 94115)

STEWART, Aurora May 9/17/67 California (Santa Barbara, California 93103)

STEWART, Terry Frederick, Jr. 3/21/69 California

STOEN, John Victor 1/25/72 Santa Rosa, California (San Francisco, California)

STONE, Sharon Lee (AKA Stone, Tobi) 12/13/42 California (San Francisco, California 94117)

Stone, Tobi, see STONE, Sharon Lee

STONE, Tobiana Johanna Dilorenzo 11/1/69 Mother (Sharon Lee Stone aka Tobi Stone)

STONE, Tracy Lamont 2/4/67 Mother (Sharon Lee Stone aka Tobi Stone)

STRIDER, Adeleine Mae 12/15/04 California (Ukiah, California)

SWANEY, Nathaniel Brown 7/5/22 Ohio (Redwood Valley, California 95470)

SWINNEY, Cleave Lonso 4/5/11 Missouri (Redwood Valley, California 95470)

Swinney, Darren (see Darren Eugene WERNER)

Swinney, Joyce, see TOUCHETTE, Joyce

SWINNEY, Timothy Maurice 9/28/38 Indiana (Redwood Valley, California 95470)

SWINNEY, Wanda Shirley 8/20/47 Wyoming (Redwood Valley, California 95470)

Talley, Christine, see BOWERS, Christine Shannon

Talley, Maureen, see FITCH, Maureen Cynthia

TALLEY, Ronald Wayne 10/15/45 California (Ukiah, California 95482)

TALLEY, Vera Marie 2/3/03 Texas (Ukiah, California 95480)

TARDY, Armella 2/12/46 Mississippi (San Francisco, California 94115)

Tardy, Bernell Maurice, see HINES, Bernell Maurice

TARDY, Eliot Wade 4/18/68 Mother (Armella Tardy)

TAYLOR, Lillian Marie 12/7/1905

TAYLOR, Lucille Beatrice 2/3/98 Tennessee (Redwood Valley, California 95470)

TAYLOR, Virginia Vera 7/29/94 Ohio (San Francisco, California 94109)

Thea, Pat, see HOLLEY, Patricia Ann

Thomas, Alma, see COLEY, Alma

THOMAS, Bernice 1/7/10 Louisiana (San Francisco, California 94103)

THOMAS, Carolyn Ann 12/3/49 Texas (San Francisco, California 94102)

THOMAS, Ernst 10/20/19 Louisiana (Los Angeles, California 90022)

THOMAS, Evelyn 11/1/44 California (San Pablo, California)

THOMAS, Gabriel 3/13/19 (Peoples Temple records say birthdate is 4/13/19) Arkansas (San Francisco, California)

THOMAS, Lavonne Shannel 12/30/70 Mother (Carolyn Thomas)

THOMAS, Scott, Jr. 6/19/57 Louisiana (San Francisco, California 94124)

THOMAS, Willie Ater 7/28/60 California (San Francisco, California 94115)

THOMPSON, Etta 2/22/04 Texas (Ukiah, California)

Thompson, Samuel Lee, see JOHNSON, Samuel Lee

THOMPSON, Vinnie (Peoples Temple records say first name is "Vennie") 4/3/02 Louisiana (San Francisco, California 94121)

TOM, Camille Tiffany 2/7/76 Mother (Marcie Simon)

TOUCHETTE, Albert Ardell 9/13/54 Indiana (Redwood Valley, California 95470)

Touchette, Carol Joyce, see TOUCHETTE, Joyce

TOUCHETTE, Joyce (AKA Touchette, Carol Joyce; Swinney, Joyce) 5/14/33 Indiana (Redwood Valley, California 95470)

TOUCHETTE, Michelle Elaine 7/21/58 Indiana (Redwood Valley, California 95470)

TOWNES, Le Flora 8/7/22

TOWNS, Essie Mae 7/3/03 Oklahoma (Los Angeles, California 90029)

TROPP, Harriet Sarah 4/16/50 New York (San Francisco, California 94117)

TROPP, Richard David 10/9/42 New York (Redwood Valley, California 95470)

TRUSS, Cornelius Lee, Jr. 9/20/60 California (Oakland, California 94619)

TSCHETTER, Alfred Walter 6/19/21 South Dakota (Ukiah, California 95482)

TSCHETTER, Betty Jean (AKA Yoon Ai, Kim) 8/17/59 Korea (Ukiah, California 95482)

TSCHETTER, Mary Alice 6/7/28 Indiana (Ukiah, California 95482)

TUCKER, Alleane 4/1/29 Tennessee (Ukiah, California 95482)

TUPPER, Janet Marie 7/31/63 Mother (Rita Tupper)

TUPPER, Larry Howard 12/5/64 California (Redwood Valley, California)

TUPPER, Mary Elizabeth 12/16/60 California (Redwood Valley, California 95470)

TUPPER, Rita Jeanette 6/14/33 Iowa (Redwood Valley, California 95470)

TUPPER, Ruth Ann 11/4/56 Iowa (Redwood Valley, California 95470)

TURNER, Bruce Edward 4/11/54 Texas (Redwood Valley, California)

TURNER, James Elmer, Jr. 5/5/59 California (Los Angeles, California 90059)

TURNER, Martha Elizabeth 9/23/1911 (Peoples Temple records say birthyear is 1910)

TURNER, Roosevelt W. 8/4/26 Oklahoma (Long Beach, California 90813)

TURNER, Syola Williams (AKA Williams, Siola) 6/27/12 Texas (Los Angeles, California 90016)

TYLER, Gary Lee 8/3/58 California (San Francisco, California)

VENTO, Celeste Marie (AKA Davis, Celeste) 11/2/67

VICTOR, Lillie Mae 2/2/58 California (San Francisco, California 94115)

WADE, Roberta Lee 12/12/10 Texas (Richmond, California 94801)

WADE, Terrence O'Keith 9/6/61 Mother (Lue Ester Lewis)

WAGNER, Inez Jeanette 12/13/27 Oklahoma (San Francisco, California 94112)

WAGNER, Mark Stacey 1/7/62 California (San Francisco, California 94112)

WAGNER, Michelle 5/18/54 California

WALKER, Barbara Jean 10/25/53 (Peoples Temple records say birthyear is 1952)

Walker, Dietrich (see Marlon PORTER)

WALKER, Gloria Dawn 11/4/37 Kansas (Inglewood, California 90301)

WALKER, Jerrica Racquel 12/23/70 Mother (Barbara Walker)

WALKER, Mary Nellie 2/17/04 Arkansas

Walker, Newhuanda Rhenelle, see DARNES, Newhuanda

Walker, Shawn (see Bethany Shawnee PARKER)

WALKER, Tony Gerard 12/29/57 California (Inglewood, California 90301)

WARREN, Brenda Anne 11/9/61 Mississippi (San Francisco, California 94115)

WARREN, Gloria Faye (AKA Griffith, Gloria) 1/9/59 Mississippi (San Francisco, California 94115)

WARREN, Janie Marie 3/23/60 Mississippi (San Francisco, California 94115)

WASHINGTON, Annie Bell 5/24/12 Alabama (Los Angeles, California 90006)

WASHINGTON, Grover 6/27/27 South Carolina (Pittsburg, California 94565)

WASHINGTON, Huldah Eddie 7/27/01 Texas (Los Angeles, California 90011)

Watkins, Erin Leroy, see EICHLER, Erin Jahna

WATKINS, Gregory Lewis 11/9/55 Mississippi (San Francisco, California)

WATKINS, William Allan 4/28/70 Mother (Betty Moore)

WERNER, Darren Eugene aka Darren Swinney 9/8/68 Mother (Wanda Swinney)

WESLEY, Bessie Mae 10/8/15 Alabama (Richmond, California)

WHEELER, Darius Daniel 9/28/70

WHEELER, Jeff L. 7/30/65

WHEELER, Marlene Diane 2/11/47 California (Redwood Valley, California 95470)

WHITMIRE, Lisa Ann 3/30/66 California (Santa Barbara, California 93103)

Wideman, Oliver Marie, see SMITH, Oliver Marie

WILHITE, Cheryl Gail 8/10/55 California (San Francisco, California 94115)

Wilkinson, Deanna, see MOTON, Deanna Kay

WILLIAMS, Charles Wesley 9/8/42 Texas (San Francisco, California 94115)

WILLIAMS, Lisa Renee 6/27/66 Mother (Lue Ester Lewis)

WILLIAMS, Louise Teska Lee 1/31/13 Texas (San Francisco, California 94117)

Williams, Siola, see TURNER, Syola Williams

WILLIAMS, Theo, Jr. 12/6/1915

WILLIS, Mary Pearl 12/21/40 Louisiana (Los Angeles, California)

WILSEY, Janice L. 9/23/49 California (San Francisco, California)

WILSON, Jerry (AKA Baisey, Jerry) 2/14/61 California (San Francisco, California 94112)

WILSON, Jewell Lee 6/24/29 Arkansas (San Francisco, California 94109)

WILSON, Joseph Lafayette 6/29/54 Georgia (Redwood Valley, California 95470)

WILSON, Shirley Mae (AKA Baisey, Shirley May) 1/14/45 Arkansas (San Francisco, California 94109)

WILSON, Wanda, aka Wanda Baisey 9/16/63 Mother (Shirley Mae Wilson aka Shirley Mae Baisey)

WINTERS, Curtis Laurine 1/9/25 Indiana (Redwood Valley, California)

WORLEY, Dorothy Lee (AKA Brady, Dorothy) 8/11/14

WOTHERSPOON, Mary Beth 10/26/49 Michigan (Ukiah, California 95482)

WOTHERSPOON, Mary Margaret 11/7/70 California (Ukiah, California 95482)

WOTHERSPOON, Jeff Andrew 5/5/47 Chile (Ukiah, California 95482)

WRIGHT, Arlisa Lavette (AKA Wright, Lisa) 7/23/61 California (Los Angeles, California 94117)

WRIGHT, Keith Arnold 6/15/62 Mother (Leomy Wright aka Valaray Henderson) and siblings (Arlissa Wright aka Lisa Wright, Stanley Wright, and Charles (Chuckie) Henderson)

WRIGHT, Leomy (AKA Henderson, Valaray) 5/22/21 Texas (Los Angeles, California 90037)

Wright, Lisa, see WRIGHT, Arlisa

WRIGHT, Stanley Glenn 6/11/60 (Los Angeles, California 90037)

Yoon Ai, Kim, see TSCHETTER, Betty Jean

YOUNG, Elois Christine (AKA Cobb, Elois Christine) 3/29/28 Indiana (San Francisco, California)

NEVER TO BE FORGOTTEN..